D-DAY
TANK
HUNTER

D-DAY
TANK
HUNTER

The World War II memoirs of a frontline officer from North Africa to the bloody soil of Normandy

HANS HOELLER

Hans Hoeller
D-Day Tank Hunter: The World War II memoirs of a frontline
officer from North Africa to the bloody soil of Normandy

© Markus Reisner and Andreas Hartinger
ISBN 979-8-4283-3410-4
Cover: Creative Factory
Translated from the German by Alexander Gruber

All photographs, unless specified otherwise, were made by Hans
Hoeller himself or taken out of his personal collection.

Contact: DDayTankHunter@protonmail.com

Dedicated to the youth of today
to help understand these times
as well as to my beloved wife Helena,
who in these dire straits
stood faithfully by my side.

CONTENTS

AUTHOR'S NOTE

To be honest, I had already put my wartime memories behind me. For decades I did not want to have anything to do with them, such was my disappointment with myself about having succumbed to the mental undertow of that time. A time born in the injustice of a peace treaty after the end of the First World War, which did not bring peace to Europe but eventually led to its destruction again. After the war had ended, I only told a select few about this time and what I had witnessed. Only many years later, during several trips to the places I had been in action, I connected to the events that had shaped me subconsciously for my entire life. Ultimately, these trips were the starting point for writing down my memoirs.

When I was sitting at the desk, pen in hand, and remembering Africa, Normandy, or the Falaise Pocket, the impressions that surfaced simply overwhelmed me. Time and again I had to put the pen aside, and sometimes I was lying awake at night, unable to find any rest. Those impressions returned; they were there and could not be repressed. They were as intense as the day I had experienced them.

Oh how naive we had been. With all our energy, we had supported a system that hurled us all into the abyss. Without consideration, mercilessly and brutally. The demon of war we worshiped had grasped our souls, drawing us into a maelstrom of death and destruction. There was no escape, and only few of us made it back to the surface. The others never returned, all memories of them faded, their names and their deaths mere footnotes of history. Their graves are forgotten, and their deaths were pushed into oblivion.

So why write my World War II memoirs? I wrote them to come

to terms with that time. To give a name to all those soldiers who had died next to me, under my command, or even because of my actions. To deliver to posterity how it came that we vigorously plunged ourselves into ruin, even cheering for each other in free fall until finally, facing gravity, we hit the ground and got torn apart without remorse.

I want to thank my wife Helena for her renewed sympathy for me voyaging back into this time and I thank the publishers for making this book available to a broad audience. And finally, my dear comrades and friends I had to leave behind, forgive me and accept these words of mine as a monument to your remembrance.

Hans Hoeller
Pottschach, March 2022

PUBLISHER'S NOTE

When the Second World War broke out in September 1939, neither of us had been born yet. It would take decades until we would come to grips with this time as adolescent young men. And when we thought to have understood the war in its entirety, it was the stories told by contemporary witnesses that brought home to us how unimaginable and inescapable these times had been to them.

One witness of this generation is Hans Hoeller. We met him by chance. We had been invited to give a lecture about our own deployments to Afghanistan and Iraq and in the middle of our deliberations a man quickly caught our attention, asking pointed and thought-out questions. Our conversation with him after the lecture was utterly mesmerizing. We were captivated not because of his wartime experiences – no, because what he told us made us understand how one was to survive in such a time. How one could sincerely believe to be fighting for justice and good, eyes pridefully on the horizon, and eventually had to realize that everything had been in vain. We sat down, listened to him and realized that his narratives, the stories of him witnessing fierce and bloody battles in the deserts of Africa and on the coast of Normandy need to be passed on to posterity. This is his story.

Dr. Markus Reisner, PhD and Dr. Andreas Hartinger
Wiener Neustadt, March 2022

"THEY HAVE LANDED"

was rudely awoken by somebody shaking my shoulder. I blinked and looked at my watch; it was just after midnight, so this had to be something important. Lance Corporal Atteneder, my trusted runner, was standing at my bedside, reporting in a low voice, "Lieutenant, sir, a general alert has been issued. Enemy paratroopers have supposedly landed along the coast forward of our location."

I looked at him in surprise. "Perhaps an exercise alert?" it shot through my head. I briskly jumped out of bed, feeling a little sad about having to leave the soft pillows on which I had slept so soundly. I told my runner, "Atteneder, alert the men. I want immediate readiness to move!"

He answered at once "Yes sir!", turned, and hurried out of my room.

I had the privilege of being accommodated in French private quarters in Cairon, about 8 km from the Channel coast. It was a little room in a nice small cottage. The owners were an elderly couple who, despite the reality of German occupation, had always been friendly to me and my men. They were standing in the garden in their nightgowns and looked at me with large eyes as I came out of the cottage fully dressed a few minutes later. I must have really looked frightening. I was standing there in heavy boots, camouflage battle dress, blackened face, submachine gun in hand, and was staring up into the sky from under the rim of my steel helmet.

It was June 6, 1944, just after midnight, and it seemed as if the end of the world had come upon peaceful Cairon. Already while getting dressed,

I had heard the emergence of droning sounds. Enemy bombers! And it sounded like there were lots of them. I looked tensely up into the dark sky where the roaring was becoming louder and louder. A deep, thundering noise sounded from the direction of nearby Caen. It was shaking the earth. The city was being bombed by heavy Allied aircraft formations. Detonation flashes of the bombs were turning night into day, with the loud droning of countless four-engine bombers constantly returning as they passed over us. The sky over Caen was glowing red. Our anti-aircraft guns had commenced their defensive fire.

The intermittent detonations in the sky were, however, showing little effect. Caen, the old Norman city with its beautiful monastery, was covered in dark clouds of smoke, which were again and again punctuated by lightning. They looked like a distant, solid wall. It was both a threatening and impressive sight for us in nearby Cairon.

Atteneder reported the details of the situation and the alarm in short sentences. Our headquarters had ordered readiness to move. We would have to act quickly now. My platoon was quartered in the garden of a chateau next to the cottage. I rapidly issued the necessary orders to get us moving. The fires raging in Caen provided so much light that we did not need any flashlights. The baggage was quickly packed and prepared for transportation. We would leave it for the supply detachment to pick up. Who knew if we were ever coming back, so it was better to be ready for redeployment.

My platoon was equipped with three modified French half-tracks which had been fitted with 75 mm anti-tank guns. My fellows were quick, and my track commanders soon reported, "Ready to move." My self-propelled guns were standing before me, fully fueled and armed.

I was just about to mount up when my hosts came running towards me. They were laden with foodstuffs and beverages and had tears in their eyes. I was surprised; I would never have expected this. They shoved the presents into my arms and wished all the best to "their lieutenant" and his men. I had become endeared to them.

Alas, I had to be off, so we mounted up to move off towards the rally point of our 8th (Heavy) Company, II Battalion, 192nd *Panzergrenadier* (mechanized infantry) Regiment, 21st Panzer Division. I raised my arm to give the signal to commence moving, and the tracks set off with a thundering noise. We rapidly left the chateau behind us. "Will we ever see it again?" I wondered.

When we arrived at the location of First Lieutenant Braatz, the company commander, I reported to him. Everybody was nervous. His command post was a hive of activity, and messengers were continuously bringing in situation reports. The situation at the Channel coast was, however, still unclear, which meant we could do nothing but wait. It felt like an eternity. Finally, First Lieutenant Braatz began a short issue of orders. "British paratroopers have airlanded to the northeast of Caen at Benouville and have seized the bridges over the Caen Canal and river Orne located there. Our 8th Company is to attack, secure Benouville, and take back the bridges!"

Short and precise, just as it was supposed to be. He did not have any additional information, just that the situation was dire. Heavy fighting had been reported from the coastline, as had the capture of several British paratroopers. I had been ordered to command the leading vehicle, so we mounted up after a brief issue of orders, made ourselves combat ready and "Close in with the enemy!" Just as we had trained for months in the royal gardens of Versailles, in the Bretagne, and here in Cairon. As we moved off, I began to prepare my battle plan. I looked at my watch; just after 03:00.

If this was the big Allied landing that all of us had not wanted to believe in yet somehow anticipated, we would have to act quickly. We would have to retake the bridges and do it soon. The fate of many soldiers might depend on it. We moved out with our vehicles. During the final stage of our approach, as we were carefully leapfrogging our half-tracks toward the objective, I heard a loud swishing sound above our heads. I looked up and was able to discern an aircraft. But where was the engine noise? All of a sudden, I understood: enemy gliders.

Just as field marshal Erwin Rommel, the commanding general in Normandy, had predicted during an inspection of our Panzer division a week ago. Now I could actually hear the engines of the transport aircraft which had released the gliders. Behind us, Caen burned and was still rocked by explosions, while in front of us, towards the coast, the sky was crisscrossed by tracer rounds. These were ascending in long lines towards the sky and were now finding their marks in the bellies of gliders full of soldiers.

It was just before 04:00, and my nerves were extremely tense. I was staring intently into the darkness before me and was trying to discern the first row of buildings of Benouville. We had halted and turned off the engines and could now hear the rest of the company following us. I was angry at the noise of their tracked vehicles being so loud. In spite of the detonations in the sky, we could be heard from a long way off.

After a while, the engines to the rear of us also fell silent. The entire company had now assembled behind us. Well, it could not be helped, I could not see anything. Dawn had already started to set in, but dense fog was hanging in the air above the meadows. That meant that I would have to reconnoiter. I briefly explained the plan to my crew. We were to scout on foot to get an overview, to ascertain whether the enemy was already in the village before us. I saw in their faces that they did not think highly of such an endeavor. They much preferred staying mounted up on their self-propelled anti-tank gun, protected against shrapnel and direct fire by its steel armor plates. No can do. If we were to probe forward with our half-tracks without accompanying infantry, we could become easy prey for enemy anti-tank gunners.

I had been riding on one of my half-tracks during the approach march, while my *Kübelwagen*, the German jeep equivalent, had followed with my two runners inside. I waived Atteneder, the driver of the *Kübelwagen,* and the second runner forward to my position. I would have to advance and would be taking them with me. I briefly instructed the commander of my half-track and then ran over to the other two self-propelled anti-tank guns with my head kept low to do the same. I explained my intent to scout on foot to every vehicle commander. I put my deputy in charge and told him how long I expected him to wait for me and from which direction I was intending to return.

To myself, I was thinking, "if I ever return!" I ordered him to send a messenger to the company and at the same time resented the fact that we had no radios. We were standing on the southern road leading to Benouville. To our right, there was a stone wall which followed the road towards the northeast and then made a turn towards the canal. I knew from the map that this had to be the boundary wall of Chateau de Benouville. We would only have to follow this wall in order to reach the village's town square. I took a deep breath before turning towards my runners and, in a low voice, shared my plan with them.

I did not know at the time that the British 6th Airborne Division was bringing a third wave of 70 gliders into a landing zone near Ranville to the east of Benouville. I also did not know that the first wave, consisting of a task force from the English 2nd (Airborne) Battalion, Oxfordshire and Buckinghamshire Light Infantry under the command of Major John Howard had already seized the two bridges at Benouville, including the one that would later be famously named "Pegasus Bridge," and that the landing forces of British 3rd Infantry Division were just beginning to go ashore on the beaches north of Caen, in the Sword landing sector.

What I also could not know was that I would become embroiled in extremely violent fighting over the days and weeks that followed, and that I would only barely manage to escape death's grasp multiple times. These events would make all the struggle I had experienced in the deserts of North Africa look meaningless in comparison.

Me on the morning of July 6, 1944, after our first attack on Benouville.

CHAPTER 1

BORN IN STORMY WATERS

On January 30, 1933, Adolf Hitler was appointed Reichskanzler (high chancellor), bringing the Nazi Party to power in Germany. On July 20 of that same year I celebrated my twelfth birthday on a date which would be of importance eleven years later. Today I sometimes wonder if I had already known the name of Adolf Hitler back then. Well, I heard the name for the first time in the radio around that time, but in 1933's Austria, my family and I had other things to worry about.

When I was born in Pottschach near Neunkirchen, Lower Austria on June 20, 1921, World War I had ended just three years before. My father had served in the Austro-Hungarian Navy at Pola for two years prior to the war. During the war itself, he had been conscripted into working at the Austro-Daimler works in the town of Wiener Neustadt, being a trained engine fitter and lathe operator.

After World War I, during the early 1920s, my father began engaging in local community work. He became a staunch member of the Social Democratic Workers' Party, dedicating all his energy to social welfare in our village. Soon he realized that the concerns of the poorest were only rarely cared about by the politicians of these harsh times. Quite the contrary: many abused their political positions to their personal advantage. Upon realizing this, my father became so frustrated that he vacated his office and left the party as a bitter man.

Oh, how bad this time was for our family! Misery, hardship, and unemployment left the greater part of the people completely hopeless. My father was tirelessly getting and losing jobs, searching constantly for sources of income to feed his family. At the time, weirs were built in the river Schwarza near our village, and many men, including him, were laboring without a break. Such work, however, was usually based on short-term projects, thus throwing the workers back into unemployment after it was done. Our family was always threatened by the dreaded word *Aussteuerung*. This meant that any social support that my father would gain during unemployment would be canceled. Poverty and despondency were omnipresent. Beggars and solicitors went from door to door, trying to get anything for themselves and their families, just to barely avoid starvation.

Even though I was a young boy at the time who did not understand what was happening in the adults' world, I was still captured by the spirit of my parents. Never will I forget how my father came home time and again, feeling so ashamed and desperate he did not have the heart to tell my mother that he had lost yet another job. Of course my mother would register and start crying. They would sit at the table, trying to bolster each other up. And me, the little nipper, would play around them, knowing that something was wrong, anxious to cheer them up. Never will I forget how my mother would then pick me up full of love, embracing me tightly. I swore to myself that I would do anything to change these conditions when I grew up. I did not want my parents to be sad. I wanted to see them happy and laughing. *Ausgesteuerte*, those were the ones walking through the streets begging for a charitable gift. No, I did not want to ever end up like that.

It is hard to imagine times like these today, but this is how they were: harsh, unminding, and without pity. When I was frolicking around with the neighbors' kids, we sometimes encountered a knot of people gathered around a house. And when they carried stretchers with covered up bodies on them out of the building, we realized that once again someone had taken their own life. There was no money for a funeral, and suicide was considered a big sin, so people were buried with haste but no honors whatsoever. Witnessing this was so degrading that the experience branded me. What had broken these people so badly that they willingly ended their life?

When I was five, I joined the Pottschach branch of the *Deutscher Turner-Bund (1919)* (DTB, "German League for Physical Exercise") at the instigation of my father. This German-nationalistic association was in fact a harbor for many eventual national socialists. Why my father, being a social democrat himself, put me into this club of all things remains a mystery to me. Perhaps because the association's club house was near our home and he wanted to start my physical education at a young age. As far as I can remember, there was no sign of ideological indoctrination at the DTB. Everything was completely about sports. What beliefs our demonstrators held we hardly ever noticed, as we were too young and not really interested in this world that the adults lived in. They were persons to be respected unconditionally, making them unapproachable.

On one of his jobs, my father had bartered a radio from an unemployed radio engineer. To me this was an astounding sensation. I was fascinated by this device that heralded news from cities and countries that I could hardly imagine. Of course I had a rough idea of Germany, so for the first time I noticed how in the early thirties a new development took place in that country. One name got mentioned over and over again: Adolf Hitler. His device of *"Arbeit und Brot für jeden"* ("work and bread for all") seemed reasonable to me, and it seemed to fall on fertile ground with the people of Germany. Both Germany and Austria were mere travesties of their former empires, but many of the populace still had upheld the national pride of old. This was just the itch that Adolf Hitler's propositions seemed to scratch. While other political parties were arguing, he managed to appeal to the people, thus winning them over. And the people did not ponder for long. Every kind of lasting improvement was better than the current life. The dictate of the Treaty of Versailles, cessions of vast territories, occupied areas and extensive war reparations did their part to cause resentment.

In Austria, these topics were discussed as well. Today I know that some leading politicians like Dr. Karl Renner deemed Austria nonviable, viewing an *Anschluss* with Germany as the only reasonable option and thus propagating it. Nobody believed in this "Rest of Austria." The right of self-determination that President Wilson had proclaimed in his Fourteen points seemingly did not apply to the Austrian people. Quite the opposite, it appeared as if the rest of the world wanted to have its share of the prize. Not just non-German speaking regions, but also areas like South Tirol were ripped out of Austria. All these circumstances, from unemployment and misery to discontent over the victorious powers' conduct, were evocative of an impending catastrophe at that time already.

Adolf Hitler capitalized on all this. He found just the right words, and the German people saw him as their savior from all the nightmarish hardship that had surrounded them. Unemployment rates started to drop, a spirit of optimism set in, and life in general seemed worth living again. The radio heralded it. The world had changed inside Germany. The wind of change was blowing there. I spent a lot of time sitting by the radio, not getting enough of the music and the news. What else was I to do? While us boys were always afoot, the radio told of things far, far away.

My friends and me (standing at the right) at a local lake.

After I graduated from Pottschach elementary school, I entered the Gloggnitz middle school which I attended until 1935. During this time, fateful developments took place within Austria as well. It was the time of the Austrian Civil War. We young boys had also caught word of clashes between the different parties. All groups had their own armed formations at the time. Above all, the *Heimwehr* (Home Guard) and the *Republikanischer Schutzbund* (Republican Protection League) tried to best each other during their marches. Eventually it came to the events of February 1934. We only heard of the violent clashes in Vienna over the radio. But a short time later, I would have to face their consequences directly.

In the summer of 1934, my parents and my aunt had agreed on me staying with her in Vienna for a few days. So I took a train to the Vienna western railroad station, where my aunt was already waiting. She was keeping house for a Jewish family, and I lived with them. The family was very nice to me, the country-bred boy, and I could not complain about not getting enough to eat. My aunt showed me around the city, and we spent most of the time visiting every corner of Vienna. When this Jewish family eventually emigrated in 1937, perhaps acknowledging the signs of the times, my aunt followed them to England in 1939.

In Vienna I was confronted by the consequences of the February 1934 events. I saw ruined houses and house fronts peppered with bullet holes. For the 13-year-old boy that I was, this was of course a big deal, and I reverently walked past the destroyed buildings, not really understanding what had happened here. In Vienna, too, the spirit of the times was almost tangible. People were crestfallen and cheerless. Hardly anyone was laughing. I saw beggars and men wearing signs asking for work. Time and again people would talk about Germany like it was a faraway land where everything was better. Great desperation here, great hope there.

After I was able to graduate middle school with honors in the summer of 1935, my class teacher Mister Krausch talked to my parents and recommended that I receive some higher technical education, having recognized my enthusiasm and talent in that field. However, my father had lost his job at the Semperit corporation during my final year at school, making him unemployed again. So I also had to bring home some money. You had to pay tuition fees back then, and even though these fees were reduced for low-income households, it had to be paid regularly. My father called on the municipality to get me a spot, but he was met with rejection. Thus I had no other choice but to stay at home for a year and try to earn some coin with the occasional job.

In September of 1937, I was finally able to move to engineering school. For two years I had worked hard to reach that goal, and I had succeeded on my own. By now there was also enough money to pay the reduced tuition fees for myself. I was granted a second chance to get closer to my dream job, and I was determined to not waste that opportunity. When the German Wehrmacht marched into Austria less than a year later in March 1938, and our country was renamed Ostmark, I was 16 years old, a student at the upper high school for mechanical engineering in Wr. Neustadt, and deeply convinced that soon I would work as an engineer for the benefit of all people. I wanted to build and develop machines that would make life easier, sparing people from hard labor. Well, for the time being, things were to go differently.

CHAPTER 2

HITLER ARRIVES

The German military occupation was a surprise to nobody. Quite the opposite! It seemed that the Austrian people breathed a sigh of relief. All of Adolf Hitler's successes in Germany were met with almost unexceptional reverence in Austria. And since their attempt at seizing power via a coup d'état in the 1930s, the national socialists managed to prevail in Austria despite being prosecuted by the government, even increasing their sympathy among the populace.

After crossing the border, German troops were welcomed with enthusiasm, the Austrian Army stayed in its barracks, and there was no sign of armed resistance. Suddenly, swastika flags were everywhere, and the Nazis that hitherto had worked in the underground immediately rallied. It was unbelievable how so many people suddenly and keenly supported a political party that had been illegal the day before. And where did all these flags and armbands come from! It was as if some resourceful tailors had sewn them months before to be ready for this day. Everything from swastika flags to the tiniest stick pin. Everything was already there.

On the eve of March 12, 1938, the national socialists already held a big torchlight procession. Everyone was up and out. The Nazis, who had no uniforms yet and thus were recognizable only by their white knee socks, were busy organizing. Orders were issued, marching groups formed, people lined up. The village was full of swastika flags. It seemed to us that everyone was carried along. Nobody stood up and said, "Stop it!" No, quite the opposite, some tried to best each other with their praise for "our" new *Führer*, Adolf Hitler. After all, he was one of us – an Austrian, just like us. Austria, however, had now become a part of history, because now we were citizens of the German Reich. The *Führer* had brought us home into the Reich.

And we, the youth? Me and my friends? The radio had heralded these developments, of course, and I too was convinced that times would get better now. All the success in Germany, the newfound pride, the feeling of community – those were affirmative terms to me. Thus we liked our new rulers. Not enough to have joined one of those illegal organizations before, but still enough to gaze in amazement at the procession and be convinced that I was now part of a big development.

As I said, there was nobody to make us hold on and think. Those who looked pondering, who maybe had a sense of foreboding, were all too few. A storm of enthusiasm had completely occupied our minds. To ask today how this could have happened, how one could be so blind, is simply overbearing. The events had sucked us in, we were fascinated and carried away by them. That is just how it was. Too compelling was the prospect of a better life.

Soon we were marching along, screaming *"Ein Volk – ein Reich – ein Führer!"* (One People – one Reich – one Führer!), singing marching songs, and going into raptures over the prevalent atmosphere. Then, on March 15, 1938, just days after German troops had crossed the border, the word was that the Führer is coming to Vienna. In trucks we were taken to the city. No idea where they had come from, but they were there. We jumped in, and off we went. After arriving in Vienna, I saw the largest crowd of people I had ever seen in my life. Everyone was drawn to Hotel Imperial. There, the crowd was waiting in anticipation. Then, on a balcony, the Führer Adolf Hitler emerged. I could see him clearly. The throng broke out in cries of "Sieg Heil," and everyone put their right arm up. Amazed by the scene, I thought to myself, "This is unreal!" A few weeks before, the Nazis had been persecuted and now, all around me, old or young, everyone was cheering the man up there as if it had always been this way. At the Heldenplatz (Heroes' Square), Hitler gave a speech from the balcony of the Hofburg before a cheering crowd. Then the Führer rode along the Ringstraße boulevard in a large silver limousine while airplane formations zoomed over our heads. All of this was accompanied by a never-ending frenetic applause of the billowing masses. And I, at seventeen years, was in the middle of this tumult.

In the evening we went home exhausted and stirred up. I felt that I had been part of something special. Today I sometimes wonder if I must have realized something, or if I maybe had overlooked anything. Nothing comes to my mind. In Vienna at least, when I saw those heated masses of people, shouting ecstatically towards this man that neither I nor all others actually knew, it seemed clear to me. "This is alright, this is just!"

The world of the adults, an unquestionable entity back in the day, was approving of the change, so we the youth did as well. Moreover, our lack of life experience made us embrace this extraordinary spirit even more than them. When I watch interviews of contemporary witnesses stressing that they had already known it back then, I have to confess that I had not. No, quite the opposite. My environment, my family, and I were all convinced to be standing at the beginning of a new golden era. Suddenly everyone was doing better, and we should have immediately gone into opposition? Not in the slightest did I question the regime. These lines shall record the truth and will not serve as an excuse for my deeds, but if I were to write anything different here today it would be a lie. It would simply not confer the truth, but rather conform to the convictions of today.

The new rulers became a part of everyday life at an unbelievable pace. Immediately the *Nationalsozialistische Partei*, abbreviated NSDAP, took over. Everything and everyone was focused on the Führer and his will. Quick progress was made, and I joined the *Hitlerjugend* (Hitler Youth), becoming a *Hitlerjunge* (Hitler Boy). My father was given back his job at the Semperit corporation in short order. Even he, being an old-school social democrat, seemed relieved to sense a clear direction and a common goal for everyone. Joining the *Hitlerjugend* or HJ was not much of a hassle. Our symbols of recognition were a uniform consisting of a brown shirt, short black trousers, as well as belt, scarf, and an armband with a swastika on it. Soon I acquired a taste for this new feeling of companionship. We spent evenings camping, engaged in varied sports, marching a lot, and playing scouting games. All that felt like a great adventure and made you proud to be part of it.

In the summer of 1939, a large HJ camp was held in Seebenstein, south of Wr. Neustadt. Different HJ formations from our region and also farther away attended. Sports and camp life came first, but we also received some premilitary training. We were drilled, shot with small bore rifles, marched with a compass, and played scouting games where groups tried to capture each other's flags. So we got a foretaste of the soldier's life we were predetermined to live.

In the nearby city of Wr. Neustadt, the huge works and hangars of the *Wiener Neustädter Flugzeugwerke* (aircraft works) were erected seemingly overnight. The old locomotive factory was put into operation again, and the airfield was crammed full of German *Luftwaffe* airplanes that always impressed us when zooming above our heads. Simply put, everything was in motion. In short order Wr. Neustadt, the city where I was going to school, had transformed from a desolate town into one teeming with activity, and we all went with the flow.

In the summer of 1939, I took up a holiday job at the Semperit corporation. I was still there in the first days of September during the outbreak of World War II. On September 1, the entire company staff was assembled in the park on the premises, where some loudspeakers had been installed. The Führer was to give a speech, which we were awaiting tensely. And there it was, his unmistakable voice. Heralding that the persecution and bullying of Germans in Poland would no longer be tolerated, that violence would be met with violence. The Polish border had been crossed by German formations at 05:45. We were now at war with the Polish state and people. It was, so he said, time to strike back.

War – at the time something which I barely had any concept of. Back then there had been no "First" World War, just *the* World War. Sometimes the men would tell of it. Oftentimes stating that we, the Austrians and Germans, had not actually lost but fallen victim to a great treason. But what "war" itself meant, that our fathers said nothing of. The whole deal seemed like honest business in my mind: naturally gentlemanly, honorable and far away from mauled bodies, dead civilians and all the other horrors. Some had been killed, but their names were inscribed on a warrior memorial in the middle of town, which dignified the topic enough in my view to make us not forget the dead. So now we were at war with Poland. It all seemed not that bad actually, since the radio spoke of victory after victory of the advancing Wehrmacht. Declarations of war by other states such as Great Britain and France remained unnoticed at first. Later, they were acknowledged reluctantly with a spirit of "We will show you all. Now is the time for revenge!"

On a forced march with other HJ comrades. To my left, rifle shouldered, my best friend Fritz Döcker. He would become a reserve officer like me and had the luck of surviving the war. As a lieutenant he was captured by the Russians in 1944, returning only in 1947.

Our weekly highlight was visiting the *Wochenschau* (newsreel). Uplifting music sounded, soldiers marched with a winning smirk towards an unseen enemy, Panzers menacingly broke out of the bushes and dive bombers, called Stuka, plunged down with a deafening howl. In our minds we HJ boys were of course already there, seeing ourselves shouting orders as a tank commander or with both hands on the control stick of a Messerschmitt fighter plane. After the viewing, we excitedly discussed what we had seen, talked about different vehicles, knowing everything about types and armaments and having nothing but contempt, ridicule, or sometimes pity for our enemies. We did not know them after all. I had never met a Pole, known no French, and imagined every Englishman to be a pretentious lord. Anxious to miss anything, we absorbed everything associated with the war and our German Wehrmacht.

Soon I had proven my skills as a leader, and so in spring 1940, I was sent to *HJ-Gebietsführerschule* (local leader academy) in Waidhofen an der Ybbs. There, I was delighted to meet more of my kind. We were dedicated to our tasks. Physical education was of utmost importance. Every morning we were mustered at the flag before doing a cross-country run. On top of that, there were additional exercises during the day. Eventually we all qualified for the HJ sports badge, which was quite an achievement – you had to perform really well to earn it. And of course there were all sorts of competitions. Winning these was deemed essential, driving our ambitions and making us give our best. In the time between, we were drilled or attended theoretical lectures. All in preparation for our duty as leaders. I never closely examined the purpose of these lessons; all that counted was that I earned trust, that my accomplishments were acknowledged, and that I was expected to pass on my knowledge to younger comrades.

To younger *comrades*, not *children*. "Hard as Krupp steel, tough as leather, and swift as greyhounds" was how our Führer wanted his Hitler Youth, and we were not want to disappoint. *Our* Führer, not *the* Führer, that was how we called Adolf Hitler. So-called "worldview lessons" made sure things stayed that way and that we were convinced of our doing – even of the German *Volk* as a whole – more and more.

In the summer of 1940, after the Wehrmacht had steamrolled France – an enemy hitherto thought all too superior – in just six incredible weeks, I graduated from engineering school with flying colors.

During the summer ahead of the final year, I had done a special kind of holiday work together with three fellow students at the Borsig corporation, located in Berlin-Tegel, so in the "Old Reich." The point was to get an impression of the capability of the German industry. Leaving my Ostmark home for the first time and going to Germany was truly exciting. We all took the same train to Berlin and were met with kindness at every moment. It appeared to me that we from the Ostmark were especially welcome, even though I sometimes was under the impression that we were traveling from the back country to the big city. At least a few "Reich Germans" gave me that feeling when they talked big about Berlin.

At the corporation, we quickly made new friends, casting all reservations between Germans and "Ostmarkians" aside. Naturally, our new friends were keen to show us around. Equally naturally, us "New Germans" being struck with amazement filled them with pride. Of course the Berliners enjoyed being seen as the privileged citizens of a new Greater German capital city. These weeks went by in a flash, and it was time to go home. We asked our supervisor if the way home could be arranged in a more lavish fashion, that is to say, we wanted to take a detour to several large cities along the way. Not only was that request granted immediately, everything was paid for as well. So we traveled by train via Munich, Königssee, Salzburg, the Tauern mountains, and Bad Gastein to Klagenfurt in southern Austria, and finally across the Semmering pass back to our home region. I will never forget this journey in which so many impressions were left on me in such a short time. I saw the Alps for the first time and got to know various regions and their people – always just for a short time but long enough to keep everlasting memories. Back at home, we were understandably met with a lot of curiosity, having to tell at great length about our discovery of Berlin and the long voyage home. Our empurpled tales added to the enjoyment of our listeners.

The year 1940 came and passed. Winter began, and by the start of 1941, the time had come. After I had finished my education as mechanical engineer, I received my draft notice. In July of 1940, I had celebrated my 19th birthday. Many of my friends who had not attended a higher school or had already earned their diploma were now deployed to the front. To be honest, I felt a bit guilty about still staying at home at 19 years. The

Wehrmacht was rushing from victory to victory, and I was still sitting at home. My brother on the other hand, being eight years older than me, had participated in the invasion of Poland. With excitement he had told me about the campaign of our troops. And never did he seem to be pondering or gloomy about it. Now was apparently the time to prove my worth. At least in my opinion, since my parents were not too delighted of the draft notice I was shoving in their faces. They would rather have seen their second son become an engineer "essential to the war effort."

My views were different. Even more so, my draft papers enlisted me for the artillery unit stationed in Siegen, Westfalen. *Artillery?* That was too far in the back for my taste. Without hesitation I went to the district military headquarters in Wiener Neustadt and expressed my concerns. My willingness was delightfully noted, and I was allocated to a *Panzerjägerabteilung* (anti-tank detachment) in Ludwigshafen at the river Rhine, near Mannheim.

At the mustering, I had already stated fervently that I wanted to become reserve officer. If I were to serve the fatherland, I would do so from the front and as an officer. And I was not the only one. My best friend Fritz Döcker had the same conviction, and I mentioned him during the visit. Gleefully I told him that our requests had been acknowledged. We even drank a glass of schnapps to the occasion. And my parents? In the days that followed, I caught my mother looking at me for longer than usual. With a lot of love but also sadness in her eyes. "Oh well, it won't be too bad," I thought to myself. None of the young men from the neighborhood had been killed in action yet, and the few local strangers that had were then even buried at the local cemetery. So their remains had been brought home.

CHAPTER 3

MAKING OF A
TANK HUNTER

On February 16, 1941, we both reported to *Panzerjägerersatzabteilung 33* (33rd Reserve Anti-Tank Battalion) in Ludwigshafen am Rhein. The distance of 800 km (500 mi) from home did not bother me. From friends that had been drafted earlier, I knew that there was hardly any free time during basic training, so what better use of that little time than to explore an entirely new town. When Fritz and I had first mentioned our draft notices, there was a big fuss – our friends congratulated us, patting our backs. We were both filled with pride and of course envisioned ourselves strolling through town as handsome lieutenants in magnificent uniforms, admired by everyone around.

The only drop of bitterness among this euphoric mood was the fact that I had met a girl I liked. Helena was her name, just as in the Greek myth, and so beautiful was she that not even Ulysses would have been able to resist her. I actually had known her for some time, but only shortly before had she lit the fire of a young love in my heart.

Duty called, however, and it was time to tell her goodbye. We promised to write to each other to lighten the longing. With the thought of my Helena and best wishes from caring parents in my heart, I began the journey northwards to do my part in achieving the *Endsieg* (final victory) of the German Wehrmacht.

Our arrival at our new home was disillusioning. *Panzerjägerersatzabteilung 33* was stationed at Ludwigshafen near Mannheim am Rhein and also used the training grounds of the nearby Schwetzingen Panzer barracks, roughly 15 km (9 mi) to the southeast of Mannheim. Apparently the barracks personnel were just waiting for reserve officer trainees like us. Now I was completely in the hands of the German Army. Being used to leading *Hitlerjungen*, it was now my turn to follow orders. First on the agenda was infantry training, which meant field exercises in the surrounding area, wearing either our dress or field uniforms. The dress uniforms served as training garments in order to spare our field uniforms. After at first being bewildered by this practice, we soon realized the point of it. Time and again we had to clean our dress uniforms right after an exhausting field exercise.

The soil at the Ludwigshafen training grounds was red like brick-dust and never did it take long to cover us in dust or loam, depending on the weather. Our instructors seemingly wanted to make sure we were covered in red soil from head to toe. "Fresh dirt adorns the soldier," they remarked. I have to say that this part of training did not feel like harassment, as I was convinced that I would have to implement these skills one day. But it was not easy. The importance of infantry training was stressed extensively, and we literally felt it in our bones. And of course we were treated just like the reserve officer trainees that we were. Our main caregivers were NCOs and sergeants, while we rarely met any officers.

There were, however, exceptional men who cared for their boys. These of course left lasting impressions. Among the NCOs, there were all different types of character. Most of those who had been to the front were treating us much more humanely than those who were "in the rear with the gear," who wanted to distinguish themselves with their dashing performance as drill instructors. Aside from field exercises we marched or fired our *Karabiner 98* (K98), the Wehrmacht's service rifle at the time. Usually we marched the long way to the shooting range and then marched back to the barracks late in the evening. Marches up to or even over 40 km (25 mi) in full gear were not a rarity. These were extremely demanding for many, and several men just collapsed from exhaustion.

And after finally arriving at the barracks all dirty, sweaty and at the end of our tethers, we were not allowed off duty – no, it was time to clean our equipment. The instructors would then check our gear and oftentimes impose more thorough cleaning work or extra duty on us. If you had blisters on your feet, you had to tend to them after duty by yourself. Only the worst cases were treated at the sickbay in order to prevent a sepsis. The staff there was not eager to admit patients.

Seeing the point in these measures was more difficult. Especially so right before the weekend. Under alleged objections to our performance, our duty could be prolonged until only a fraction of our free time was left. One particularly popular game was the "fancy-dress ball," where we were mustered multiple times in short succession, each time wearing different gear. This would often occur on Saturdays, with up to fifteen different dresses within an hour before lunch, followed by some drill and an air alert, and then we were busy cleaning everything once again. The only calm time was during lunch, which we had to attend in a perfectly neat uniform, of course. All this ate away at our nerves; only our sense of comradery helped us cope. In these barracks, living together on a limited space, sharing the same hardships, challenges, and strains, we formed a strong bond.

Basic training offered some pleasant surprises as well. During our runner exercises, we had to draw maps of the surrounding terrain and navigate the area using a compass. Eventually we had to find a lonely homestead, where our instructors awaited us with a glass of schnapps. That we surely did not expect. When it came to individual training, we were encouraged to show a top performance through all sorts of competitions. And we all were up to the challenge. Our swearing-in ceremony was especially imposing. The whole event was meant to leave a lasting impression with us young recruits – successfully, I might add. At the top of our voice we spoke the oath:

"Ich schwöre bei Gott diesen heiligen Eid, dass ich dem Führer des Deutschen Reiches und Volkes, Adolf Hitler, dem Oberbefehlshaber der Wehrmacht, unbedingten Gehorsam leisten und als tapferer Soldat bereit sein will, jederzeit für diesen Eid mein Leben einzusetzen."

("I swear by god this sacred oath, to the Führer of the German Reich and People, Adolf Hitler, supreme commander of the Wehrmacht, I will serve with unquestioning obedience and, as a valiant soldier, I will be ready to honor this oath with my own life.")

What astounded me was that there was no mention of a fatherland or homeland. We were sworn in on the Führer, Adolf Hitler himself. Well, we did not waste a second thought on that. Happy to complete our basic training, us reserve officer trainees were looking forward to the future. After the tough and demanding weeks of basic training, we were subject to specialist weapons training. For us, this meant getting to know the *3.7-cm-Panzerabwehrkanone 35/36* (3.7 cm Pak 35/36) anti-tank gun. At the start of the war, this gun had been the Wehrmacht's primary means of combating tanks. By now it had mostly been phased out of front-line duty.

During the French campaign of 1940, its caliber proved too small to penetrate the thicker armor of French *Char* and British *Matilda* tanks. Soon, larger caliber guns like the 50mm Pak 38 or the 75 mm Pak 40 were deployed. Since the Pak 35/36 was similar to the Pak 38, the former continued to be in service, mostly for training purposes.

Over the course of the war, the gun earned the nickname *Panzeranklopfgerät* (lit. tank knocking device). That name spoke for itself. Only a new type of ammunition, the *Stielhohlladungsgranate* (a shaped-charge shell), helped a bit after its introduction in 1942. It could penetrate up to 180 mm (6 ½ in) of steel armor, but its range was rather low, so you had to let an enemy tank close in to around 200 yds. Not the best option during a firefight.

The Pak 35/36 was a drawn gun, consisting essentially of a barrel and breech, a sloped gun shield of 5 mm (0.2 in) thickness, a split-trail with two round beams and two wheels. Two soldiers were enough to successfully operate the gun. We soon realized the true meaning of "drawn" during the weeks that followed, not only getting to know all the weapon's ins and outs but putting the gun into position manually countless times. Always pressed for time, of course, since "enemy tank ahead!" was a recurring theme. With its combat weight of 330 kg (725 lbs.), the gun was still light enough for us to complete all these tasks in a timely fashion. In secret, however, we were happy not to serve in the heavy artillery.

After the first shots with live ammunition, we also lost all interest in serving with the Panzer troops. We witnessed the effect that even a small 3.7 cm projectile could have on a practice target. The shell's tungsten core had bored right through the steel target – and the effect on anything behind it was ominous to us.

Driving a tank into concentrated fire of a whole anti-tank platoon seemed like suicide. Surviving inside a tank always depended on the thickness of its armor ... as well as individual luck. Time and again we realized that there was no single spot on the battlefield that offered better chances of surviving the fight than any other. Whether on land, at sea, or in the air, death had all kinds of faces and your odds were equally good (or bad) everywhere. The solution offered to us was strict drills and demanding a lot from yourself, which was presented as life-prolonging, We exercised each and every step until it became second nature. Eventually we were dreaming of them. And of course we were brushed up on our infantry training from time to time. A gun crew consisted of four men, who all were soon committed to each other and "ready to take on all that may come!", or so we thought.

After training with the gun, some of us were chosen for additional driving lessons. I was one of the lucky few, and earned a license for motorcycles, passenger cars, as well as trucks. By late April 1941, still during our gun training with the Pak 35/36, we were subject to strict examinations testing our tropical fitness. This gave us an idea of where our first deployment to the front would be. Those who passed would have their trial by fire in Africa. And we wanted it.

In fact our *Panzerjägerersatzabteilung 33* formed the reserve for *Panzerjägerabteilung 33* (PzJgAbt33, 33rd Anti-Tank Battalion). Which meant that any losses suffered by *Panzerjägerabteilung 33* were compensated by new recruits from our *Ersatz* unit at home. After completing their training, the *Ersatz* was immediately sent to the front.

In April 1941, Panzerjägerabteilung 33 was assigned to the 15th Panzer Division. Originally formed in November 1940 from parts of the 33rd Infantry Division, it was shifted to Africa starting April 1941. The first German troops there, commanded by Major General Erwin Rommel, had appeared on February 11, 1941, just days before the beginning of my service.

One of the rare calm minutes during basic training. Our group (I stand right at the back) with our NCO instructor (front left). He wore a wound stripe, meaning he had already been to the front, and was one of the more likable instructors.

German newsreels had made a big fuzz, and there were rumors about how Rommel had ordered his troops to drive multiple rounds through Tripoli in a big parade in order to make local British spies believe that a much larger force was present. We young soldiers could not know if there was any truth to that rumor, but nevertheless the story was impressive. Starting in early April 1941, the 15th Panzer Division was shipped from Italian Naples across the Mediterranean Sea to Libya. Once there, it was to be deployed at Tobruk, a coastal town staunchly defended by the British and relentlessly attacked by the Germans. Brigadier General Heinrich von Prittwitz und Gaffron, then commander of the 15th Panzer Division, had been killed on April 10th during forward reconnaissance by a direct hit from an Australian anti-tank gun. So, men from a unit like mine, but on the other side, had killed my division's commanding officer even before the unit had arrived in the theater of war. After us young recruits had figured out which unit's *Ersatz* we were in February 1941, we always watched those parts of the German newsreels concerning developments in Africa with increased interest. After passing the examinations on tropical fitness, we knew full well: We're going to Africa!

CHAPTER 4

AFRIKA KORPS

After completing my three-month training, my comrades (including, to my great joy, my friend Fritz) and I were housed in private quarters at Enkenbach near Kaiserslautern, Germany. Those were pleasurable circumstances for us since we were able to escape the daily grind inside the barracks into a civil environment. We were not idle, however, receiving tropical uniforms and a lot of other equipment.

The officers, as well as the "*Spieß*", meaning the highest-ranking NCO of the company, began making dispositions and organizing the preparations for a redeployment to Africa. Getting new uniforms and gear made us sporty, and we had our own little fancy balls. In addition, there were lots of lessons aimed at preparing us for the environmental conditions of the continent as well as African people and their customs. We learned about scorpions and sandstorms, about Bedouins and about how much water the human body needs to survive. There were also small booklets handed to us for further reading, containing everything about the lands and peoples of North Africa. And of course, we kept moving out to refresh or improve our infantry skills in the field.

In May and July 1941, Rommel's lucky star had risen over Africa. My parent unit, *Panzerjägerabteilung 33*, had been involved in the fighting and suffered its first losses. At that time, the detachment was composed of a headquarters company for logistics, a signal platoon for communications and three *Panzerabwehrkompanien* (1ˢᵗ to 3ʳᵈ PzAbwKp). Each of these anti-tank companies consisted of three platoons, each fielding four 37 mm Pak 35/36.

Due to casualties of dead and wounded during the fighting around Sollum and Halfaya Pass in June it was high time to ferry in replacements from Germany. So, leaving our private quarters in late June, our whole detachment was put on trains and sent across the Alps and through all of Italy to Tarent. When we arrived there, the surprise was great. In front of us in the harbor were three huge cruise ships. Full of astonishment we learned the names of the three giants: *Ozeania, Neptunia,* and *Marco Polo.* The ships *Ozeania* and *Neptunia* were two sister ships grossing around 20,000 GRT each. It was agreed with the Italians that each crossing was to consist of half German and half Italian troops and supplies each.

The ships were actually passenger ships which had been converted to troopships. For this purpose they had been equipped with 105 mm guns for submarine defense at the bow and stern, and 20 mm twin flak guns against air attack distributed over the whole ship. With mixed feelings we went on board. On deck while we already received life jackets, rumors quickly spread and we learned that the Mediterranean was teeming with British submarines. Just in April a complete convoy consisting of five freighters was destroyed by those. Altogether more than 1,500 soldiers and sailors had drowned. This didn't necessarily comfort us.

Once on board, we witnessed the ships being loaded. Thousands of soldiers like us were streaming on board, and heavy cranes lifted all sorts of goods packed in large crates, but also vehicles and guns on board to disappear in the ships' bellies. There was an incredible amount of activity, and with interest we observed the Italian dockworkers, who carried out the loading with a lot of gesticulation, but skillfully. At the onset of the evening we got to our bunks, lying as tight as sardines in a can. After one night inside the cramped ship, we departed on the next day. On deck, leaning against the railing, we watched the spectacle unfold. Ahead of us our escort, consisting of some sleek Italian destroyers, began to move, and our converted cruise ships followed lumberingly. One lonely German Ju 88 warplane appeared in the sky to spot surfacing submarine in time to warn our Italian companions. The ships started going on a zigzag course for increased safety.

After some time we went on to befriending the Italian anti-aircraft gun crews. They immediately proved to be very approachable. To overcome the language barrier, we tried communicating with hands and feet, as the German saying goes. They let us man the guns and soon we eagerly performed targeting practice. Patting each other's backs, we managed to ease the tension. We found our Italian allies to be quite nice fellows who told us about their homeland with a lot of emotion in their voice. The tension during departure as well was our training on those AA guns was soon replaced by the monotony of travel over sea, however, and after a chilly breeze had set in we eventually decided to go below deck, where we also spent the night. The next day nothing but the same thing, with nothing happening. Finally we reached Tripoli harbor, Libya, after two days at sea without special incidents.

Targeting practice with our Italian brothers in arms (left) on a 20 mm anti-air gun aboard *Neptunia*. This helped distract and give us confidence during the journey.

Upon arrival in Tripoli, we were immediately charmed by the Mediterranean coastal city. Flat-roofed houses with tall minarets in between dominated the townscape. The shore was flat and the streets framed by palm trees. In the harbor there was a frenzy of activity in expectation of our ships' arrival. Something that also welcomed us immediately, however, was incredible heat. Having not felt its full force at sea thanks to a cool salt-breeze, the sun was beating down on us relentlessly as soon as we slowed down to enter the harbor. We began sweating inside our uniforms, and the sweat ran into our eyes below our uniform caps.

Immediately the unloading commenced. We went ashore and assembled in front of the harbor office building, where trucks were already standing ready for us. There I saw the distinctive symbol of the German Afrika Korps for the first time: a palm tree with the trunk halved by the swastika. Both were simply painted onto the former field gray doors, with the whole truck around them being hastily covered in sand-colored paint.

Disembarking from the ship and carrying our gear was already enough to cover us in sweat. We quickly realized that any unnecessary movement was to be avoided. But to no avail, the tail lifts were dropped, we started loading and eventually mounted the trucks. The ride commenced, and instantly we discovered another inconvenience even worse than the heat: dust. It got to us on the load bed from the sides as well as from behind, and everyone rummaged around for a handkerchief to hastily tie around mouth and nose. Our ride led through Tripoli and, along a straight asphalt road, eastward. Upon leaving the harbor we saw the first locals populating the streets in their customary attire. We also noticed veiled women for the first time. Donkeys and a few camels strolled by on the street and were enveloped by our cloud of dust. After some time we reached "Km 5." *Kilometer 5* was the name of the reception and acclimatization camp established in the desert. Being located in the desert roughly 5 kilometers (3 miles) east of Tripoli, it was named that way for a lack of any nearby prominent terrain feature.

This camp was now to be our home for the first days in Africa. Here I also received the news that from now on I was assigned to headquarters company of *Panzerjägerabteilung* 33 as a driver and messenger. Our first mission as newbies was to get accustomed to the climate of the theater of operations as well as familiarize with the car pool. The first days went by smoothly. We established contact with other German soldiers who had been here for longer and tried drawing from their experience and, most of all, to hear the latest news from the front lines. Sollum and Halfaya Pass had been defended successfully, and the latest reports indicated the British being on the retreat.

I immediately noticed how faithfully the soldiers were talking about Rommel. His vigorous decision making after he first arrived in Africa had found much appreciation among the lower ranks, and the victories achieved had convinced them of his skill as a leader. The entire Afrika Korps was in high spirits after it managed to beat the British and "… sent it into the desert!" Our units had developed into a powerful force with great morale.

Rommel and his officers were leading from the front, a fact thanks to which many important decisions could be made without delay. As a sign of affiliation, the Afrika Korps armband was introduced for all men of the German Afrika Korps – a strip of fabric with the word AFRIKAKORPS stitched in silver on a green background, which every soldier was wearing on his lower left sleeve. This of course contributed to a sense of unity among the men and everyone, including me, proudly wore that stripe on his uniform.

Any Italians we encountered were also regaining some visible confidence. Here, the difference between officers, non-commissioned officers (NCOs) and enlisted men was greater, especially when it came to morale and fighting spirit. While our officers, NCOs and enlisted men all shared the same rations, the Italian Army handled this very differently. They had four different kinds of menu, strictly divided into officer, sergeant, NCO and enlisted men rations. Officers were served three-course meals while the lowest ranks often suffered from starvation. We were surprised to find that the humble soldier was not considered to be of much worth in the Italian Army. This helped us better understand the reports of lacking combat prowess of our southern allies. There were exceptions to be pointed out as well, however, and time and again we heard stories of Italian soldiers showing great courage during the bitter fighting in June. The different alignments among the Italians were also interesting to me. There were followers of Mussolini as well as the Italian king. Men aligned with *Il Duce* were fighting more doggedly, while men true to the king somewhat lacked enthusiasm in the field. All of them admired us Germans, however, and I had heard that when the Italians were fighting directly at our side, their fighting spirit improved considerably.

On African soil, shortly before deploying to the front line.

Back in the military camp, the daily challenges of the desert climate embraced us again. Soon we got to know several annoying fellows: sand fleas, scorpions as well as sand vipers and adders. The camp's close surroundings featured expansive cactus fields, which were home to all kinds of critters. Sand fleas and scorpions proved to be the most annoying. The camp was made up of barracks and tents erected right on the desert soil. Consequently, we had to welcome various "guests" on the floor every morning. Every day, soldiers were stung by scorpions and had to be treated at the medics' tent. So we quickly developed a habit of tying our shoes' shafts closed after doffing them in the evening or shaking them out in the morning. This applied to all things and items in general which were left unattended for a short while – all kinds of wildlife could have crawled inside.

In addition, the sun was of course very discomforting. If we were to deploy to the front-lines right after arriving, we probably would have collapsed after a short while. Acclimatization was of utmost necessity and importance. We realized that in the midday sun every kind of movement was excruciating, and that the interior of any vehicle became as hot as an oven. Water was to be consumed at any opportunity in order to avoid dehydration. Here in the rear echelon, behind the front line, there was still enough of it. Providing some form of shade, be it by putting up tarpaulins or camo netting, was paramount and our highest priority during every rest and at the beginning of every short stop.

Our desert equipment unfortunately proved to be of limited adequacy to these conditions. The uniforms had been designed based on experiences in German colonies during World War I; however, they were mostly unfit for use in the Libyan desert. Unlike British uniforms, which were made from wool, ours were made from cotton. This meant that they were cold at night, gave warmth during the day and absorbed humidity in the morning. Only our high boots proved highly useful against sharp thorns and spikes of dry desert vegetation. The tropical helmet, which had seemed very handsome back in Germany, soon turned out unsuitable. The combination caps that were handed out were much more practical. Once in combat, you would wear your steel helmet to fend off shrapnel.

As time went on, everyone collected his own custom inventory of varying uniform parts, ranging from British shorts to Wehrmacht coats and Italian uniform jackets. Our superiors, who had to endure the exact same hardships, graciously turned a blind eye to their men becoming more and more colorful. At first, however, we had to make do with the uniforms we had brought with us from Germany. We soon commenced trading a wide variety of uniform parts with Italian soldiers. To have more water available, an additional canteen proved very useful, too. These aluminum flasks, if you were lucky, were covered in soft felt which could be soaked in order to keep the inside cool through evaporation. Additionally, everyone soon had a good scarf to protect against dust as well as sunglasses to help with bright sunlight. Being in this life-hostile environment made us learn quickly.

CHAPTER 5

BAPTISM OF FIRE

In July 1941, I made my first long supply trip from Tripoli to Sollum. Half-track vehicles, which were mainly used as tractors for our light anti-tank guns, had also come with us. These had proved themselves in the hot climate without any problems. During pauses, the column was spaced out very far to offer no concentrated target, while at night we went in close formation to make the escorts' job easier as well as reducing the chance of someone getting left behind in the desert, which had happened several times before. More than just a few German and Italian soldiers were swallowed up by the desert during the fighting in North Africa, never to be seen again.

German and Italian field engineers had constructed a roughly 80 km (50 mi) long road circumventing the siege of Tobruk, so the only thing we noticed while bypassing the scene was the thundering rumble of artillery duels raging around the town. Also of note was the border between Libya and Egypt, which was demarcated by a 50 km (30 mi) long fence of barbed wire starting at the coast, crossing the road and then leading into the desert.

After our arrival at Sollum and unloading I was ordered to report to the command post of *Panzerjägerabteilung 33*. It consisted of one of the flat buildings typical for the region and a few tents. I reported and was immediately sent directly to one of the officers. He was standing in front of a tent talking to some NCOs. By his shoulder pieces I recognized him as an *Oberleutnant* (first lieutenant).

I stood to attention and reported, "Lieutenant, Private Hoeller reporting as ordered!"

He looked me over and said, "Hoeller, very good. My name is Lieutenant Meder. I am a staff officer for special deployment. I've been informed you're my new driver?"

"Yes, Lieutenant!" I confirmed.

"Very well, in the fighting of the last weeks I lost my messenger. From now on you are assigned to me and thus my new attendant. Report to the *Kraftfahroffizier* (motor pool officer), he will assign you to a motorcycle. Welcome to the front, Hoeller," he said and shook my hand. In light of this friendly gesture I must have looked quite surprised, because the non-commissioned officers who had listened to our conversation were all smiling. So, this was it. From now on I was a *Krad* messenger for the staff of *Panzerjägerabteilung 33*. The staff essentially enabled the detachment's commander to lead his force. It also had several messengers like me. This assignment meant that I would not return to Tripoli, but rather stay here.

On our way to the front lines. The man sitting on top served as air spotter to detect approaching enemy attack planes.

"Very well," I thought, "now I won't have to endure the long journey back, and also I was eager to get to the front lines." My first impression of First Lieutenant Meder had been of a positive nature, and sergeants as well as NCOs seemed likable. The motor pool officer gave me a short briefing and noted my data – in case my relatives needed to be informed of my demise. He also showed me my new quarters for the time being: a small tent on the desert floor. The ground had not been prepared much, just a few layers of rocks had been piled up in a circle around the tent. "Against the shrapnel," the officer proclaimed.

From an NCO, who was responsible for the staff's vehicles, I received my machine – a heavy BMW with a sidecar. I parked it right in front of my tent, fully fueled, to be ready at a moment's notice. My Kar 98 carbine I swapped for an MP 40 submachine gun, which was handier and less of an inconvenience while driving. It was easy to handle, but I was told to maintain it with special care in this dusty desert climate. Which meant cleaning it over and over again and oiling it as little as possible. Oil absorbed the dust, causing unwelcome jamming – not the best of things to happen when face to face with the enemy. Close to our camp was one of the three anti-tank companies. Its assortment of vehicles and ordnance was not bad at all. The Pak 35/36 that I knew well formed its main armament, for which there were half-track tractors, *leichte Zugkraftwagen Sonderkraftfahrzeug 10* (SdKfz 10), available. In addition I spotted a few Opel *Blitz* trucks, Horch medium personnel transports as well as several VW *Kübelwagen* offroad cars, called "Kübel."

Over the following days I familiarized myself with the Sollum area, getting to know some other men of the detachment as well. They hailed from all kinds of places, even Ostmärkers like me were among them, which stirred up some homelike feelings. The three anti-tank platoons of the company close to us were deployed at the pass roads near Sollum as well as Halfaya Pass; a focus of anti-tank capability between the infantry of I Battalion, *Schützenregiment 104* (104th Rifle Regiment). These soldiers had captured the pass in May, 1941 and in June, they had successfully defended it against British tank attacks. The successful defense had been made possible by the use of several 88 mm AA gun batteries in the

Sollum area. As I found out, those heavy gun batteries belonged to the first detachments of either Flakregiment 18 (AA-Regiment 18) as well as Flakregiment 33. Talking to other soldiers, I learned that Flakregiment 18 had been deployed for combat in Africa after moving over Sicily from its home garrison in Wiener Neustadt, Ostmark. Their positions were well fortified and their crews were full of confidence owing to their recent success against the British heavy tanks. All in all, the batteries deployed had disabled 91 (!) British tanks.

Soon I was ordered to report at the detachment command post, ready to start. First Lieutenant Meder was already waiting for me. "Well, Hoeller, up to the front it is. Today we're going to inspect our detachment's furthermost positions. Just take us where I point to, I already know the way by heart," he said. Off we went, racing away.

As he had announced, he pointed in some direction and we raced through the desert, passing dunes of sand and rocks shaped into bizarre patterns by the wind. Time and again I looked to the edge of my goggles to take a peek at my passenger in the sidecar. Despite the darkness setting in more and more, he seemed perfectly confident that the direction we were heading was correct. Eventually we reached our positions at Halfaya Pass. The sun had already sunk below the horizon, leaving behind a twilight in the sky. The only sign of having reached our destination was the fact that the First Lieutenant ordered me to halt. As we were standing there, the engine chugging away idling, and I took a hard look through the dusty goggles into the dark, I spotted a silhouette parting from the rocks and closing in purposefully. It was our contact. I felt relieved and secretly admired the First Lieutenant for his sense of direction. Thanks to months of experience in the North African desert he had found the way to the forward positions almost blindly.

Our front line essentially consisted of drawn-out anti-tank gun, machine gun and infantry positions nestling to the plateau's edge. A serpentine road led from the coast below up to the plateau. Halfaya Pass was the opening between the two. In the bright moonlight I had a fantastic view from the edge. One could clearly make out the sea. I reckoned that during the day this elevated area would be unbearably hot.

In our positions I recognized the familiar Pak 35/36 as well as MG 34 carriages. The dugouts were surrounded by walls of piled-up stones and only little actual digging had taken place. The rocky ground was simply too hard to get deep. The soldiers' tents were close by, utilizing each and every depression in the ground to protect against shrapnel. There was no artificial source of light to be seen, the front line men blending into the surrounding rocks and dry bushes.

Disabled British Matilda Mk II tank at the plateau behind our positions at Halfaya Pass. The number 38 had been painted on by our successful gunners to help count the British tanks that had been taken out.

Immediately, the First Lieutenant began checking on each position. Following him, I seized the opportunity to speak to soldiers from the company. They were quite welcoming and asked what was new in nearby Sollum. Well, me as a newcomer had little to talk about, so they told me about the fierce battle they had made it through in June, just a few weeks ago.

We were on our way to the next position as a sudden thunder tore through the air, followed by a surging rustle. We halted and I looked at my first lieutenant, who in turn looked at me. With his jaw dropped as if gasping for air, he screamed "Take cover!" Arms ahead I leaped as quickly as possible behind the nearest boulder, and just then the impacts commenced. With loud bangs the enemy artillery shells detonated amidst our positions. Immediately the area was illuminated as bright as day from all the explosion flashes. There were so many detonations in such a short time that it sounded like a relentlessly coherent, deafening roar. With a bright flash, a shell went down less than 20 meters (65 ft) ahead, and I could feel the shockwave generated by the blast. There was loud whirring all around, and I realized that its cause was shrapnel virtually filling the air. I observed red-hot splinters hitting nearby rocks, coming to rest in the sand and smoking. All of this took mere seconds and was over as fast as it had begun. After a moment of absolute silence, painful screaming tore through the night, followed closely by cries for a medic. You could hear the shock in this shrill voice. The screams were coming out of the darkness immediately ahead. From the position that we wanted to visit next. A semblance of "curses, we have casualties!" flashed through my mind. Since we could not hear any more gunfire, the First Lieutenant and I sprang up and ran towards the position ahead.

It was a horrific scene which was only bearable thanks to the dark. Medics were already at the site, trying to save what was left to save under a dim flashlight. The medics struggled to rescue the wounded and fallen soldiers. Two maimed bodies lay motionless while a third was writhing in pain, sobbing convulsively. The smell of burnt powder filled the air and only a twisted wreck remained in the AT gun position. Two men had been killed instantly, one had been badly wounded by shrapnel. The British shell had hit the 3.7 cm AT gun's position directly as well as its unfortunate crew in the nearby tent. A lucky shot for the Brits, a disaster for the gun crew. The low rock wall had not offered enough protection so that the tent was simply blown away.

I was standing at the site, taken aback by the sight. As the First Lieutenant was energetically directing the rescue efforts, I tried to help bring the wounded to the back into a safer area. "That went quite fast," I thought to myself. One moment we were chatting under a quiet dome of stars, the next we were caught by the reality of war and its utter cruelty. I found myself shaking a bit once the adrenaline started fading. This fire attack had caught me red-handed, while it had also been my trial of fire – although I had had different expectations of the latter.

The following weeks went by smoothly. British artillery strikes became somewhat of a routine and yes, one could actually get used to them. Only rarely did a shell hit one of our positions directly in the way I had witnessed. Most of them detonated at some distance away, which of course was anything but harmless; each shell created a downpour of shrapnel. Our own artillery answered only rarely, namely once a British position or battery had been clearly identified. We did not have enough ammunition to fire off blindly in the general direction of the enemy. For the most part, the purpose of both sides' artillery fire was to not give the opponent any peace as well as disrupting enemy activity. As always, the military had a term for this: "*Stör- oder Streufeuer*" (harassing fire or zone fire).

In mid-August of 1941 we were redeployed from Upper to Lower Sollum, closer to the coast. Lower Sollum's main feature was its large wadi – a wide dried out riverbed leading into a large bay on the coast. This area would provide additional protection against the British long-range artillery fire. The wadi also offered more green than the plateau, and with great joy we discovered some fig trees bearing ripe fruits. Fishing at sea was also possible, and we did so with minimal effort. We would simply throw a hand grenade into the water, let it detonate and then gather the fish killed by the shock wave.

Fruits and fish were a welcome improvement of our rations. Food, rations, and fresh water were a thing of their own altogether. Most of the food consisted of all kinds of canned fodder. All possible kinds. Very often sardines in oil, which in the heat often agitated one's stomach. Usually we also drank the oil to get some additional hydration. In addition, those canned sardines were a barter good coveted by the Bedouins who gave us pumpkins, dates, or other fruit in return. Italian rations were also part of the daily menu, which mostly consisted of "AM cans." We sarcastically called them *Armer Mussolini* ("poor Mussolini")–up to this day I have no idea what "AM" actually stood for. They contained fibrous donkey meat, as well as rock-hard cheese and crispbread. And, of course, sand which always found its way into the mouth, grinding between the teeth. In the newsreels they showed how in the searing heat eggs were cooked on the steel plating of our tanks. That may very well have been possible, as it was clearly hot enough, but I cannot say for sure since I never saw a single egg in all of Africa. On that same note, I hardly saw any of our tanks in the summer of 1941. So we entertained ourselves by painting white *Balkenkreuze* on the back of turtles we found near the sea. I wonder if the British found any of them during their later advance in November and, if so, what they may have thought of their discovery.

Water was always in short supply, or what was there was salty. Coffee, for example, was brewed with salt water; it tasted awful, but one got used to it. But the thirst grew more and more, and I caught myself daydreaming about drinking from the cold, clear water of the Saubach stream springing from the foot of mount Schneeberg back at home, where we used to catch trout as kids. This happened at night, too; you would reach for your full canteen to take a sip, but it never became real. We later learned a handy trick from the Italians. They put a dash of anise schnapps in their canteens. This made the water taste terrible, but the taste of anise covered up the sensation of thirst for a while. Word of this soon got around and anise schnapps became hard to get. Water from the wells, which often lay close to the sea, was often salty as well. Many of us paid for this prolonged dehydration in later years with kidney stones. This happened to me, too.

After a few months almost everyone was suffering from chronic inflammation of the kidneys and gastroenteritis. Profuse sweating during the daytime left crusts of salt on the uniform. This was exacerbated on the rare occasions when we took a bath in the sea or when we washed our uniforms in the seawater. The salt remained in the uniform's fabric. In the cold nights, a salt-rich uniform drew humidity from the sea breeze, which soon made for a wet uniform you had to wear in the cool night. The consequences were colds as well as inflammations of kidney and bladder. Everyone wore something extra around their belly at night, but colds and diarrhea were still a common problem.

Oftentimes people would carry a spade with them, to dig a small hole before relieving themselves. This was quite important, as it prevented infectious germs from getting spread by wind and dust. But sometimes one of the men had such a sudden urge that he did not have any time to dig a hole or even drop his trousers. Getting said trousers clean again without water available was another story. The Bedouins taught us to wash ourselves with sand.

People had watery diarrhea for weeks or even months on end. This was caused not by the aforementioned hypothermia, but mostly by the widespread dysentery. Once you had that, it was hard to get rid of; your condition deteriorated and the immune system weakened more and more. As if that was not enough, your liver would soon take its toll. By the end of summer, almost everyone at the front suffered from jaundice. You could see it in your comrade's eyes. We attributed our bad health to the rations and permanent inflammations within our lower bodies. I languished so much that I was almost brought to my knees. But there was not much to do about it, those who fell and would not stand up again were brought to the sickbay while the rest held their positions in more or less of a good condition.

In August 1941, there were signs everywhere that our own offensive was being prepared for. First rumors came up saying that Rommel planned attacking at the next opportunity. Only a shortage of supplies had forced him to bide his time for so long. Despite all early victories he had to accept that his next attack had to be deferred. In the meantime more and more new materiel had been brought to the front. We received new, stronger Pak 38 anti-tank guns which fired 50 mm rounds instead of the old 37 mm ones. The shells themselves had been developed to promise success even against thickly armored fighting vehicles. The new guns were somewhat larger than the old Pak 35/36, weighing a little over 900 kg (2000 lbs.). Their range was already over 9,000 meters (5.6 miles). While you could not effectively track any target at that distance, the higher muzzle velocity leading to this maximum range improved the accuracy at medium distances. Over a 1,000 meters (1,090 yd) away, their armor-piercing shells were still able to penetrate almost 50 mm (2 in) of steel. Those were good prospects when targeting British Matilda and Crusader tanks.

Initially, one of our three platoons was equipped with four Pak 38. We all commenced training with those guns immediately and straightaway noticed the difference in weight of almost 600 kg (1300 lbs.). The number of men in each gun crew was increased and training hours were mostly in the evening, when moving around was more bearable thanks to lower temperatures. In combat every man had to do his part, which meant that in a pinch the messengers were expected to also be able to handle an AT gun.

Our new 50 mm Pak 38 in action.

It was mid-August 1941, one early evening when we were just visiting one of the positions, when suddenly the alarms were sounded. One of our observation posts had detected suspicious movement. All tensed up we gazed into the desert ahead. The gun crews were readying shells, and the clacking of ammo crates revealed that the MG positions were preparing for an assault as well. The First Lieutenant's presence had a reassuring effect on the men. After some time, with the sun already setting, he decided to send a scouting party towards where the movement was supposed to have been detected. A short briefing followed; some men left our forward positions and vanished in the twilight. Anxiously, we waited. Meder readied his flare gun and its ammo, so he could light up the field ahead in the event of a firefight.

Alarm! All men had taken up their positions, tensely watching the forefront. A reconnaissance party was sent scouting. On the right, the anti-tank gun platoon's commander observes the area ahead with binoculars. My camera caught this moment as well.

Finally, after what seemed like forever, it was reported that the scouting party had returned. Darkness had already set in, and we had feared the worst. Upon returning, however, they brought a big surprise with them: four captured Englishmen. They had been ordered to recon our positions, and one of them had slipped off a rock, injuring his leg badly, perhaps even breaking it. This fall, along with the resulting unusual movement through what should have been motionless desert, was then detected by our observation post. The British had planned to wait for darkness and then bring their injured comrade back to their own lines, but our scouting party had caught them by surprise. They were so occupied with rescuing their comrade that they did not notice our men approaching. Even with the help of our soldiers, together all of them took a substantial amount of time to reach our lines. The prisoners were brought to a tent and subject to a first interrogation by Meder. This gave me plenty of time to have a good look at our opponents.

To my surprise, they looked just like us. Well, what had I expected? An English lord, strolling around the desert with cane and bowler hat? Even their uniforms were similar to ours. Only their distinctive flat Brodie helmets and knee-high stockings gave them a different appearance. They looked quite exhausted and gratefully accepted the water we offered. The fellow with a broken leg was in great pain; one could see that he was barely able to keep his composure. The medics did their best to bring him into a more comfortable position, but mostly in vain. After some time, the interrogation had just ended and the First Lieutenant wanted to organize the prisoners' transportation, the radio in a neighboring tent sounded the well-known song of Lili Marlene:

Vor der Kaserne bei dem großen Tor
Stand eine Laterne und steht sie noch davor
So wollen wir uns wiederseh'n
Bei der Laterne wollen wir steh'n
Wie einst Lili Marlen'

Outside the barracks, by the corner light
I'll always stand and wait for you at night
We will create a world for two
I'll wait for you the whole night through
For you, Lili Marlene

All of us went silent, and the British began humming along softly. Their leader, a sergeant, bid the First Lieutenant to wait until the song's end. Meder nodded, and so we all raptly listened to the whole song.

And for the first time, in this frankly incidental and harmless situation, exhausted, tired and face to face with the enemy, I asked myself if this war we were fighting made sense. I was smitten by these events and felt an unprecedented connection to the British. There they were sitting now, young fellows, just as gaunt and weary as us, but just as full of dreams. In this moment, all of us were closer to each other than ever before.

In fact, that song was something special. Sung by Lale Anderson in four verses, Lili Marlene had become famous on both sides of the front. Such that the British had translated it to English using the same melody. Each day shortly before 10 PM it was aired on all German military stations to wrap up the day's broadcast. These could also be received by the British, of course. Whenever the circumstances permitted, each of us tried to not miss that moment. The radios were set to the according frequency, and for a few minutes all of us had their heads anywhere but in the war. If one was to walk through the camp then, the song would softly sound from every tent, every dugout, every tank and every command vehicle.

Oftentimes I would see someone with tears in their eyes, which some would hastily wipe away when they felt caught. The song stirred up feelings of longing and touching sentiment opposed to the unbearably dreadful reality all around. We never had any artillery strikes or any other kind of attack during this time. It was a kind of unofficial ceasefire. This may seem glorifying to today's reader, but in times of war there are countless such incidents; some happenstance that, for a short while, unites all parties involved in common longing for home and family. Just to continue slaughtering each other shortly thereafter with the same old hatred and vigor.

CHAPTER 6

UNPLANNED DEPARTURE

In late August 1941, Rommel decided to capture the fortress of Tobruk, which was still occupied by the British and stuck like a thorn in our side, once and for all. The British had built up the city's defenses further and even managed to reinforce it by sea with men and materiel despite fierce German air attacks. So, starting in early September, Rommel tried to tighten the noose around Tobruk. His headquarters were relocated to Gazala, to the west of Tobruk, and commenced preparations for the assault. Since attacking from Halfaya Pass eastwards toward Cairo was not feasible, then at least the important harbor of Tobruk was to be captured. Rommel had used all arriving supplies to continually reinforce active combat formations. Consequentially, the 5th Light Division was transformed into the 21st Panzer Division in August. This division was to decide my fate over the course of the war. With the 15th as well as the 21st, Rommel had two full armored divisions in addition to the Italian ones in the African theater of war by late Summer 1941. He seemed to have enough forces available to dare the risky attack.

In mid-September, during the preparations for this offensive, our detachment was ordered to hand over our positions to other units in order to support the planned attack. Our journey led us to the east of Tobruk – we were happy to notice that this was once again close to the sea. Here we took up positions between the coast and Via Balbia. If the assault on Tobruk was to be successful, the British were expected to attempt a breakout towards the east, which would make them run into our anti-tank gun fire, leading to their ultimate destruction.

First Lieutenant Meder took care to survey our planned positions with appropriate diligence. The companies quickly dug in, and 88 mm Flak guns were also deployed in our area once again. Something that benefited us during the buildup of our positions there was the fact that we had absolute air supremacy – unlike around Sollum and Halfaya Pass, we did not have to watch out for British fighter and fighter-bomber planes. On the contrary, we could witness our *Stukas* drop bombs on Tobruk almost all day long. For us on the ground, such a dive bomber attack was always a sight to behold.

When the Tobruk perimeter had been tightened, the area we later deployed to had seen intense fighting. I discovered multiple provisional graves, but also something just as gruesome. A few of the graves had been scavenged by jackals. Because of the hard ground, the graves were quite shallow, so they were covered with piles of rock to keep the carrion feeders from consuming the dead. Those carrion feeders were really tenacious, however, digging through to the remains. Time and again these desert jackals were roving about near the graves, trying to reach the decomposing corpses, scratching and scraping. The rocky terrain offered them plenty of hiding spots. On their search for something to eat, they would daringly sneak up on us, only driven off by having rocks thrown at them. Most unnerving, however, was their typical howling at night. On guard duty at night, this could become quite annoying. I was no exception to this, and during these lonely nights I thought with consternation about the graves of the fallen, who could not find peace even in death.

Already during the transfer from Sollum to the Tobruk area, I noticed that something was wrong with me. The usual exhaustion had intensified for me. I was even more tired than usual and now, at the Tobruk frontline, the first attacks of fever and diarrhea were coming. My fever got worse and worse, eventually rising to 40 degrees centigrade (104 °F). I was just barely able to stand and so our medic decided to have me admitted to the hospital. High fever, abdominal pain and diarrhea led him to suspect typhoid fever. In addition, I showed clear signs of jaundice. When he informed me of his decision I was shocked. I didn't want to leave my comrades and go into the uncertainty of a military hospital stay. This typhoid disease, a kind of bacterial infection, I only knew from hearsay. Now I was to have it? However, our medic was convinced and described what drastic consequences an outbreak of the disease in our unit could have. And so, totally exhausted as I was, I surrendered to my fate.

Southwards of Tobruk, near Al Adem, there was a large field hospital of the German Afrika Korps, where I was brought to in the medical vehicle. Upon taking a brief look at me, the doctors did not hesitate to confirm our paramedic's suspicions. The field hospital, however, was already above its capacities. My condition did not improve notably at Al Adem, and the attacks of fever and stomach cramps took a heavy toll on me. In contrast to how I had earlier objected to leaving the frontline, I was now so exhausted and suffering that I was wishing to get better from the bottom of my heart. Nothing else mattered to me. With a high fever and intense stomach cramps I lay on a cot, hoping for my condition to change.

Eventually I was moved from Al Adem to a hospital at Derna, where the Afrika Korps had stationed a special disease control unit shortly before. This had proved to be necessary after casualties from infectious diseases had risen dramatically over the past months. I have barely any recollections about the journey to Derna. The hospital was overcrowded with sick German and Italian soldiers, some of which were in comparably bad shape as myself. As such, I was quickly sent off again. A Junkers Ju 52 transport plane carried me to Crete and, from there, to Athens. The only thing I remember about these flights were the giant red crosses painted on the airplanes' sides, which I perceived during the embarkation. On top of my exhaustion, the engines of Auntie Ju droned so soothingly that I fell asleep almost immediately.

After more than four months of deployment in Africa, I now left the continent. In hindsight I can say that leaving the North African theater of operations on November 8, 1941 was a lucky coincidence for me, as the following months saw heavy fighting. On both sides, thousands of men lost their lives. Until early November, 1941, Tobruk was fiercely sieged by German and Italian troops. Then came the big surprise which the Germans had not seen coming: on November 18, the British commenced Operation Crusader. After the last operation in June had failed, there had been a change of leadership among the Commonwealth forces. General Archibald Wavell, who had not been able to defeat Rommel, was replaced by General Claude Auchinleck. After months of preparation, he initiated a counteroffensive. Rommel's plans to attack Tobruk had become known to the British, as decoding the German Afrika Korps' radio messages had resulted in effective intelligence.

Operation Crusader was a success, and the forces defending Tobruk even managed to mount a breakout attempt. This attempt, however, ended in a disaster for the British, as they lost 113 of 141 tanks committed to the action. Our anti-tank efforts had brought great success, with our 88 mm Flak guns contributing in no small measure. The British forces advancing from Egypt pressured Rommel more and more, however, and after a series of engagements inside the Libyan desert the prevalence of supplies as well as the concentration of force eventually decided the battle. Rommel, who was caught red-handed after initially believing the offensive to be just a reconnaissance in force, had to withdraw. The siege of Tobruk was lifted by the British in mid-December 1941, and only in late December, 1941 the German Afrika Korps was able to form a defensive line near El Agheila – right where Rommel's successful advance had begun in March. The front line was now back where it had been eight months ago.

During the fighting in November 1941, German and Italian Axis troops lost almost 33,000 men in total, whereas the British lost around 18,000 soldiers. German units encircled at Sollum and Halfaya Pass held on until January 17, 1942. Then they had to capitulate as well. By December 1941, the British were convinced that Rommel had been put in his place once and for all. Just like after their success against the Italians in February, they began pulling their troops out of the theater. Rommel, however, kept receiving supplies and reinforcements, initiating another surprising offensive on January 21, 1942. Surprising indeed, as neither the British nor German OKH had anticipated it.

One more anecdote regarding my first deployment to Africa in 1941. In the spring of 1942, after my return from Africa, the Italians awarded me, among many thousands of German soldiers, the "German-Italian campaign medal" (*Deutsch-Italienische Feldzugsmedaille*) to honor my commitment. On one side, this medal featured two gladiators (symbolizing Italy and Germany) who together fought a crocodile (symbolizing the UK). The other side featured a depiction of the *Arco dei Fileni*, the Italian triumphal arch located in the Libyan desert. I would wear this decoration next to my *AFRIKAKORPS* uniform stripe from then on. When Italy renounced her alliance with the German Reich in 1943, Wehrmacht soldiers were prohibited from wearing Italian decorations. The two nations' brotherhood in arms had not endured for long. As for me, I kept wearing the medal in 1944 during my deployment in France – in remembrance of my Italian comrades, who I kept in good memory in defiance of all later events.

CHAPTER 7
OFFICER'S TRAINING

The rapidly growing number of Wehrmacht divisions led to an ever increasing demand for commanding officers on all levels of command. Thus the officer corps underwent an unprecedented multiplication of its numbers. In order to not water down the quality of future leaders, the corps' training regime was adapted multiple times between 1933 and 1945. Until the end of 1942, when I was withdrawn from the front line, the ideal officer's career looked as follows: A basic requirement for officer training was being eligible for university training, although this was dropped later in the war. After six months of training in the reserve forces followed by three months of front line duty, the cadets would return to the officer's academy for three further months. Then two to four months at the front again, after which they were promoted to full-fledged officers. The whole system was designed to produce battle-proven leaders instead of theoreticians. Service at the front was simply regarded at the best mentor.

Before I was to become officer myself, however, I needed to recover to full health. Once in Athens, I was first put in quarantine for 14 days. During this time, the fever attacks became weaker and weaker, and my general condition improved considerably. After thorough examination, the doctors decided to dismiss me and send me back to Germany. I received my travel orders and began the journey, accompanied by an NCO who had the same destination.

Only after a bumpy truck ride that brought us to Lamia we were able to board the train to Belgrade. From there we went through Vienna and further into Germany. Once in Germany I realized that quite a lot had changed while I had been away. My old unit, *Panzerjägerersatzabteilung 33*, had moved from Ludwigshafen to Landau in the Palatinate, which was 50 kilometers (30 miles) further southeast. Right after arriving at the Landau barracks I received note that I was reallocated to *Schützenersatzbataillon 104* (104th Reserve Rifle Battalion), which provided replacements for *Panzergrenadierregiment 104* (104th Mechanized Infantry Regiment) of the 15th Panzer Division. My sergeant major had great news for me. I was to go on sick leave at home. So I packed up my belongings again, boarded another train and commenced the journey back home to my loved ones. Thus I spent the days between December 11, 1941 and January 8, 1942 at home. My parents saw to aiding in my recovery, and my dear Helena excitedly welcomed her "repatriate." What I was especially happy about was the privilege of spending Christmas at home. The weeks went by quickly and before I knew it, I was with my unit at Landau again. The winter there was harsh, and snow piled up over a meter (3 ft) high. I quickly resumed everyday life at the barracks. Measures needed to be taken to further my officer training, which resulted in me being posted for basic training duty.

After a few weeks in Landau, I also spotted a very familiar face on the barracks grounds: First Lieutenant Meder. Once we had recognized each other, we cordially shook hands. Meder told me about the heavy fighting which our unit had had to endure in November 1941. The positions at Halfaya Pass and around Sollum had been enveloped by the British, and the units there had eventually capitulated. We both agreed that we had been lucky to have been redeployed to Tobruk.

Meder was quite surprised to find me here and made a promise to help forward my officer training. Almost immediately, I was assigned to a class of reserve officer candidates; a course ahead of actual officer's training in order to specialize into a distinct services branch. This served as preparation for me attending the *Panzertruppenschule* (tank forces academy) in Wünsdorf. If needed, course participants could also be posted for basic training duty. Both regular lessons as well as training duty mostly happened at the Schwetzingen parade grounds – a military training area which I already knew from my own basic training, including some of its weapon inventory. Among other things, we trained recruits in handling the Pak 38 50 mm AT gun, which I was quite familiar with. But there was also a gun which was new for me: the 75 mm Pak 40. This was, in essence, a derivative of the Pak 38.

Thanks to its larger caliber of 7.5 centimeters (2.95 in) it could effectively combat the Soviet T-34 and KV-1 tank models which had emerged on the Russian front, causing a lot of trouble for the German troops. With the old "tank knocking device" they had been powerless, but this new 75 mm Pak 40 was able to disable these modern tanks even at a greater distance. What was special about our guns was that they had already been mounted on a self-propelled chassis. Some obsolete tank bodies had been modified with a mounting which accepted the Pak 40 guns. In our case, a *Panzerkampfwagen II* (Mark 2 Tank) body had been used. This type had seen combat in Poland and France during the early war and by now was helplessly obsolete. By installing a 75 mm AT gun it was hoped to produce a capable tank destroyer. First the old superstructure had been removed, which was then replaced with a gun mounting that could be adjusted horizontally and vertically, with the 75 mm gun surrounded by some 15 mm (0.6 in) of steel plating. This formed a fighting compartment, which remained open to the rear and top sides, thus offering little protection against shrapnel or direct fire coming from those directions. The chassis' front was not well armored either, having around 30 mm (1.2 in). This, however, in conjunction with tank tracks, provided excellent mobility and made for an anti-tank weapon capable of rapid redeployment. As such it could be used to quickly create anti-tank bulwarks at threatened front line sectors or following an enemy armor breakthrough. An important capability if we wanted to combat dreaded enemy tank formations, especially in the far reaches of Russia. In addition, it was possible to rapidly shift to an alternate position after firing. The newly constructed vehicle was termed *Sonderkraftfahrzeug 131* (SdKfz131, special purpose vehicle) or simply *"Marder II"*. With its 140 horsepower engine, this "Marten mark II" reached a road speed of 45 kph (28 mph) and still as much as 19 kph (12 mph) cross-country.

After one more month of training duty I was eventually promoted to sergeant on April 1, 1942. From then on, things moved rapidly. A few weeks later, during May, I was sent on vacation – special leave, that is, due to my upcoming reassignment to officer school at Wünsdorf. This special leave lasted from May 22 to May 27, just six days. Naturally, I wanted to spend that time at home, so I boarded another train. This time I returned much more proud; I was a sergeant now, after all, and not a simple rifleman anymore. I favorably noticed how the lower-ranking men were now saluting me with a lot of respect. My Africa Korps armband also generated quite a lot of admiration.

By the end of May, my officer training at *"Panzertruppenschule I"* (1st Panzer Forces Academy) in Wünsdorf had commenced. This school, also called *"Schule für schnelle Truppen I"* (1st rapid forces academy), was located 50 kilometers (30 mi) south of Berlin.

Having a break during training at Panzer Forces Academy, Wünsdorf. I sit first from the left.

Training of German Wehrmacht officers on a low level, meaning lieutenants, followed a simple tenet: Lead from the front. At every point, be it in the lecture room during tactics lessons or while commanding men in the field, we were drilled to be forward near our men and stand our ground in battle. This was the best way to stay on top of things and make the right decisions without delay. Furthermore, one was to "lead by mission" instead of "leading by orders." This granted more freedom in execution. Which meant for us: the given objective was to be achieved, but how you achieved it was completely up to you. And, since you were at the front during combat, you lived in the situation and could thus make the right decisions quickly. Inflexible orders from the rear would hardly ever allow for that. In short, we were taught *what* to do, but had the freedom to decide *how* to do it. In addition to our theoretical and practical lessons in leadership there were courses regarding military knowledge – for example, lectures about education and military science, about military law and the composition of the German Wehrmacht. German history, too, was not left out and a fixed part of the agenda. Furthermore, we were taught the duties of the German soldier as well as rules for work and life. A brief excerpt of these professional standards reads as follows:

> *Always be a role model, especially in times of crisis.*
> *[...]*
> *Before you start giving orders, have a good look at your men and try to recognize the person they are inside. Knowing people is prerequisite to treating people correctly.*
> *Orders only make sense if they are convincing.*
> *[...]*
> *Always act with reason and heart when you are responsible for human lives, especially in war.*
> *[...]*
> *Uphold until your last breath the faith in the Greater German Idea and in God; this faith also lends inner strength especially in crises of life and during war, when human strength is often tested. An age as grand as ours is only mastered with unwavering faith.*

Furthermore we received Wehrmacht High Command's *Mitteilungen für die Truppe* (messages for the troops). These pamphlets were distributed among Wehrmacht ranks down to company level and were also handed to us. With articles such as "How Roosevelt deliberately steered towards war" or "Lies, deception, terror – weapons of British politics" it was made sure that we knew how nobody but us and our soldiers were fighting for the right cause, not our enemies. We were raised and instructed to represent the future elite of the German Wehrmacht. Our lecturers never tired of repeating this sentiment. What counted for us were the here and now, to prove ourselves as capable commanders, and the victories we wanted to achieve on the battlefield.

Today, much of this may be hard to relate to for the reader. We were indoctrinated into hardly ever asking questions – questions were asked only while directly confronted by the horrors of war. Just like I had experienced in Africa. Behind the front lines, one tended to get worked up into feeling invincible again. This would change for me only over the course of my later deployments where, in the face of suffering and death, I would start to question situations and orders.

September 30, 1942 was the day before our graduation from Panzer troops academy and promotion to lieutenant. On that occasion, we were allowed to witness an extraordinary event. All available academy personnel along with us cadets were taken to the *Reichssporthalle* (Berlin Olympic Stadium). There we were to attend a speech by the Führer. Early in the morning we jumped on trucks that took us to Berlin. A huge crowd of people in uniform was already there, moving onto their allocated seats in an orderly fashion despite their great number. Thousands upon thousands of Wehrmacht and party personnel gathered to listen to the Führer of the German Reich. As soon as we all had found our seats amidst the vast crowd, Adolf Hitler entered the stage. Ineffable cheering broke out, everyone stood up and kept shouting "Sieg Heil!" The whole crowd billowed in excitement; the atmosphere was beyond comprehension.

The German Reich was at the height of its power. France was occupied or "allied" to us, Great Britain had been put in its place, we were in possession of the High North, in Russia our armies had advanced up to

Leningrad, Stalingrad and the Caucasus, the entire Balkans were occupied, while in North Africa we were standing at the border to Egypt. The world trembled before the German people and its Wehrmacht. With the speech that was to follow, Hitler made us feel all that. He spoke about the opening of the eastern regions, how the general supply and food situation would improve for all fellow Germans. Hitler was of the opinion that the next year would bring the deciding victory. And we all believed him.

On the next day, the time had finally come. I was promoted to lieutenant and became reserve officer of the German Wehrmacht. All of us mustered at the academy to receive their rank insignia, and our commander gave a rousing speech wishing us all the best for our front-line deployments. This we would be needing for sure, as the life expectancy of a young lieutenant was on average around seven days of front-line service – not more than a week. A company commander already had an expectancy of fourteen days, while a battalion commander even made it to thirty days on average. Of course we were never officially told these numbers, and I would come to know them only after the war; however, rumors of a short lifespan for lieutenants never ceased to circulate within our ranks. Well, all of us assumed that this would not be the case for themselves.

For me, there was just one thing: I wanted to get back to the front, if again in Africa then all the better. Since my departure from there, a lot had happened. In an initial offensive starting in January, 1942, the German Afrika Korps had managed to advance as far as Gazala and El Adem near Tobruk until the end of May. In June, the German-Italian joint operation *Theseus* marked the beginning of large-scale attacks on Tobruk itself. Two weeks later the defense perimeter had been breached and Rommel's forces stood inside the town. In total, around 32,000

Finally officer.

Allied soldiers became German POWs, with the Afrika Korps capturing roughly 10,000 tons of fuel and 5,000 tons of other supplies. Rommel was rewarded immediately: Hitler promoted him to the rank of General Field Marshal. German newsreels were full of joyful reports about this success. As for the Desert Fox himself, he kept on pushing forward even though his forces were somewhat weakened after having captured Tobruk. He chased the retreating Commonwealth forces until they committed to battle again in July 1942 near El Alamein.

British Prime Minister Winston Churchill now demanded that General Auchinleck conduct a counter-offensive just like Rommel would have done, but Auchinleck refused. Consequently, he was relieved from command on Churchill's orders and replaced by General Montgomery, who took over the British 8th Army with one clear goal: to banish Rommel and his forces from Africa once and for all. Montgomery kept bolstering up his forces over the months that followed until his superiority was guaranteed.

Finally, on October 23, 1942, the expected large-scale attack at El Alamein began. For a total of five hours the British shelled the German and Italian front lines on a ten kilometer (6 mi) wide section between Bir el Atash and Bir Abu Sifai. A murderous barrage from which there was no escape. On the evening of November 2, 1942, Rommel decided to retreat the following day and radioed this intention to Germany. However, Hitler and the Führer's headquarters forbade the withdrawal, and so Rommel hesitated for another 24 hours before eventually, on November 4, he returned to his initial decision in defiance of Hitler's orders. Thus began the retreat of German and Italian troops from Egypt through Libya.

My comrades and I had anxiously followed the events in Africa. Every newsreel we rooted for Rommel and his men. However, we also suspected that our side did not enjoy quite as much supply, while the British could draw on much more resources. Well, once I was promoted lieutenant, I was bursting to get back to Africa. Such was the confidence instilled by my training, such the pride after achieving an officer rank, that I – and my peers as well – believed we could turn the fortunes of war through our deployment there alone. Once we arrived at the front lines, we thought, things would go in our favor again. In the evenings when we sat together – for once – over a beer in the mess hall after training, we still reinforced each other's opinion. Well, we were more than mistaken.

CHAPTER 8

CLOSE COMBAT

The situation developed quickly. In order to permanently turn the tide in Africa in favor of the Allies, British and American troops mounted an extensive landing operation on the northwest African coast, *Operation Torch*, on November 8, 1942. Within a short time, the Western Allies succeeded in capturing a majority of key ports from Morocco to Algeria.

While these events were unfolding, I was already in Italy. Immediately after my promotion to lieutenant, we were assembled at Pirmasens, Germany and transferred by rail to Naples. As with my first African deployment, we went over Brenner Pass and through South Tyrol toward Sicily. A total of five companies had been formed from 104th Panzergrenadier Training Battalion at Landau as replacements for 15th Panzer Division at El Alamein. Each company was led by two officers; the first was the company commander, with the other leading first platoon while at the same time being second in command. As a newly commissioned lieutenant, I took over an infantry platoon with Captain Riedel as my company commander. Riedel, was just barely older than myself, but had already gained some experience in fierce battles at the Russian front. Upon arrival in Naples, we were temporarily quartered in Italian barracks. Here, we did not yet notice much of the unfavorable war developments in Northwest Africa. The Italian officers and soldiers present kept things running as if in deepest peace.

Nevertheless, we did not remain idle, conducting training with our men. These training sessions were intended to serve our forthcoming deployment and were therefore treated very seriously by the soldiers. In total, my infantry platoon, including myself, consisted of 36 men (also see the list in the appendix). The three infantry groups each comprised a group leader, his second in command, two machine gun teams with a gunner and loader each, and four riflemen. To lead these three groups I had a platoon command squad available, which consisted of the platoon squad leader (simultaneously my deputy commander), three messengers and a medic for first aid. As for armament, my platoon had six 7.92 mm MG 42 machine guns and 29 standard issue 8 mm Kar 98k carbines. I carried a 9 mm MP 40 submachine gun.

Being an officer, I also carried a 7.65 mm Sauer 1938 (H)) pistol. Out of all these guns, the six MGs were the most important. Their high rate of fire of up to 1,500 rounds per minute made them fearsome weapons when utilized correctly. Consequently, our enemies soon gave it the nickname of "Hitler's Buzzsaw." I first encountered the MG 42 during reserve officer training. Compared to the older MG 34, it had significantly better performance and was easier to handle as well. One soldier termed *MG-Schütze 1* (MG rifleman 1) would aim and fire the weapon, while another, *MG-Schütze 2*, was responsible for feeding in the ammunition. In addition, the latter carried a folding tripod which could be used to turn the light machine gun (*lMG*) into a heavy one (*sMG*). This stable arrangement considerably increased the gun's effective range.

Leader of my command squad as well as my right-hand man was Sergeant Wilhelm Rupp, born in 1910 and a man of the first hour. He had been in this since the Poland campaign. We immediately got along well, and I realized that I had a very capable man supporting me. My three group leaders, Corporals Peter Klauck (1st group), Otto Aust (2nd) and Wilhelm Hegewald (3rd), were all experienced soldiers as well, who had been in the military since the beginning of the war. Each of them had been at the front just like me, some of them had even fought in Poland and France.

With our enlisted men, however, the situation was entirely different.

Almost all of them had entered the Wehrmacht in summer 1942, just a few months ago. This was to be their first combat mission. The youngest men were just 19 years old while the oldest, my medic, Private Josef Hartmann, was 35. Their private professions were of all different kinds; from miner over fitter to baker, a variety of craftsmen were present. The sole professional soldier was Sergeant Rupp, my second in command.

During these November days in Naples, more and more other units joined us in a short period of time. You could see how the reinforcements were coming in. Eventually the order was given to form five so-called *Feldbataillone Tunesien* (Tunisia Field Battalions), abbreviated *Tunesien 1* to *Tunesien 5* (or, even shorter, T1 to T5). Each of these consisted of a staff section and five companies. Our company was assigned to T4, commanded by Captain Karl Koch. Now that it was clear that we were going to the front lines, the atmosphere grew tense. Everyone knew about the situation in Africa and it was foreseeable that many would not return home. We were to prevail or perish. Sentiments like these circulated among the men. And as it had been for millennia, the soldiers attempted to find solace on the eve of battle by drinking. There was nothing left to do shortly before our departure, and the battalion commander knew what was going to happen. And, as long as things did not get out of control, he would not prevent it. Some resourceful soldiers soon acquired wine and booze. Most of all, the heavier Italian wine quickly showed its effects. For many of the men it did not take any more than that to raise their spirits again. Such "encouragement" made them deal with their fate much better.

The next day, on November 25, reality quickly caught up to us. The order to redeploy was given. We were to fly from Naples directly to Tunisia and reinforce 10th Panzer Division there. In full gear we were brought to the near airfield. Dozens of Ju 52 transport planes were waiting for us. Each of our platoons was assigned one aircraft. Feelings of tension rose once the engines started running, and the soldiers went aboard with mixed feelings. The individual planes, each of them loaded to the brim, formed a line, and rolled towards the runway. Soon it was our turn; the pilots markedly revved up the engines, and we rose up into the air lumberingly. The weather over the sea was bad and we were shaken pretty well. Nonetheless, after some time in the air I wandered forward to our two pilots and spend some time looking over their shoulder.

The cockpit offered a beautiful view. I could observe other Ju 52s zooming in formation just 50 to 100 meters (55-110 yds) above the water. This low altitude was necessary to reduce the possibility of British interceptors spotting us. Most of all, British Beaufighter long-range fighter aircraft wreaked havoc among our cumbersome transports. The lone gunner and his MG sitting in our aircraft would have hardly any chance of fending them off. While thinking about this, I was unnerved by the fact that I could not see any fighters of our own accompanying us. I attempted to ask the pilots about it, but they just shook their heads. All in all, I was glad about flying in bad weather. This way British interceptors would have a hard time spotting us.

View from the cockpit on the Mediterranean and some other Ju 52s of our formation.

All of a sudden the pilots started to discuss something, gesturing wildly, and a little later one of them pointed towards the middle engine.

It stuttered for a bit before the propeller blades slowed down until they were just rotating in the wind. Now things got dicey. For a normally laden Ju 52, a single failing engine was not necessarily a big deal, but we were overloaded and the weather was all but good. The co-pilot turned towards me and signaled that we were to divert in the direction of Sicily. I nodded knowingly, even though I had not a clue what exactly was going on. When I wanted to turn back around, he dragged me close to him and yelled into my ear that we should throw anything overboard that could help make the craft lighter. I nodded and signaled my understanding. What was clear to me, however, was that an emergency ditching would in all likelihood mean the death of us all. Either we would die in the crash or drown in the stormy sea.

I returned to my men and made them understand that we would land in Sicily due to technical problems. I could see in their faces how their fear of crashing was greater than their joy about not having to go into combat so soon. The plane turned left, following a course towards Sicily. The gunner opened the side door via its emergency handle, and in short order most of our equipment went overboard. The MG ammunition boxes were the very first to sink to the bottom of the ocean. In this flurry of activity, through the roaring airstream, one of my NCOs screamed a question toward me about whether we were to jump off the plane as well. I looked at him, utterly dumbfounded. Immediately I shook my head, and morale among the men improved somewhat.

I signaled to the pilots that we had thrown everything away. The other planes vanished from sight, and after just a short while the coast of Sicily and the inner countryside became clearly visible. We soon spotted an airfield. I took a sigh of relief. My men, too, were visibly relieved, patting each other's shoulders in joy. After one preliminary traffic circuit, we touched the airstrip with a gentle bump and climbed out of the craft. Now, for the time being, it was time to wait. The pilots, along with some airfield technicians, warily inspected the engine. After some screw driving and knocking they seemed satisfied and let the engine be.

In the meantime darkness had set in, so continuing the journey was out of the question and we accommodated ourselves for the coming night. We had landed at Trapani on the western tip of Sicily, and the few existing shelters were overloaded thanks to countless redeploying German troops. Thus we accommodated ourselves in quite a spartan fashion.

The next day, we were assigned to another formation of Ju 52 transports. At 07:00 we went up into the air and joined the convoy. Along with around 50 other Ju 52s, we managed to complete the trip to Africa without any further complications. Shortly before our arrival, Tunis had been bombarded by the Americans. Consequently, some of our aircraft had trouble landing due to the high number of bomb craters. On November 26, 1942, I set foot on African soil once again after almost thirteen months. This time, I was an officer responsible for the lives of 35 men under my command.

We had landed in Tunis, however, while the rest of our unit had been brought to Bizerte. As such, there was some confusion as to what to do with me and my platoon. There was a general atmosphere of rushing as if the Americans were right at our doorstep, and the landed troops were transported off the airfield without delay. Communication with Captain Koch or Captain Riedel was not possible for me. They had entered the front lines immediately after their arrival at Bizerte.

After some back-and-forth discussion and me explaining our situation, someone took things into their hands, and a paratrooper sergeant who coordinated the moving of airborne units out of the airfield gave me a marching order. We were to move into the "Marshal Foch" barracks in Tunis via truck in order to join the paratroopers of Lieutenant Colonel Koch of *Fallschirmjäger Regiment 5*, who coincidentally had the same name as my battalion commander. Two Opel Blitz trucks and a Kübelwagen were quickly made available to us, we mounted up and the journey continued. Soon after the outskirts of Tunis came into view.

Upon arriving in the barracks we were immediately taken in and I was told that we were now effectively attached to the paratroopers. There was also a mission just for us. An attack was planned to commence in a few days, where our new unit would join the 10th Panzer Division in advancing from the Djedeida area towards Tebourba. On the day of our arrival, the Americans had almost reached Tunis coming from Djedeida and Tebourba. This threat was now to be neutralized. All available forces were being brought forward for the counterattack.

We spent the next day in these barracks, during which I received additional details about the attack, which was scheduled for December 1, 1942, in a short briefing. The plan was as follows: The Americans and British were to be attacked at Tebourba from both flanks as well as the front – 10th Panzer Division from the north at Chouigui Pass (*Kampfgruppe Lueder* and *Kampfgruppe Hudel*, two Battlegroups) and paratroopers of *Fallschirmjäger Regiment 5* (*Kampfgruppe Koch*) from the south at El Bathan. These pincer movements were to facilitate an encirclement of the Allied forces around Tebourba. A fourth combined German formation, *Kampfgruppe Djedeida*, was to also attack Allied positions west of Djedeida one day later, December 2. These simultaneous attacks and the resulting encirclement leading to the destruction of Allied forces were to relieve the pressure on Tunis itself.

Our departure towards the front lines was scheduled for the next day already. Before that I tried my best to gather additional information for my NCOs and soldiers – Nothing is worse than being an uninformed soldier. Before you know the wildest rumors are spread, the men feel left in the dark and become uneasy. I wanted to avoid that and give them the impression that they knew what was going on at the front lines. Up to date reports and information made them feel like they are living in the situation and thus are not helplessly subject to large-scale developments. Trust in one's superiors could make the difference between success and failure in combat. This was instilled in me at Wünsdorf Panzer Forces Academy, and I had witnessed the meaning of this sentiment on my first missions in Africa, 1941.

In the Marshal Foch barracks we stocked up on ammunition from German supply transports while also treating ourselves to some hand grenades. Eventually everything was done, and after a wakeful night and some final preparations we left the barracks at noon on November 28. Soon we arrived at Djedeida. I reported to the local command post and was briefed by a Major. The paratroopers in this area had been subject to intense pressure over the last few days, so we were to reinforce them until our attack would commence. Once I had an overview of the situation, I was informed of the mission envisioned for me and my men during the coming offensive.

We were to immediately redeploy to the first lines at Djedeida and get ready. While the flanking maneuvers were to start on December 1 due to the greater distance between opposing forces, we were to wait for one additional day and then initiate the frontal assault as spearhead of the combined forces of "Battlegroup Djedeida" on December 2. On hearing that, I had to swallow nervously. The British had been in their positions for several days, which meant their foxholes had been fortified and expanded, heavy weapons and MGs positioned and, most likely, artillery brought forward and ranged in.

The Major had used a map during my briefing, which allowed me to get a better understanding of the terrain west of Djedeida. The map located the British around 3 km (2 mi) west of the town on a low hill. Our positions lay opposed to them in a shallow basin, which meant that our assault on the British would go uphill. All this went through my head within seconds. As the Major stated, our combined forces of Battlegroup Djedeida in essence comprised two infantry march battalions, a mixed armored company of 10th Panzer Division, Luftwaffe AA units with 20 mm and 88 mm guns, and finally the paratroopers that were already stationed in the furthermost lines. 10th Panzer Division, among their more common German Panzer III tanks, also had a new type of vehicle available, the Panzer VI "Tiger," later called "Tiger I."

What the Major promised me was a preliminary bombardment by our own artillery, which would soften up British positions right before the attack. This gave me some reassurance. We would not have to run up against the British completely unprepared. Nevertheless would this assault mean forlorn hope for me and my platoon, posing an enormous challenge for my inexperienced young soldiers. On the way back to my men I thought about our options. I assembled the soldiers and described the situation as well as our mission to them. From the faces of the more experienced NCOs, I immediately noticed that they were judging the situation the same way I did. I emphasized the preliminary artillery strike. Tensely the men listened to me. Many probably could not begin to imagine what this attack could mean for them.

Inwardly, I first thought to myself that most likely some would not survive this attack, indeed perhaps I myself could be dead soon. I banished the thought and tried to present our mission as clearly as possible. In closing, I announced that I would determine the detailed plan of attack on the spot later in the field. The NCOs nodded in agreement, and I was relieved by this feedback. I had their support. This was essential to make it through the assault.

By foot, we marched on into our designated combat zone, which we arrived at shortly before darkness set in. On our way we could see the damage caused by the American armored offensive and the resulting fighting around Djedeida. We reached the edge of a grove of eucalyptus and olive trees spreading over a large portion of the area ahead. There we were received by a platoon of paratroopers. As dusk had already passed, we joined them in their positions, resolving to take over our own positions the next day. Before I went to sleep, the paratroopers told me how they had to endure fierce fighting against the Americans and British. Two days before, November 26, they had come close to being destroyed by the American armored spearhead. However, they had also been able to destroy a few tanks in turn.

The next morning I had my first look at the surrounding terrain accompanied by the paratrooper platoon commander. The *Fallschirmjäger* already knew the place quite well, leading me on a tour through our positions. The terrain was much like I had surmised. Our positions were essentially on, or directly next to, a tiny ridge roughly 2 km (1.2 mi) west of Djedeida. Around 600 meters (660 yd) ahead another ridge rose up, behind which the British had dug in. This was our objective. Between these features, in a shallow depression, was a vast grove of eucalyptus and olive trees. It had been planted artificially, such that all the trees were neatly arranged in parallel rows. This resulted in long swaths of open ground leading across the field. To the left, the grove was bordered by a railroad track and the Mejderda river; to the right lay the road leading from Djedeida towards Tebourba, along which the American tanks had advanced a few days ago, forcing our paratroopers into the woods. In the process, eight German Panzer III and Panzer IV tanks had been disabled. These were crucial losses that were now sorely needed in the upcoming attack.

The eucalyptus trees had been completely tousled by the fighting. I counted a total of fifteen tree rows going north from the railroad. Among these trees, the paratroopers had dug their positions. Before their foxholes still lay some dead. British and German soldiers that were killed during the initial skirmishes. In a small ditch, a hidden place for the wounded was concealed by some twigs. There, a wounded British soldier lay as well. He had been captured during one of the attacks and it seemed that he thought this to be his last day. Impassively he lay below the branches. When I bent down to him he looked at me with tired eyes. The paratrooper commander explained to me that they had planned to bring the man behind the lines after my unit had taken over.

Interrogation of another captured British soldier had revealed that our opponents were part of 2nd Battalion, Royal Hampshire Regiment. Just like us, they had been brought up to the front lines recently. In another place cleared for the wounded which we visited, British and German soldiers were sitting next to each other in togetherness.

Getting briefed by paratroopers at the eucalyptus grove west of Djedeida.

Until noon we had relieved the paratroopers, who assembled in our rear. I wished them well and hoped to see them again during the planned attack. My runners had contact to the command post further back, and we were now on our own. Just when I wanted to get some rest, several dull bangs could be heard, and moments later the first shells detonated in front of our positions. The explosions quickly drew closer. Our arrival and relief seemed to have been noticed. We put our heads down inside the foxholes and were grateful that the paratroopers had already dug them.

While the detonations drew closer, I could hear the characteristic hum of shrapnel cutting through the air, and the trees around us had to endure the storm. Pieces of wood and leaves rippled down on us. A short while later the action was over again, I sent out my runners and was very relieved to receive note that we had suffered no casualties. I then personally inspected our positions and convinced myself of this. Leaves and twigs littered the floor everywhere. All soldiers were in good spirits, although it was apparent that this first attack had left them full of adrenaline. For many, this had been their baptism by fire, and they looked at me eyes wide open.

However, the attack let my men make another discovery. While visiting one of the foxholes, a soldier pointed towards a body lying roughly 50 meters (55 yds) ahead. One of the men had observed this body moving during the artillery strike. I guessed that it was a wounded Englishman lying in no man's land. Just as I wanted to go ahead and take a look, there was more rushing and whistling in the air above, and we were forced back into our foxholes. An intense smell of powder and eucalyptus filled the air. I decided to wait until dusk before looking for the Englishman. The trees offered not enough cover to move out undetected. In the evening, once another British bombardment seemed unlikely, me and two other soldiers, my medic being one of them, cautiously went forward. On the approach we could already see that, just as surmised, it was a wounded British soldier.

Carefully we moved closer to the "Tommy," as we jokingly called the British back then. His faint rattle showed that he was seriously wounded. I bent over to him very slowly so as not scare him. He looked at me eyes wide open, his mouth stained with blood, and I could see a large wound in his chest that let out foamy blood with each rattling breath he took. A bullet or a piece of shrapnel must have hit his lung. The Englishman whimpered softly, his eyes begging from deep inside his already pale face. I took his hand, squeezed it firmly, and said in English, "We will help you. We will bring you to the field hospital." He moaned faintly and squeezed my hand back a bit to signify that he understood. My medic, Private Hartmann, bandaged him provisionally, and together we brought him back to our positions, covering each other's movements. Once there, I gave orders to make sure the Englishman would be brought to the next assembly point for the wounded in the rear. My medic and a few other soldiers picked him up and carried him to the rear. To this day I do not know whether he survived. I very much hope so. He was not much older than my young soldiers.

The night from November 29 to November 30 went by without further events, but the next morning we were greeted by yet another artillery strike. This time the shells struck significantly closer to our positions. They had to have an observer in the area to direct the guns – I could not see any other explanation. It was past time to do something about that. I sent my runners to the rear, requesting our own artillery strike focused on the single house. And indeed support was granted, not by artillery fire, however. Instead, several *Luftwaffe* soldiers towing a 20 mm AA cannon arrived at noon, which they set up on the small hill behind us. They began firing at the house with explosive and tracer ammunition. I also told one of my MGs to fire at will, so we let loose a few bursts of fire towards the building. The first salvos already struck the target and smoke emerging from the house indicated that it had started to burn. The *Luftwaffe* soldiers fired a few more salvos before withdrawing with their cannon. For a while I kept looking at the house through my binoculars, but nothing seemed to happen. Well, I may have been right, because the afternoon went by calmly and there were no more artillery strikes.

It was only a day later that another artillery strike forced us deep into our foxholes. This was the fourth time, and it was more intense than the ones before. Almost like a miracle, none of my soldiers had been wounded by all these British shells. And especially in woodlands artillery could be terribly effective, where shells with impact fuses could hit a tree and thus detonate above ground. We had been lucky, however, even though this last attack showered us not only in leaves and branches, but also chunks of earth and rocks. It was just a matter of time until the British shells would strike home. At some point our luck would run out, that we all knew.

The night before December 1 was also quiet, and the morning greeted us with another British artillery strike. These recurring attacks slowly wore my men down, and I enjoyed the thought that we would leave our positions the following morning. Even though the reason for that was our assault. Still, better to make a move than having to bear one artillery strike after the other.

Around noon, the paratroopers arrived, and we went through the mission details together. Tomorrow morning, December 2, 1942, at 07:00, I was to assault the British positions on the other side of the ridge after a preliminary bombardment. The paratroopers of Battlegroup Koch wanted to execute the decisive advance on El Bathan further south. Once the paratroopers had departed in the evening, I gave some final orders. I went through all the details again, trying to convey trust and conviction. Finally everyone returned to their positions, and it was time to wait for dawn. This would be my first real assault, and I was responsible for a whole platoon to boot. My head was full of thoughts about this and that, going through all our options time and again. What if our artillery did not fire? What if enemy defensive fire caused heavy casualties and we were halted right in front of their positions? Pinned

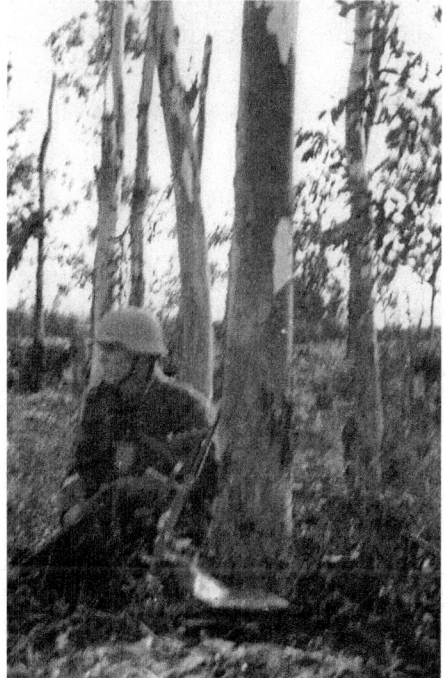

Waiting for the attack to begin.

down without any way around? So many questions that I could not answer. I lay in my foxhole in the fading heat of the day, contemplating the coming attack and what it might spell for us.

In the early morning hours, when I had just caught a little sleep, a shot suddenly whipped through the night. I startled up immediately. The men of my platoon command squad, who had their foxholes right next to mine, were wide awake as well. Just like me they had been barely able to sleep. I sent out the runners to check all our positions and find out what had happened.

After a short time, I knew it. Disaster had struck. One rifleman of 3rd squad, 30-year-old Georg Siegl, had ventured too far away from his foxhole and on his return was shot by one of his comrades. I rushed to the squad. There he lay, a bullet hole in his chest, already dead. His squad's commander, Sergeant Hegewald, was distraught and wanted to find out how it could have happened. Still in shock, the rifleman who had fired tried to explain how he had seen a figure approach his foxhole from the front, thinking it was part of a British reconnaissance patrol. What rifleman Siegl was doing in front of our line we did not know. Perhaps he had wanted to relieve himself and got lost. I asked the shooter to calm down. It was not his fault; it had simply happened. I ordered Sergeant Hegewald to calm the men down, adjuring him to not let any unrest emerge shortly before our attack.

The dead man was to be put behind our line. We would retrieve his body after the assault. Hegewald nodded and I rushed back. Inside I was aghast. Why did this have to happen just now? Was this a dire portent? Shortly before 06:00 I ordered the alarm and we began our advance through the grove along the whole line. I wanted to take up a favorable starting position before waiting for our artillery strike. Everything went smoothly. We secured a position in a shallow ditch undetected. Quietly we hunkered in the undergrowth. I was sure everyone knew what had happened shortly before even though nobody let it show. Now the attack was occupying their minds. The MG 42 near the railroad embankment was to cover our first advance. I wanted to move along the embankment and the swathes of trees as projected by our plan. Tensely we lay between the tree rows, covering all directions. I took a look at my watch. "06:45, so it won't be long!" I thought.

All of a sudden I heard an unmistakable sound. A faint chink of tracks and vibrations in the ground heralded the approach of war machines. The engine noise came from behind us; our Panzers were on the advance. The humming of engines and metallic clank of tracks in their bogie wheels grew louder and louder, until suddenly the first tank appeared on the railroad embankment. A German Panzer III, as I expertly recognized, behind it another – but what kind of monstrosity was among them? It had to be a Tiger. It was almost twice the size of a Pz III, and its wide tracks lumbered along on both sides of the railroad track. In the lead vehicle I could spot a head with headphones sticking out of the turret hatch. I moved a bit out of the protective undergrowth and held my MP 40 up high. With a jolt the Panzer came to a halt, and the tank commander raised his hand as well. The Panzer directly behind him kept going for a bit while the Tiger came down from the embankment, closing up to the leading vehicle. It now stood in a shallow ditch that offered some cover, its engine chugging along, its fearsome 88 mm gun menacingly pointed in our direction.

I could feel my adrenaline level rising. Looking at my men's faces I recognized guarded joy stemming from the unexpected arrival of these tanks. Again I looked at my watch: just before 07:00. Now all that was left was for our artillery to keep its promise and fire in time. And indeed, muffled bangs sounded and just like that shells whizzed over our heads. A mushroom cloud rose from the hillside before us, and then another right next to it. But I immediately realized, "They're firing too short!" Shell upon shell now detonated ahead of us on the hill. Not on the ridge or shortly behind it, however, where the British had their positions. I counted twelve impacts, then the show stopped. So that was all the ammunition they had in stock for us. Behind us the engines roared up, and I gave the sign to attack. I gripped my submachine gun and we swarmed the grove in a line formation, staying close to the ground. We took the first 20 yards … 60 yards … to our left, one of the Panzer IIIs ground along the railroad on top of the embankment. I was animating the men and we had almost reached the ridge when all of a sudden hell broke loose. A machine gun rattled directly ahead, projectiles whizzed past us, bangs of small arms fire filled the air. Next to me one of my men slumped down; in front of me another was carried off his feet. Enemy bullets tore through our ranks. We dropped prone, gasping for air. I looked at the Panzers. The leading Pz III jolted to a halt, its hatches swung open, and its crew dropped out onto the ground. "AT hit," it crossed my mind.

The second Pz III now started firing, while the Tiger was still standing in its ditch. All of that happened in mere seconds. Impacts around me brutally put me back into my own situation. Enemy fire intensified. We were almost on top of the ridge, our enemies behind it. Crossing the ridge seemed impossible to me. Their fire was too intense. I yelled at my men around me, pointing towards the embankment. We had to reach it and take cover there. Two of my MGs opened fire and we threw ourselves towards the embankment. While I was running, I was looking around: we were around 25 men left, which meant that I had lost around ten men already. One or two more leaps later we reached the embankment. I felt the hot whizzing of projectiles flying past us. With a shriek one of my soldiers, a runner, fell to the ground. We ran past the firing Pz III's rear and lied down on the other side. The runner had made it as well. Blood squirted out his upper leg, and he hunched with pain. Sweat poured over my face and into my eyes, I panted, the bang of the close-by tank gun hurt in my ears.

Sergeant Rupp lay down next to me. "How many are left?" I yelled. "Almost 20!" was his response.

"Forward … here, along the embankment! The tank will support us!" I screamed and ran along the slope. The soldiers followed, some of them overturning me on the assault. Again the fire intensified, and we dropped on the slope after around 110 yards. To our left I discovered a house. Figures were emerging from it, hands up. Englishmen! I gestured towards the rear. Without giving us any further attention, they ran back.

Directly ahead I saw a culvert in the embankment. Perhaps a dried-out irrigation canal between the river and the eucalyptus and olive grove. Something was moving in the culvert. It seemed to be a wounded

Englishman. Apparently we were now on a level with the British positions on the far hillside. I sent one of my men to capture him. Carefully the former approached him, upon which the Englishman suddenly drew his carbine and shot him in the belly. The bullet went out of his back and my soldier dropped to the side. I yelled at the next man, "Hand grenade!" He understood, readied one, pulled the pin, and threw it into the culvert. With a dull bang it exploded. I raised my MP 40 to get the men's attention … but all of a sudden stinging pain flashed through my lower right arm. The MP 40 dropped to the ground, and I gazed at my arm. I was shocked to see blood dripping out of my sleeve. Apparently, I had been shot through my lower arm.

A shell detonated close by. Shrapnel whizzed above our heads. It seemed that we were being targeted by cannon fire. Perhaps the AT guns that had taken out our Panzer? We hunkered into the slope. Suddenly it was as if the embankment was torn apart to my left. I was sprayed with rocks and chunks of dirt. Almost the same instant sergeant Rupp bumped into me, burying me under him.

Almost stunned, I pushed him away with my left, and I lost my breath. A shell had struck right next to us. Sergeant Rupp bore the brunt of the shrapnel, and his body had protected mine. What had landed on me were his mutilated remains. His right side was unrecognizable. Everywhere blood streamed out of his torn-up body. We had to move away if we wanted to survive. I looked around; we were no more than ten to twelve men. With my left hand I drew my pistol, looked to my left and right, and yelled "Assault, forward!" I dragged myself up, and together with what was left of my platoon I advanced over the railroad embankment towards the British positions ahead.

With one leap we left the embankment behind. The first British foxholes appeared ahead. Inside them British soldiers, unmistakable thanks to the flat steel helmets on their heads. They were pointing their weapons at us, bayonets fixed. I screamed in English, "Hands up! Come on, hands up!" and ran towards them, my pistol drawn up to them. The first Englishmen dropped their guns and raised their arms. I slowed down. Out of the corner of my eye I saw how right next to me, in front of one of my men, an Englishman yanked up his hands … and my man shot him with his carbine. Realizing his mistake, my soldier immediately lowered his rifle.

Suddenly I saw movement. Less than three yards away, an Englishman drew a bead on me with his bayoneted rifle. I raised my pistol and in the same moment I felt an impact in my lower body. I could see the recoil pushing the Englishman's shoulder back. Tumbling forward, I shot at him multiple times. The bullets hit his body. He collapsed, burying his rifle under him. I fell on him. I had been hit again, that I could feel, but I was not in pain. I rolled to the side and dragged myself to a sitting position. My pistol, it turned out, was emptied. The rest of my platoon assembled around me. I saw only a few soldiers. "Where are my other men?" I thought. "Where is my platoon?"

Things went quiet. The shooting had ended. We had almost wiped each other out. Two thirds of my platoon were either dead or wounded, with myself being severely wounded by shots through my lower arm and hip. This had been the price of this assault. My medic, private Hartmann, who had made it unharmed in whatever way, leaned towards me. I wanted to stand up, but he gently pushed me to the ground. He gestured towards two Englishmen, and together they picked me up and supported me. I ordered my men to bring the captured "Tommies" to the rear and secure our new positions. Then I commenced the march back with Hartmann, the lightly wounded and our prisoners.

We arrived at our staging area. There a vehicle, a customized Opel P 4, was ready to transport the wounded. I was not yet ready to leave, however. I indicated to one of the British that I wanted my coat picked up, which I had left behind before the assault. I took off my steel helmet and donned my uniform cap. Then I took my camera out of the coat, showed the Englishman how to use it and asked him to take a picture of us. The man gave me a puzzled look at first, but then bunched us together and took the picture. The resulting photograph shows a group of people who, just minutes ago, had wanted to kill each other and were now standing in togetherness. After taking the picture, I was loaded into the Opel P 4, and together with two other wounded from my platoon as well as "my two Tommies" we went to the medic station.

The photograph taken right after me being wounded on December 2, 1942. I stand left, my uniform cap tilted on my head. In the middle, with a flatter steel helmet, stands one of the two unknown Englishmen, a corporal who carried me to the rear.

Now, in the car, the adrenaline subsided and the pain started. My trousers and my sleeve were full of blood. In the arm it seemed that no bones had been hit, but my hip was hurting immensely. With my lips pressed against one another I made it through the ride. My two British prisoners looked at me compassionately, without hatred. The British soldiers asked me whether they would now become German prisoners of war (POWs). I said no, since in Africa Allied POWs were principally handled by the Italians. They looked saddened and asked if we could maybe make an exception for them. Despite the pain this request made me smirk. Again I declined and told them that in Africa there was only Italian imprisonment. The car rumbled along, and the pain made my forehead sweaty. The pain became unbearable.

In the Tunis hospital I was treated professionally. The arm wound was a clean penetration between ulna and radius. Things were worse with my hip wound. The bullet had entered my groin and exited on the other side. The wound was sanitized, and I got a cast to remain absolutely still.

The pain did not subside, however, and after a few days the wound began festering. The doctors realized that there was little to do about it here in Africa. Consequently, I was to be brought back to Europe. I was also told that our offensive had been successful, with all objectives reached by December 3. The Americans and British only barely managed to escape complete destruction. On the battlefield they left 134 destroyed tanks, most of them from the regiments of the American 1st Armored Division.

When my belongings were packed, I was directly handed my German-Italian dictionary and pay book. I quickly saw why. Both had been in my trousers' back pocket, and now they both had a small hole. The bullet that had penetrated my hip had also passed through both booklets on its way out. It was not only those that had been damaged, however, but also the photograph of my beloved Helena, which I had put inside the pay book, had a bullet hole.

On December 7, 1942, I was brought to Tunis airfield. Other wounded were put next to me, until the plane was eventually full. The doors were shut and before I knew it the aircraft took off. Pain in my hip was still enormous, and I could barely move with that cast. Africa had not kept me for long this time. Just a few days and I was already on my way back home.

My German-Italian dictionary and picture of my girlfriend Helena. Both fell victim to a British rifle bullet.

CHAPTER 9

A NEW ASSIGNMENT

My flight with Auntie Ju carried me from Tunis to Catania, Sicily. The medical personnel carrying me out of the plane and into an ambulance tried to handle me as gently as possible. Some degree of bumping and shaking was unavoidable, however, and I had to bite my lips in order to not moan. Once I was lying next to other fellow wounded strapped down in the ambulance, the doors were closed and we were driven to the Wehrmacht hospital in Palermo. There I was not kept for long, as after thorough examination by the doctors, it was decided to transfer me to Germany. After more than a week on the train we finally arrived at Tuttlingen reserve hospital on December 17, 1942. I was completely exhausted. The constant pain had taken a toll on me, and all I wanted was one thing: relief. Everything else I did not care about.

Luckily, the doctors at Tuttlingen seemed to employ an effective therapy. Just three days after my arrival and after taking appropriate medication, I was feeling significantly better. For the first time in a long while I fell into deep, dreamless sleep, out of which I awakened somewhat recuperated. The doctors told me that the infection was starting to heal and that my leg was saved. They did not know yet, however, if I would regain full mobility. That was up to the progress of the coming weeks.

With these worries in the back of my head I observed Christmas of 1942. I was cheered up by mail from home. I had as soon as possible sent a short telegram to my parents, carefully telling them that I had returned to Europe battered, but still alive. They wished me all the best for my recovery and pleaded for me to write back soon. My dear Helena, too, sent me a letter full of heartfelt wishes. These messages by my loved ones at home gave me strength and made me look forward in defiance of the pain. Christmas celebrations were prepared and held by the hospital staff with quite some enthusiasm. Many patients were not in the mood to celebrate because of their, in part, very serious injuries. Our caregivers were very well aware of this and as such went out of their way to pull us out of our lethargy.

Right after the cast was taken off, I began restoring my old mobility. This was not so easy, however, but I kept a stiff upper lip. With deliberate movements like bicycle exercises, for example, things were improving slowly but steadily. As soon as I was able to walk again, I forced myself on ever farther excursions. Without concern I went as far as I could and only then turned back. Upon seeing this doggedness, doctors and nurses just shook their heads, but as long as I was not harming myself they refrained from gently forcing me back into my accursed sickbed.

In mid-February 1943, I had recovered up to the point where I could be dismissed from the hospital and could finally go on my long-desired cure leave. Before I was released, however, there was another surprise. All of a sudden a delegation appeared at my bed, and with some dramatic rhetoric I was awarded the *Verwundetenabzeichen* (wound badge) in black as well as the Iron Cross 2nd Class, abbreviated *EK II*. Black was the lowest tier of the wound badge, indicating that I had been wounded once or twice in combat. The EK II was awarded to me "in the name of the Führer and supreme commander of the Wehrmacht" for my efforts during the assault on the British positions in Tunisia. Thus I became one of the roughly 2.3 million German soldiers that would receive this order during the war.

I was very proud of receiving these awards at the time. From that day on, everyone could clearly see that I had been to the front and earned my merits in combat. So I diligently attached them to my uniform jacket. Shortly thereafter, I made my farewells to the hospital staff.

I was full of hope, and the train ride seemed to last for an eternity thanks to all the anticipation I had for seeing my loved ones. The Bavarian landscape passed by, we crossed Salzburg and Vienna, and then the moment finally came. I arrived at my beloved hometown of Pottschach, able to embrace my family again. But all of that was still nothing compared to the moment I was finally holding Helena in my arms. After a few days, I also had the chance to meet my older brother Otto again. I had not seen him for a long time as well. He had been drafted before me, and just like me he had seen quite a lot. At the time he was serving in Panzer Regiment 4 of the 13th Panzer Division. As commander of a Panzer IV tank, he had lived through several dangerous encounters. On multiple occasions he had been barely able to cheat death. In January of 1943, his Panzer Division under the command of Army Group A had stood at the Caucasus, so he had close experience of events at the Volga. Up to that day, my brother Otto had made it through the ranks of the Wehrmacht, rising from a humble rifleman to corporal. In honor of his accomplishments he had also been awarded the EK II, and for his combat service in Russia in the winter before he had received the *Winterschlacht im Osten 1941/42* (Winter Battle in the East, 1941/42) medal – which was jokingly called the "frozen meat medal." When I told him about the new Tiger tanks I had seen in Africa, he listened with deep interest, although neither of us could have known that only months later he would command one of these behemoths himself. In September of 1943, the Panzer regiment that Otto served in was converted to a heavy tank detachment called *Schwere Panzerabteilung 507* and equipped with fresh Tiger tanks. This unit was then deployed at the hot spots of the Eastern Front, and Otto would stay with it until the end of the war.

My brother and I did not want to spend all of our short leave talking about the war, and so we found much joy in the fact that we could embrace each other and that we were both well. Not to mention our parents, who could hardly believe their luck when, after several years of war, both of their sons were back under their roof not just merely alive, but even in good health. I could also see, however, that my mother already dreaded the moment we had to leave her again. Because of this, Otto and I did our best to hearten our parents, spending more time with them than we had in a long while. We all knew that it could be the last opportunity in a long time.

On the left me and Helena in joyful togetherness. On the right me and my brother Otto.

During my cure leave I worked primarily on regaining my old mobility. I did a lot of gymnastics, but also broke out my skis and immediately "attacked" towards the Rax and Schneeberg mountains. On my first downhill run at the Rax, the unwonted jerky movements during turns made me clench my teeth in pain, but I did not slacken off, turning even harder. The bullet wound in my lower right arm had completely healed, although I probably had suffered some nerve damage; certain parts of the arm became irritated upon touching them. Luckily, I am left-handed, so this was not much of a detriment. Slowly but steadily things were back in order again. Everything else was done by my mother's cooking, which my body happily accepted. I could feel my old strength returning.

After a short month, however, this wonderful time in Pottschach came to an end, and in mid-March of 1943 I was to return to my barracks at Landau. Upon arrival I was immediately posted on basic training duty.

Now that I was a leader and drill instructor myself, I wanted to pass on what I had learned. I designed my training to be demanding, but I did not employ any of the oftentimes pointless chicaneries which I had seen during my own basic training. That I had sworn to myself back then – if I ever was to come to such a position, I would delete such pointless lessons without substitution. And when I looked into the eyes of my recruits, I knew that they were secretly thankful. Feedback like that did not require many words.

On May 13, 1943, we at Landau received more bad news over the radio. German and Italian forces in North Africa had surrendered. After Stalingrad, this was the second great defeat of the German Reich. The term "second Stalingrad" soon made the rounds. Hitler had rejected shipping German and Italian troops back to Sicily until the very end. A pointless show of stubbornness; up to 250,000 soldiers were marching into Allied POW camps. With pithy rhetoric the Wehrmacht report informed about the demise of Army Group Africa.

During that time I was assigned to a newly-formed Panzer division in France. On the quiet I had already heard of plans to establish such a unit. Rumor had it that one of the Panzer Divisions destroyed in Africa was to be rebuilt. When I received the order and skimmed through the lines of text, I felt a burning ambition to get back to the front. My thoughts were occupied by the war again. I was actually happy about these news. A short while before I had been certified fit for active service, from which point on I was fired up for returning to a combat unit. Sedate life at Landau was not exciting enough to me. Any doubts that had silently emerged after the surrenders at Stalingrad and in Africa, any peaceful thoughts I had had during the time with my loved ones, all of that was swept away. It was at the front that we were needed, not here at base. It was especially among us officers that we had encouraged each other, with propaganda coming through newsreels and newspapers doing the rest. "Now more than ever!" we thought.

Such being the case, the days at Landau soon came to an end. In early June, 1943, I boarded the train to Versailles near Paris, France. Someone was already waiting there when I arrived. A sergeant reported to me, and we walked up to a parked *Kübelwagen* car in which we went to my new unit's base. I was then utterly amazed when I realized that we were heading straight towards the famous Palace of Versailles. In its spacious palace gardens, which the famous Sun King Louis XIV had created in the 17th century, our Division was to be formed. That I could not have expected.

Once arrived at the Versailles command post of *Schnelle Division West*, the future 21st Panzer Division, I was welcomed by my new battalion commander, Major Zippe. After some hearty greetings, he informed me that I was to be assigned commander of a tank destroyer platoon in his II Battalion. One company of his unit was being built up as a heavy company equipped with anti-tank guns mounted on customized French armored chassis. Major Zippe welcomed me as an "old African" and wished me all the best for the coming months before finally dismissing me with a firm handshake.

Being in good spirits, I went ahead to my new unit. It was housed in a barracks formerly used by the French Foreign Legion, not far from Castle Versailles. There at the barracks I was welcomed by my new company commander, First Lieutenant Braatz. He, too, gave me a warm welcome before briefing me on the location and my new platoon. I quickly assessed that this ongoing buildup of 21st Panzer Division was something special. Due to the present general shortage of materiel as well as ever-increasing demand for new combat units, the rebuilding of 21st Panzer Division went different from what had been the norm. For example, Braatz explained to me that it had been explicitly ordered that "… required gear and vehicles are to be requisitioned exclusively from French captured goods or through provision by the 'Commander in Chief West'."

After the defeat of France in 1940, the German Army had established huge collection points for captured weapons across the country. This equipment was now to be used. To this end, captain Alfred Becker, World War I veteran and future commander of 21st Panzer Division's newly formed *Sturmgeschützabteilung 200* (200th Assault Gun Detachment), was tasked with retrofitting captured French vehicles to accept and be equipped with German guns. He founded *Baustab Becker* (*Baustab* meaning "construction cadre") and, with a lot of improvisation, began fulfilling his mission. He knew how to realize the potential of this war materiel to its greatest effect. Eventually, almost 450 armored vehicles and motor tractors had been converted to tank destroyers, self-propelled artillery, and other kinds of combat vehicles by June 1944. These vehicles were the backbone of our 21st Panzer Division.

Our heavy company consisted of an anti-tank platoon, an anti-aircraft platoon and a grenade launcher platoon. Each of these units was equipped with three converted French self-propelled guns. My anti-tank platoon had three half-tracked vehicles with an anti-tank gun on top, converted from French Somua MCG artillery tractors. Each of them now bore a German 75 mm Pak 40 anti-tank gun. Back in 1942, I had been trained on a similar vehicle, a Marder II, at the Panzer Forces Academy. In essence, it was an anti-tank gun with additional mobility bestowed upon it; as such, the vehicle was extremely well-suited for attacking enemy armored groups from the flank, but not for an offensive role. It was also unsuitable for urban combat since the fighting compartment had no roof, making it vulnerable to hand grenades thrown from above. So getting cover from accompanying infantry was a necessity.

Modified Somua MCG half-track with German 75 mm Pak 40 anti-tank gun. I had three of these vehicles in my platoon.

A vehicle's crew comprised five men: driver, assistant driver, gunner, loader, and commander. In addition to the three half-tracks, I also had a medium-sized Renault truck available as ammunition carrier, whose crew of one NCO and three riflemen could also serve as emergency infantry protection. For myself there was a Type 82 *Kübelwagen* with a driver/messenger and another messenger. With this car I could deliver orders myself or establish communications. For the most time, however, I was riding along on one of the gun carriers. In total, my platoon had a strength of 22 soldiers of different ranks.

Some of the men in my platoon were experienced soldiers who had seen a couple of battles. Some had fought in Africa just like me. Once they learned that I had served in Africa twice they happily accepted me without any prejudice. To my great joy I soon found that I had gotten a glorious bunch of fellows to lead. Immediately starting to better get to know my soldiers, I also pushed on with training the vehicle crews.

Most of our training time was dedicated to handling and operating the half-tracks' 75 mm guns, taking up positions, calling and allocating targets as well as shifting to a new position. Especially the latter had to be done as quickly as possible if one wanted to survive the first salvos on the battlefield. Consequently, I let the crews take up a position time and again until they could go through the procedure in their sleep. Unfortunately, it turned out that my three self-propelled guns had no radio equipment whatsoever, so I gave commands over short distances exclusively via hand signs. If I wanted to give a lengthy order or introduce one of my guns to an unusual firing position, however, I had to either take my *Kübelwagen* from one gun to the next or, should we already be in position, go there on foot. This kept me on the run a lot, and more than a few of my men probably had to smirk when they saw me dart from one gun to the next over and over.

The following weeks of training at Versailles quickly flew by, and on July 7, 1943 we were assembled and told that our formation was now officially called 21st Panzer Division again. From that point on, me and my men belonged to 8th Company, II Battalion, 192nd Panzergrenadier Regiment. My battalion commander, Major Zippe, now had a total of seven companies: three *Panzergrenadier* armored infantry companies, one heavy company, one infantry gun company, one *Reihenwerfer* barrage mortar company and one supply company. Considerable fighting power.

Taking a rest during field exercises in the Rennes-Laval area. Near the center sits my company commander, first lieutenant Braatz.

Assigned commander of our regiment was Lieutenant Colonel Josef Rauch, while command of 21st Panzer Division as a whole went to Brigadier General Edgar Feuchtinger on August 1, 1943. He had already led Schnelle Division West at the rank of colonel before its conversion to an armored division; now this man was to command 21st Panzer Division, and over the coming months it would turn out that his ways of employing the formation were not accepted without controversy.

Feuchtinger was not a "tank head," but originally an artilleryman who became a known figure in the 1930s for organizing the *Reichsparteitage* (Reich party rallies) at Nuremberg. On these occasions, he had gotten acquainted to Adolf Hitler, and many opined that his connections to the Führer were the sole reason for him being assigned commander of 21st Panzer Division. Along with other company officers I was housed in private quarters directly next to Castle Versailles. Thanks to that I soon came into contact with French locals. Towards us, they were quite reserved, but not unfriendly. It seemed as if they had come to terms with us occupants. Our food was bought at local markets, with the French farmers and merchants probably being somewhat grateful for getting to do more business; after all, our presence came with greatly increased demand for foodstuffs. There was no semblance of supply shortages at the time.

In mid-August of 1943, our regiment was redeployed to the Rennes-Laval area in Brittany. Here there was a large training area where cooperation of the regiment's individual units was to be refined. My platoon and I were quartered in a small tranquil Breton village. While my men were housed in two buildings, I enjoyed the privilege of having a room at the local Catholic priest's home.

The priest, as I would soon discover, had a very national attitude and, in broken English, repeatedly tried to engage me in conversation about the war's proceedings. At that, he was always very kind and quite obliging towards me in general. By initially talking about religion, he wanted to earn my trust; for instance, he inquired whether I knew the sectarian composition of my soldiers and whether I had consideration for that. I answered that this was taken for granted as long as it did not interfere with military considerations. It would soon turn out that his curiosity was of a different nature.

When he discovered my *Afrika* cuff title and I told him that I had served in Libya, Egypt, and Tunisia, he became increasingly pressing. He now also directly mentioned our 21st Panzer Division. To his regret, however, I did not respond to that, which increasingly irritated him. I soon found out that he was secretly searching my room, rummaging through my private belongings and documents – when I left them in the morning, they were in a slightly different place when I returned in the evening. Since I nevertheless took to him, I refrained from reporting this behavior. On the contrary, I was attentive in not saying anything negative about France in his presence. He had great interest in our activities and intentions. During a meeting with First Lieutenant Braatz and several locals we conferred about our future quartering. On that occasion we found the priest, index finger raised, talking to the villagers about us "Hitler officers." I had to smile; After all, I knew that this opinion came to be through his daily "political" discussions with me.

We were anxious to not alienate the local population. Consequently, lack of discipline towards civilians by our men was not tolerated. One evening, a local girl was halted by some of our soldiers and prevented from leaving. After the mayor filed a complaint to company command, the soldiers in question were admonished by First Lieutenant Braatz, with apologies offered to the mayor, the girl, and her family. Then a warning in light of other events was issued to the regiment. Two soldiers of a neighboring unit had been found in one of the region's numerous forest ponds, their dead bodies drifting in the water. It was determined that they had been shot while bathing – apparently an act of the Resistance. This left me much more cautious near the priest.

One man of my platoon hailed from Alsace and thus spoke perfect French. He would often serve as our translator. He was a quiet type and known loner. When he talked, he talked mostly about his brother who served at the Eastern Front and who he had not heard from for a long time. The French had quickly found out about his background, and he was presumably contacted by Resistance members. One morning, eventually, he could not be found. Even after a long search he was still gone. He had apparently deserted. Now it became clear to me why he had been so quiet. Perhaps he had struggled to find a way out of his situation, eventually deciding against us. You never knew what was actually going on and what could happen.

After almost a month in the Rennes area, I was shocked to find my legs making more and more trouble. I was not in pain, but it started with some feeling of numbness in both feet that spread upwards. Eventually it became so bad that during field exercises, I needed help getting up into the gun compartments. Stubborn as I was, I did not want to admit that something was wrong. Then, during one of these exercises, our battalion physician watched me getting helped while climbing up one of the gun vehicles. He went on to ask me about my condition, and I told him about my hip wound. The physician insisted on examining me, finding that I had no more reflexes in my legs. He immediately took me off duty. I was transferred to Suresnes military hospital near Paris, where the doctors at first could not find any cause for my apparent paralysis.

My condition got worse by the day until I was finally unable to move my legs at all. I lay in bed, utterly desperate. The doctors suspected that my gunshot wound and the severe infection that followed had led to some sort of nerve palsy. They explained to me that recovery could take a long time, and that there was some uncertainty about how and if I would recover at all.

In late September, 1943, it was decided that I would leave the Paris hospital heading for Germany. An ambulance train took me to Trier, a town at the Moselle river near the border with Luxembourg. Apparently there were some nerve paralysis specialists. Nevertheless, in my case they were at first quite puzzled. After a short while I was treated with light electric shocks which indeed made me very slowly regain control of my legs. Encouraged by that, I commenced exercising my mobility again. It was extremely arduous, however, because I had to learn walking like a small child. Just like after my wounding in Tunisia, I doggedly worked on getting back on my feet again. Time passed by and I spent another Christmas and another New Year's Eve in hospital. Just like the year before in Tuttlingen, here and now, 1943/44 in Trier, people went out of their way to make us patients' holidays as livable as possible.

By April 1944, I had come to the point where I could walk normally without a stick. During my recovery I had followed German newsreel reports with interest and come to realize that, since last summer at least, we had been on the defensive everywhere. In September 1943, the Allies had successfully landed on the Italian mainland, the Italians had deposed their *Duce* Benito Mussolini and abandoned the Axis; our forces had occupied Rome and my former Italian brothers in arms entered captivity in the thousands. In the winter of 1943/44, fierce fighting erupted around Monte Cassino and in January, the Allies landed at Anzio and Nettuno south of Rome, establishing beachheads that were furiously attacked by our troops.

On the Eastern Front, things were in no way better. In early April of 1944, Russian forces invaded Romania, marking the first time in three years that they left Russian soil. As a consequence, 34 Wehrmacht divisions were sent from Germany to the front in an attempt to stop the Soviet armies. A futile endeavor, as it would soon turn out. German troops were on the retreat westward. In the Reich itself, the German armament industry as well as the civilian populace were under increasing pressure. American bomber formations were flying precision attacks on military factories by day, while the British Royal Air Force engulfed German cities in firestorms by night. On August 13, 1943, even Wiener Neustadt, my former school town, was attacked by American bombers for the first time. More raids on the town and its industrial facilities followed until the end of the year, and in March of 1944, American bombers first reached Vienna and dropped their deadly cargo there.

At the end of my recovery, I could look forward to a short home leave. I seized that opportunity to finally do what I had been planning for months: asking Helena to marry me. The fact that she said *yes*, made me the happiest man on earth.

CHAPTER 10
A STORM IS COMING

n late April, 1944, I was to return to 21st Panzer Division. In the weeks before, the division had been deployed to Hungary for a short time. It was feared that the Hungarian Government could secede from the Axis. The intention was to prevent a "second Italy", and so on March 19, 1944, a total of eight German divisions had marched into Hungary during Operation *Margarethe*.

There was no trace of resistance, and Hungarian head of state Nikolas Horty, a former *k.u.k. Kriegsmarine* (Austria-Hungarian Navy) admiral, was allowed to remain in office. In reality, however, the Germans took power by installing a new Germany-aligned government comprising Hungarian fascists. So our eastern allies also began seeing the signs of the times, seeking to distance themselves from the declining German Reich. They wanted to avoid the undertow of the coming maelstrom of death and destruction. But it was far too late. Whether on Germany's or the opposing side, the people of all European nations now had to drain the cup of sorrow to the dregs.

After its return from Hungary, my division was relocated to the Caen area, the capital of Normandy. In early 1944, things still seemed calm in France. Some evidence of a coming large-scale Allied naval invasion was starting to corroborate, however. French Resistance activities to prepare for such landings along with intensifying attacks on French transportation hubs by Allied bombers did not go unnoticed by German leadership and the *Abwehr* (German intelligence). In early summer of 1944, a storm was brewing in France, and I would soon witness its thunder.

On May 2, 1944, I reported back to Lieutenant Colonel Rauch at the regimental command post in Thury-Harcourt south of Caen. From there, I went on to the battalion in Le Mesnil to my battalion commander, Major Zippe. He was visibly happy to see me, showing me the way to our company in person. We left the command post in a *Kübelwagen* headed for Cairon, a small village roughly eight kilometers (five miles) northwest of Caen. My return was a pleasant surprise for all. They had not expected me to ever return to France. First Lieutenant Braatz, greeted me as friendly as months before, and the men of my platoon were happy as well. *Oberfeldwebel* (master sergeant) Tanner, commander of the grenade launcher platoon and born Styrian, offered especially warm greetings. With him, I had spent many hours of training exercises around Rennes, and we had always worked well together. My second in command, also a master sergeant, had led my platoon commendably while I was away, making sure that the soldiers remained highly capable and ever vigilant. By now, our 21st Panzer Division had been deployed to the French Channel Coast with all its formations ready.

Here, behind the *Atlantic Wall*, it was to secure the important town of Caen as well as serving as a powerful mechanized reserve force in case of enemy landings in this area.

Construction of this Atlantic Wall had been started back in 1942. It reached from France all the way to Norway, stretching over more than 2.500 kilometers (1.550 mi). The purpose of this defensive line was to defend against possible Allied invasions of the European continent. In France, development of the Atlantic Wall was overseen by "Commander in Chief West" General Field Marshal Gerd von Rundstedt.

Under his command were Army Group B, commanded by General Field Marshal Erwin Rommel, as well as Army Group G, commanded by Colonel General Johannes Blaskowitz. Rommel was of the opinion that an Allied invasion could be defended against only if the troops landed could be thrown back into the sea within the first few days. Many of his measures were taken with this objective in mind. Although the Atlantic

Wall had thousands of bunkers, its defenses lacked depth. To alleviate this, Rommel ordered the offshore Channel banks covered with mined obstacles, which would hamper the advance of landing craft before they could even reach the beaches. In the hinterland, all open areas where gliders could land were littered with thousands of wooden stakes called *Rommel's asparagus.*

All of these measures were under the watchful eyes of the Allies, who photographed each and every foot of the beaches, even sending out frogmen commandos to survey the obstacles planted in the sand. As such, German preparations and defensive measures were no secret to the Allies. In January of 1944, Rommel was eventually handed command over all German forces north of the Loire river. In this function he was still subordinate to General Field Marshal von Rundstedt, and the two soon were in fierce disputes over where exactly the Allied invasion would happen. Their discussion mostly revolved around the deployment of the Wehrmacht's powerful armored formations.

While von Rundstedt wanted to keep them deeper inland, Rommel pleaded for shifting them closer to the coast. Von Rundstedt's thoughts were largely based on the judgments of General Inspector of Panzer Forces, Colonel General Heinz Guderian, as well as Panzer Forces General Leo Geyr von Schweppenburg. Both favored a massive counterattack of Axis armored forces well after Allied troops had landed. Rommel was quite judgmental of this concept. Well, Guderian and Geyr von Schweppenburg held the view that, if the all-important mechanized formations were stationed closer to the coast, they would become too spread out since the location of the landings was still unknown. In the hinterland, Panzer and Panzergrenadier divisions could be assembled for a concentrated push once the invasion commenced. Rommel on the other hand judged that the Allies would have air supremacy right from the beginning of the landings. Shifting large armored formations would then be hardly feasible. In North Africa, Rommel had witnessed first-hand how Allied air superiority could slow down troop movements to a crawl, thus paralyzing any offensive capabilities.

None of these generals, however, was in actual command of the vital divisions. Hitler reserved for himself the right to approve commitment of these important formations. Rommel's attempts to call on Hitler were only marginally successful. On May 7, 1944 eventually, on order of Commander in Chief West, he received three powerful Panzer divisions for his Army Group B to serve as its reserve: 2nd and 116th Panzer Divisions as well as our very own 21st Panzer Division.

This assignment was only *occasion-related*, meaning only for deployment against possible naval invasion. For all other purposes such as training and buildup, the three divisions still remained with Geyr von Schweppenburg's *Panzergruppenkommando West* (Panzer Group Command West). This command in turn got its orders directly from Wehrmacht High Command which, in effect, meant Hitler.

An abstruse situation that left none of the people involved satisfied. At the very least Rommel was able to independently command three Panzer divisions on the occasion – without having to ask the Commander in Chief West or Wehrmacht High Command for permission. This important fact was in compliance with his plans of an immediate counterattack. There was a catch, however. Out of those three divisions, only the 21st was stationed close to the coast, while the other two were far behind in the hinterland.

We kept on training our soldiers at Cairon and enjoyed the beginning of a French summer which, as the locals told us, promised to become especially beautiful. We were just around ten kilometers (six miles) from the sea, so we would go swimming there in our free time. We were largely exempt from having to partake in the massive fortification building at the Atlantic Wall, which was left to regular infantry divisions; our regiment only had to plant some of *Rommel's asparagus*. Apart from that, we had only established a defensive perimeter of emergency positions around Cairon. Rommel was expecting air landings, so he insisted on all-around defensive measures in the rear as well.

Our division's relocation closer to the coast had been a concession to Rommel. The area had not been chosen arbitrarily; Caen was seen as a vital industrial center, and it also lay at the river Orne, which went northeast from the town towards the Channel coast. Even if the Allies were to land at the Pas de Calais and not in Normandy, it was not unexpected for them to drop paratroopers in the latter region. Caen was a prime target for such an operation, since capturing the town and nearby crossing points over the Orne would make troop movements between the eastern and western parts of the coast practically impossible. Consequently, our 192nd Panzergrenadier Regiment was stationed north of the town and west of the Orne, while the 125th Panzergrenadier Regiment was northeast of Caen and thus on the east bank of the river.

South of the town, finally, were the Panzer regiment as well as the artillery and any other support units. Ahead of our division, directly at the coast, were the formations of 716th Infantry Division commanded by Brigadier General Wilhelm Richter. This infantry division was tasked with defending the coastline itself. Its soldiers watched over the beaches in concrete bunkers and pillboxes as well as operating machine gun, anti-tank and artillery positions further back. They had almost no mobility whatsoever.

In theory, General Field Marshal Rundstedt in his role of "Commander in Chief West" was in control of almost one and a half Million Wehrmacht soldiers, of which roughly 850,000 were part of the *Heer* (Army). In practice, the command situation was not that clear. Like the Panzer divisions, the infantry divisions had an abstrusely organized leadership; Rommel's Army Group B led the 7th and 15th German Armies. Subordinate to 7th Army, commanded by Colonel General Friedrich Dollman, was LXXXIV Army Corps, led by General of the Artillery Erich Marcks. This corps, in turn, comprised six infantry divisions, with one of those being the 716th in the Caen area.

The formations in which the infantry divisions' soldiers were serving, however, varied greatly in their combat strength. Of a total of thirty infantry divisions, the majority had only very limited transportation capabilities, with many also lacking in artillery as well as anti-tank weaponry. Since France was regarded part of the *rear*, many of the best soldiers had been relocated to the front lines in Italy and Russia. Around a fifth of the personnel of 7th Army were members of the *Osttruppen* (Eastern Forces), which were Poles or even Russian prisoners that had been conscripted as

Hilfswillige (HiWis) or who volunteered in order to escape a fate in the camps. I knew that many of the divisions stationed in France were only of limited combat value.

The truly powerful formations in northern France were six Panzer and Panzergrenadier divisions of the *Heer* and the *Waffen-SS*. These even had potent Pz V *Panther* and Pz VI *Tiger* tanks. Committing these, however, would only bring success if we had air supremacy. But how were the few available *Luftwaffe* fighter squadrons to be coordinated? Rundstedt had no control over the *Luftwaffe* or the *Kriegsmarine* (navy). This would prove exceedingly detrimental to German efforts at the beginning of the Allied invasion. Not to mention that neither *Luftwaffe* nor *Kriegsmarine* had much to offer in order to seriously oppose the Allies once they attacked. The forces available were simply too few.

Within our battalion, discipline was first-rate, and there were no problems between us and the inhabitants of the small village of Cairon. Quite the opposite – we enjoyed almost friendly relations. My platoon was housed in a small chateau, with me living in a middle-aged couple's neat little house. I could walk through the chateau park and directly enter the backyard of my private quarters. My French hosts would even invite me and my NCOs to an afternoon coffee on multiple occasions. As such, we would spend many Saturday or Sunday afternoons sitting in this lovely backyard garden.

The man of the house would often remark that, while occupation is never a good thing, "… the demeanor of the occupiers determines the framework for living together." My host was right at that, and my comrades and I assured him that he had nothing to fear from us. Nevertheless we avoided talking about the war or the occupation and instead mostly discussed everyday matters with our landlords. After all, much more than that was impossible, since all we had to communicate were our small dictionaries and hopeful gesturing. This often led to bursts of hearty laughter on both sides.

One of these afternoons, we suddenly heard loud engine noise, and before we knew it an airplane swooped over our heads only a few hundred feet above. We jumped to our feet and tried to get another look at it. The aircraft entered a steep curve and began to circle above the village. We determined the plane to be an Allied reconnaissance craft. Our 20 mm AA gun was not ready, and shooting the plane with MGs or even carbines seemed completely pointless to us. So we watched it circling and hoped for the arrival of our fighters. But nothing happened. As if he had all the time in the world, the Allied pilot photographed his targets, flew his loops and circles before eventually, after some seemingly endless minutes, turned back north.

We were shocked. An Allied recon aircraft this far behind the coast, completely undisturbed by our interceptors? That was a harsh blow to our morale. The afternoon was ruined, and we were depressed enough to not want to look our hosts in the eye we left the scene. The humiliation was simply too great.

In early 1944, American and British bomber formations attacked the German Reich from Great Britain without suffering too substantial losses. Time and again we received air raid warnings. Then we would observe the contrails of high-flying American bomber formations going east over our heads. Squadron over squadron flew towards our homeland, and the thought of what havoc their bombs might wreak there filled us with horror. American escort fighters equipped with external fuel tanks had emerged in the sky in early 1944, soon turning each interception by our own fighters into a suicide mission. In addition, there were barely any German fighter planes stationed in northern France. As such, the *Luftwaffe* could hardly do anything to oppose incoming and attacking Allied bombers.

Up to that point we had been spared, but American bombers, protected by their escorts, had already started devastating transportation hubs as well as bombing larger troop concentrations here in France. Civilian casualties were on the rise, and we could see how the French themselves were also suffering under this intense bombing campaign. They most certainly had a different idea of how their liberation would look like. Bitterly they endured this fate, secretly hoping that the Allies would soon commence their long-awaited landing operation and bring the war to an end.

Dug in and ready: Training exercises with my anti-tank platoon at the Cairon defensive perimeter.

CHAPTER 11
FINAL PREPARATIONS

Me and my comrades used to discuss all the time in what area, if at all, the Allied landings would occur. Most were ready to bet on the area of Calais. Here, the English Channel between France and Great Britain was the narrowest, thus making a ferrying operation the easiest to execute. Others argued for our position in Normandy because we would not expect it here. Most of our soldiers ultimately did not care where the Allied troops would land. Many hoped that it would happen as soon as possible – not because they yearned for the war to end, but because constantly waiting for the invasion to happen was unnerving. They were waiting for months by now. The soldiers wanted to lock horns with the unknown enemy, no matter the outcome.

During these weeks, Rommel was visiting his troops in Normandy unusually frequently. It seemed as if he had come to the conviction that the Allied landings would commence here. He personally inspected the individual defense positions at the channel coast, ordering changes and improvements to be made time and again. This did not always yield approval. The troop leaders already had enough of him appearing again and again, with his defensive measures keeping their men from commencing, in their opinion, much more important field maneuvers.

On May 30, 1944, he visited our division as well. To welcome him, parts of our regiment assembled at full strength in a small forest near Lebisey, north of Caen; not in the open field, like in past times, but hidden between trees and bushes. This showed us all quite plainly what was going on with our air superiority. A company of Sturmgeschützabteilung 200 (Assault Gun Detachment 200) had been transferred to our area a short time earlier, so they were also set up along with their self-propelled guns.

Then Rommel appeared, accompanied by our divisional Commander Brigadier General Feuchtinger and his staff. Rommel went along with Feuchtinger, the latter showing the former each and every of our units, detailing the features of our battalion with the help of his staff officers as well as regimental commander Colonel Rauch. I could also see a cluster of war reporters swarming around Rommel like busy bees, diligently taking photographs. We were standing mustered in full battle gear before our vehicles, waiting. Our men were wearing their steel helmets, we officers had field caps. Rommel took his time. You could see how he was especially interested in our adapted French *captured equipment*. Every type of vehicle was explained to him in detail. The self-propelled guns intrigued him the most. Then the time had come. He moved towards our company. Looking in his direction, I saluted. But it seemed that he had already seen enough. Purposefully, he marched past our company, meeting our gazes for a moment before disappearing again.

Rommel's appearance instilled respect for him. He walked upright, radiating confidence and conviction – which was exactly what we expected from him during the harsh hours looming. As for me personally, I was a bit disappointed; I had hoped he would be especially interested in our Panzerjägerzug (Tank Destroyer Platoon). "Whatever," I thought, waiting for my orders to reorganize and join up with the other units. The orders came straightaway, and I ordered my crews to assume march readiness. We fired up the engines of our vehicles and rolled back towards our quarters.

In the evening we learned that Rommel had been satisfied with 21st Panzer Division, but not with the expansion of the coastal defenses. Once again, he had urged the responsible commanders to use more initiative and had ordered additional measures. When he was standing at the beach in front of the 716th Infantry Division, he said in front of the assembled generals, "Gentlemen, I know the British from Africa and Italy. And I tell you, they will choose a location for their landings where we will not expect it. And right here, on this very spot, this will be."

Rommel inspecting parts of our 21st Panzer Division in the Lebisey area, May 30, 1944. This photo was taken just in the moment when he marched past my tank destroyer platoon. With my hand at the cap I am saluting him.

There is another small episode about Rommel's visit that I want to share. The photograph of Rommel, my crew and me was later published in the Nazi Party propaganda journal "Völkischer Beobachter." In 1944, this "Völkisch Observer" had a circulation of 1.7 million issues and was distributed in the whole Reich, of course including our home, the Ostmark. My beloved Helena discovered the photo of Rommel and us in the issue and was convinced that she had recognized me on it. My parents had come to the same conclusion, and together they wrote a note to the "Völkischer Beobachter" and asked for a copy of the photograph. And indeed, a few weeks later my family received a letter from the editorial office containing several prints of the photo. I myself did not know anything about this story until after the war, when I was finally able to examine the photograph for the first time.

On June 1, 1944, First Lieutenant Braatz, on orders of the battalion, tasked me with taking up an observation post with one of my guns on Hill 61, northwest of the village of Bénouville and south of Colleville. We packed the bare necessities, I loaded up my *Kübel*, and after a short drive we arrived at our observation position, or as we called it, *B-Stelle*.

From this observation post we had a wonderful view along the Caen Canal and the parallel river Orne towards the coast. That was why right next to us the command post bunker of the 736th Infantry Regiment was situated; its commander, Colonel Krug, was responsible for the defense of this sector. From the town of Caen, the river Orne flows northeast directly towards the channel coast. Just around 400 meters (440 yards) west of the Orne, the Caen Canal lies in parallel, also flowing towards the sea. The distance between Caen and the sea is roughly 10 kilometers (6 miles). A road, in parallel to the Caen Canal, leads from Caen over Bénouville to Ouistreham at the mouth of the Orne.

If you were to drive from Caen towards the sea, you would enter Bénouville after 5 kilometers (3 miles). Here, at the northern edge of Bénouville, lies a T-junction with an additional road leading eastwards over two bridges crossing the Caen Canal and the Orne river towards Ranville.

In our observation post on hill 61 near Bénouville, June 1, 1944. On the picture I am busy improving the camo of my helmet.

The two bridges over the Orne river and Caen Canal, right in the middle between Caen and the sea, had enormous operational value. Between them and Caen, there was only one other possibility of crossing the Orne and the Canal: at Colombelles, in the northern outskirts of

Caen. With the exception of these two locations, moving from east to west or vice versa between Caen and the channel coast was impossible.

The two Panzergrenadier regiments of our 21st Panzer Division, positioned north and east of Caen, were separated by the two streams, the bridges themselves guarded by units of the 716th Infantry Division. Upon examining the terrain in front of me, I immediately realized, if the Allies were to land here in Normandy, the bridges northeast of Caen would be of tremendous importance and thus heavily contested.

I was to end up being right indeed. But the time had not come yet. Allied aerial reconnaissance was active again that day, and covered by some bushes, we watched a British Spitfire recon aircraft flying low along the coast, from east to west. Bitterly we observed that today, too, this sortie went uninterrupted. Like earlier, during our afternoon coffee party, our Luftwaffe was nowhere to be seen. On the next day we concluded our observation mission and moved back to Cairon. The time in this *B-Stelle* proved to be invaluable to me; now I was able to fathom the importance of the Caen area. If the Allies were to land here, we would be right in the focus... which would be pretty uncomfortable.

The following days were a slack period for us, but reports of French Résistance sabotage acts were mounting. Time and again field cable squads had to move out in order to fix cut lines. In addition, the Allies had conducted excessive airstrikes on June 1, targeting mostly transportation hubs and the bridges across the Loire and Seine. Something was in the wind; we could all feel it. On June 5, we successfully completed a company maneuver in the close vicinity of Cairon. In the process, we observed that our exercise was eyed with interest by individual French civilians. We understood that each and every of our steps was noted down by the French resistance. Our defensive positions were not a secret either. All our minefields had been delimited by barbed wire and marked by warning signs – the risk of civilian casualties was simply too high. Consequently, as expected, the French resistance knew exactly where our troops were deployed. Unable to change these circumstances, we resignedly acknowledged those civilians and focused on training our soldiers.

A happy moment of comradeship: The men of my platoon shortly before invasion.

CHAPTER 12
D-DAY

I n the evening of June 5, 1944, an armada of unprecedented size put to sea from British ports. More than 4.000 Allied landing craft as well as 600 minesweepers, destroyers, cruisers and battleships started their crossing of the channel. South of the Isle of Wight they assembled, sailing southwards under harsh winds and rough seas. Their destinations were the beaches of Normandy between Cherbourg and Le Havre. This sector had been chosen since the Allied leadership assumed that the Germans would expect an amphibious invasion at the narrowest part of the English Channel, on the French coast near Boulogne and Calais, thus investing less resources into the defense of Normandy, which lies further away.

When the first bombs from enemy aircraft were detonating at Caen roughly 20 minutes after midnight, we were bounced out of our beds in Cairon. Dozily I rubbed my eyes while my runner, Lance Corporal Atteneder, reported to me. Judging from his wide-eyed gaze I could see that he was extremely nervous.

I quickly put on my uniform, rushed into the garden, and gave a few initial orders, accompanied by the hum of enemy airplane engines above and the flashes of heavy explosions illuminating nearby Caen as bright as day. Within a short while, my platoon was ready to deploy, and we began moving towards the rallying point of our 8th Company. Once there, we were ordered to simply wait for the time being. First Lieutenant Braatz had no clear overview of the situation yet, a fact condemning us to remaining inactive. The humming of enemy aircraft engines above us persisted, and we could make out some of our own defensive fire. Tracer rounds were shackling the sky around us in long chains. Everyone was waiting, all tensed up. Everyone checked his gear and made sure that it was ready for use in the upcoming battle. Then eventually, after almost three hours of anxious waiting, our superiors managed to make up their minds.

Braatz assembled us and relayed the battalion's order to us platoon commanders: "Company to immediately march towards Bénouville, capture the local Orne bridges and reconnoiter the unclear situation towards the coast!" We had been waiting for this order on the edge of our seats. In an instant, we had fired up our engines and were vigorously yelling commands. The men were hurrying, relieved by their time of waiting having ended.

My three self-propelled guns formed the spearhead, followed by the rest of the company somewhat behind us. First the heavy mortar platoon of staff sergeant Tanner, equipped with three self-propelled 8 cm launchers on French carriers; after them came Braatz's company command and finally the anti-aircraft platoon of Sergeant Grimm. The latter was fielding three self-propelled Unic P107 vehicles equipped with 20 mm Flak 38 cannons.

Major Sergeant Guse, our company sergeant, stayed in Cairon for the time being, along with the logistics group. The unclear situation did not allow for taking them to the front. Communications with them were held up via motorcycle messengers. While moving towards what we suspected to be the front line, we noticed an increasing number of explosions coming from the coast. The Allies had begun bombarding the beaches in preparation for the amphibious landings of their soldiers. I knew that the situation could turn hazardous very soon, so we had to move cautiously. Braatz fell behind a bit with the rest of our company, while my tank destroyer platoon slowly tiptoed towards Bénouville, the three self-propelled constantly leapfrogging – individual vehicles passing each other in their advance while the stationary ones provide cover.

In spite of the dangers looming ahead I pressed my men forward until the southern outskirts of Bénouville were finally in sight shortly before 04:00. We could make out the village roughly 330 yards ahead, the road leading dead straight towards its houses. To the left was an open field, with only a small hedgerow and a ditch lining the road. To the right lay a young forest with the trees and bushes of a park right next to it, the latter enclosed by a wall which also served as the road's right boundary. I ordered a halt and designated firing positions for my guns along the street. It was during this time that our nerves were strained to breaking point. Avoiding contact with the enemy and not getting caught off guard was paramount – a conceivably difficult goal. Advancing into the village without fire support would have been pointless, as we could have fallen prey to an ambush by British anti-tank and machine guns. Getting our company to reinforce us was vital. I ordered my men to wait until the company's other units had arrived.

After assigning a signaler, the rest of our force was soon closing up. Braatz put the anti-air platoon left of the road to protect the open area, with my tank destroyer platoon next to it spread out along the road, enjoying additional protection towards the direction of the village. The heavy mortar platoon was set up somewhat deep in the forest to the right. Its mission was to bombard targets ahead of us as soon as they were detected.

The sky above was imbued by the droning of bombers and the rustling of smaller aircraft engines. We looked up, and for the first time I could make out the silhouettes of airplanes. Gliders incoming! Obviously, the British had begun reinforcing their troops.

Making the most of each hedge and every bush's cover, our guns took up position. During this I cursed their engines' loud noise. If the British had not already known of our presence, then by now they would. After a while, all units had finally taken up their positions; quiet set in again, except for fierce combat noise coming from the town's center. Obviously, there was fighting going on in the village. Now that the rest of our company had caught up, we were able to advance further. I decided to form a reconnaissance party under my personal command in order to scout along the road leading into the village, protected by my self-propelled guns. After dismounting, I briefly informed my platoon as well as Braatz of my intentions and indicated the planned advance to my runners. Both of them had already guessed what was to come and stood ready. Keeping our heads low, the three of us sneaked along the right-hand roadside ditch until we reached a high stone wall – the boundary of Chateau de Bénouville, according to my map. Both road and wall went on until their lines disappeared in the morning mist.

It drizzled. I hoped for the rain to stay because, if the weather was to clear up, dawn would soon give way to the sun, likely dissolving the last wafts of mist through its warm rays. Now, however, dense clouds were filling the sky. Which was good for us, since it meant that Allied fighter-bombers would have a hard time spotting us.

I raised my hand and we slowly sneaked ahead. I decided to switch to the left side of the street, as the Chateau's wall would have offered no cover against enemy fire. One after the other we leaped across the road. Along the ditch and a yard-tall hedgerow, our force covering us from behind, we stealthily advanced.

The noise of battle ahead had ceased, and any detonations we heard seemed to come from far away. After around 300 yards, the street had a crossroad. To our right, the park wall ended at a gatehouse while the dense house rows of Bénouville lay straight ahead. The gatehouse with its half-round portal served as an entry point to the castle's park, a street bending to the right leading into the garden. Suddenly I became aware of a body lying motionless in the ditch, near the hedgerow's end. While I could not recognize the patchy uniform, I could see that it was a British paratrooper, judging by the size of his magazine pouches. His unnatural posture meant he was dead. We had already come damn close to the enemy.

But where was that enemy, exactly? I suspected them to have taken the rows of houses in front of us. *Tommy* seemed to be waiting just for us. I could not make out any movement, but all was suspiciously silent. Sweat running over my forehead, I checked windows and garden hedges through my binoculars. There! I spotted shapes in patchy uniforms. They were running low along a hedgerow. "That's got to be the British," I thought. Slowly I crouched back and signaled to my runners that the houses ahead had been taken by the enemy. I could see the tension in both of their faces.

In the gardens ahead I could see more British soldiers. Here at the crossroad, we were in an exposed position; the only cover came from the roadside ditch and the hedgerow, which was not taller than a yard. The droning of aircraft filled the sky, with gunfire grumbling and bombs detonating in the distance. I rightly concluded that the British warships had begun their preliminary bombardment. The day of the landings had come, and it had come right here to our region. Flat and motionless we were lying in the ditch, and I compared our surroundings to the map I had brought along.

Nearby explosions startled us. All of a sudden, an engine revved, and tracks rattled. Before we knew it, a German armored personnel carrier drew close coming from the town center, tearing past us at high speed. We caught a glimpse of its rear; through open doors several wounded could be seen, one soldier with a torn uniform lying between them on the floor.

As quickly as the APC had appeared, it vanished again. I was hoping that my gun crews were to recognize the vehicle and hold their fire. To my relief, nothing happened in the minute after that; behind us no bang of my 75 mm guns and no impact explosion was heard. I decided to turn back. Our covering fire would not support us beyond this point; advancing any further would have been forlorn hope, as we would have run straight into the arms of British paratroopers. But for the time being I wanted to get something out of the way. I wanted to leave this memorable moment to posterity. Beckoning Atteneder, I doffed my steel helmet, drew my camera from its camouflaged cover and asked him to take a picture of me. Baffled at first, he quickly understood, took the camera, and released the shutter. I stowed it away again, donned my helmet and continued looking ahead.

We went back as carefully as possible. Advancing into the village and towards the bridges with the whole company was pointless. Without adequate infantry support, our open-topped gun carriers would have been drawn into a murderous firefight with British paratroopers. Any combat inside the village would have been at their decisive advantage. A better plan was for us to hold the position we had already captured, meaning the southern village outskirts, as well as scouting through the park towards the Caen Canal bridge. Covering each other's movements, we eventually returned to my company's forward positions. Braatz was keen to hear my report. He acknowledged my view of the situation. As the retreating German soldiers had reported, the town's center was already chock-full of British paratroopers, and they had barely been able to fall back after a short but intense fight. A situation which I could give confirmation of.

The vigor with which we had taken our blocking position near Bénouville in addition to the success of my first reconnaissance patrol gave me a good feeling about everything. Our men had chosen their positions meticulously, immediately camouflaging all vehicles from aerial view. You could only spot them if you already knew where they were. The rainy weather persisted, and with the beginning forenoon we anticipated bad weather which in turn protected us from possible air attacks. With the heavy mortar platoon ready to fire, Braatz ordered Oberfeldwebel (Staff Sergeant) Tanner to take up an observation post in the front with one of his runners. Before they left, I briefed them shortly, imploring my good friend not to go beyond the crossroad. The houses behind there were already in British paratroopers' hands.

Staff Sergeant Tanner took a telephone with him, and after a few minutes we heard that British paratroopers had been spotted at the crossroad which I had scouted up to. So they had slowly advanced towards us. Calm and collected, Tanner relayed coordinates for a fire attack. Shortly afterwards the distinctive roaring of our heavy mortars sounded behind us. This gave us confidence. We could hear the grenades exploding in the village. "We're not defeated yet!" I thought, listening to our observers' reports. The first shells had already been on target, immediately driving the British into the houses. Now they knew that they were watched.

In the following hours, our two forward observers set the pace of everything happening. As I had found out earlier, the most advanced British positions lay near the crossroads. These were now being shelled by our mortars. Time was of the essence in this situation. British paratroopers had no heavy weaponry, so their defensive measures were only effective inside the confines of the village. Even then, they could not hope to resist a massed German attack for long – a vigorous push would drive them out of their positions. Preparing for a possible attack of our own was imperative. First Lieutenant Braatz had already reported our observations of the enemy and this possible opportunity to battalion command; the only response, however, had been an order to "hold any captured ground."

Enemy activities were growing progressively. Battle noise coming from the coast was getting louder and louder, with ever-increasing numbers of explosions. We knew that time was running out. Still we could not do anything. An attack with our small force alone would have been doomed to failure; we could not hope to make it far. Time passed, our mortars fired, but there was not a single sign of a counterattack of our own.

Shortly after noon, a sudden alarm message came from our forward observers: enemy tanks ahead! I promptly hurried to the most forward of my well-camouflaged gun carriers, which was guarding the road towards the village's center. Before my Bénouville reconnaissance endeavor, I had ordered my gun commanders to "fire at will upon identification," and when I was rushing towards the vehicle, a muzzle blast tore through the air, followed by a violent explosion.

The whole gun carrier jerked backwards. I climbed up the board wall and immediately received a status report. On the road ahead of us, roughly 300 meters (330yds) away, two M4 Sherman tanks had appeared. One was fired upon my men, causing the other to reverse out of sight again. I looked through the glass pane. And indeed, a Sherman was standing there, engulfed in bright flames, a thick pillar of smoke rising from the wreck. This meant the British had already brought up tank support into the village.

We had scored our first kill. I gave the gunner a pat on the back, but promptly had to think about Staff Sergeant Tanner and his observation team in the front. After a few minutes, I could see two figures scurrying through the roadside ditch: Tanner was returning from his observation post with the other observer. Still panting, he gave a report. Upon arriving at the crossroad, he had spotted the British paratroopers through his binoculars, directing our mortar fire on their positions. After the first hits they had vanished, so he proceeded ordering curtain and harassing fire between town center and bridge, based on his map. A few minutes later, an elderly man had appeared on the street, limping towards him and stopping in front of the hedgerow in which he was hiding. After looking in their direction for a short time, the man had turned around, limping back to where he had come from.

Staff Sergeant Tanner was unsure what to think about this, until a sudden burst of engine noise was heard and two British Sherman tanks were coming from the direction in which the man had vanished. Tracks clanking and barrels lowered, the vehicles were slowly crawling along the road towards their position, one offset to the side behind the other. Tanner and his subordinate had cowered low in the ditch, not even thinking of crawling away.

As the noise of the tank tracks was growing louder and louder, they had heard a crackle of gunfire, the shell detonating a few yards in front of them. When they had already seen themselves being overrun by British tanks, the one in the front had burst in a gruesome explosion.

My anti-tank gunners had done a good job. The second Sherman had stopped abruptly, rolled back, and disappeared behind a house. Tanner and his observer poised shortly before hurrying back in our direction as fast as they could. They had been quite lucky.

After this British tank advance I went to First Lieutenant Braatz and recommended sending a combat patrol through the park, and the chateau therein, towards the canal bridge. The map showed a small ridge to the north of the chateau, sloped in the same direction, i.e. towards the Orne channel. This would be the ideal elevated position for our weapons to support a counterattack through the village's center. Braatz gave permission, I grabbed both my runners as well as one of the gun commanders, and the four of us began advancing towards the park. Instead of a wall, the southern edge of the park was delineated by a tall iron fence. Sneaking along this fence, we found an iron gate after roughly a hundred yards. This gate was open, so we entered the park area and worked our way forward towards the Caen Canal.

Before long, we were standing in front of the chateau which lay at the left bank of the canal. The chateau itself was a big, multistory building towering over the park, thus promising to offer a good view over both Orne bridges. Securing each other's movements, we crossed the open space between the forest edge and the chateau, running towards the main entrance which was surrounded by impressive columns. Gasping for air, we entered the building when we suddenly got startled for a moment. A French middle-aged woman ran towards us yelling and flourishing wildly. We were all puzzled, did not understand a single word, so we just did not respond, charging further into the building. Standing in a great staircase, I wanted to risk taking a look from the roof, so we rushed upwards.

When we had climbed half the building's height, all of a sudden hell broke loose around us. The glass of the large windows shattered, large caliber projectiles battering the walls. Glass shards, splinters of wood and fist-sized chunks of the walls got sprayed all over the place. I quickly peered out the window, and to my surprise, in the middle of the canal I saw a small vessel showing the war insignia of the Reich at the stern.

"Our own! They're thinking we're the enemy!" I thought.

I shouted, "Move! Move!" and we hurried to the top. The staircase behind us looked desolate. That had been a close one. Looking around, I needed a window to the north. When I opened a door and we entered, the next surprise was awaiting us. We were standing in a whitewashed hall full of hospital beds, several nurses in white facing us, huddled together and staring at us in fear. Now we realized the chateau was being used as a hospital.

I was amazed and shocked at the same time. That was something I had not expected. I could not remember seeing a red cross on the building. For a moment, I looked at the ground awkwardly, but composed myself again. I put down my submachine gun, raising my hands in an imploring manner, hoping to not appear threatening. The nurses and patients were still eyeing us in anxious silence. Holding my hands up, I turned my head and approached the window, taking a look outside. As I had expected, the view from the chateau over the canal bridge and the houses of Bénouville was great. A perfect observation position to direct our heavy mortars. I witnessed two impacts at the bridge, seeing jets of debris rise up. Our mortars were performing blind harassing fire.

I took a look through the binoculars, and sure enough I could see movement coming from the coast over the bridge. Those had to be the British. Lined up in long rows, one after the other they moved along the canal, coming from the shore towards the crossing; armored vehicles between them, aircraft above them. It was a fantastic and at the same time depressing sight. We could see a mighty stream of enemy soldiers and their war material pouring in from the coast. When we were looking through the binoculars, the events unfolding before our eyes seemed like a Fata Morgana. I just had to take another look. The spectacle was simply overwhelming.

Our position at Château de Bénouville would have offered a superb view to direct our mortar fire, but without hesitation I abandoned that thought. This would have violated international law of war. The British would have found out where the spotters would be hiding in no time, and all hell would have broken loose here. As a matter of fact, the British opened fire on the chateau multiple times during the day, without causing severe damage or casualties among the patients. Suspecting artillery spotters and sharpshooters inside the building, they used a German 7.5 cm anti-tank gun captured at the bridge to flush out any such foe.

Just as we were running up the chateau's staircase, a Vorpostenboot (patrol boat) of the German navy had opened fire on the building. After coming from Caen and attempting to close in on the bridge, the vessel came under fire from the German anti-tank gun captured by the British paratroopers. The crew had turned their craft around, unloading their 2 cm cannons at everything that appeared like a possible enemy position. Apparently they had seen us moving in the staircase and opened fire. We had only realized that the Vorpostenboot was there when its 2 cm flak shells were hitting everything around us.

Already in the morning, shortly after the British landings had begun, two Vorpostenboots from Caen had actually sortied along the Canal towards Ouistreham. Close to the canal bridge they had been shot at by British paratroopers' PIAT (Projector, Infantry, Anti-Tank) anti-tank weapons. This led to one boat running aground and its crew getting captured right away.

The second vessel had disengaged, and in the afternoon, just as we were moving towards the chateau, its crew attempted another recon sortie towards the bridge; probably to also look for the other boat and its crew. In the process, the vessel again came under defensive fire by the paratroopers near the bridge. Our Vorpostenboot's subsequent fire during its retreat past the chateau had nearly claimed our lives. A small episode of military history which almost killed me and my three men.

Without saying a word we turned around, left the ward, stormed down the staircase as quickly as possible and left the chateau. Once outside, we ran to its western boundary and worked our way forward towards the Caen Canal. We reached the ridge, and indeed it offered a good view of the houses of Bénouville and the Caen Canal bridge.

Again I sensed shell impacts, and I could see the British running in all directions. In my mind I congratulated our heavy mortar platoon, which was hitting its harassing fire pretty accurately without a spotter, relying on the map alone. Here from this ridge we would be able to support an attack pretty well. I took a look at my watch. It was shortly before 16:00. We could hear intense battle noise coming from the coast, and airplanes were gliding through the cloudy sky. We set about our return through the park. Back at our company I reported to Braatz. He was visibly depressed. The fact that we were left hanging in the lurch so close to the objective embittered him.

Reports coming in from battalion command indicated that the Allied landings were in full swing already. Heavy fighting raged at the coast ahead. We, however, had not received any orders, and with the exception of firing our mortars there was nothing that we could do. It slowly dawned on us that in these deciding hours our leadership was almost unable to make decisions. After us getting an overview our Infantry, supported by tanks, surely would have been able to break through to the bridges. Dusk was already approaching, and we were still lying in the same positions. When I had just concluded my report, we all suddenly realized that an eerie silence had set in. All the aircraft engine droning, all the muzzle blasts and explosions had vanished in this uncanny quiet, which was right away superseded by a loud swoosh. We looked up. From north and east, hundreds of transport gliders were closing in at low altitude. A staggering sight that left us all speechless for a few seconds.

It looked like a huge flock of raptors was plummeting on us. In fact, it was a fleet of over 250 military gliders of the British 6th Airborne Division flying in the last and deciding reinforcements of the third main wave. Coming from the north over the canal's mouth, they turned in a big arch from east to south, passing right over us to the west and towards hill 61.

At a blow the firing commenced again. Our 2 cm anti-air carriers as well as our machine guns opened fire. We saw our bullets hitting the giant birds, several of them bursting into flames, breaking apart and vanishing from sight behind the trees in a nosedive. We shot until the breeches of our guns and cannons were red hot, but it was futile, there were simply too many. After having witnessed this airborne landing taking place almost without interference, we all were greatly impressed, realizing that a counterattack of our own would come too late. Clearly our enemy was superior in numbers and material available.

Braatz and I concluded that we should at least try advancing through the park up to the ridge we had discovered. An attempt to inhibit, or at least delay, British tank reinforcements had to be made; the ridge would offer a good position to do so, as it offered a great view of the road leading to the bridges. Now that night had set in, a push under cover of darkness seemed promising. The increasing number of Allied fighter-bombers cruising above our heads would be unable to detect us. For additional protection, I got some Panzergrenadiers to support us.

Taking one of my self-propelled guns, an additional observation squad for the mortars and the Grenadiers I set out for the ridge. We slowly felt our way through the park. At around 21:00, we arrived at the ridge. Night had already set in and in spite of all the fires raging at the coast and Caen it was getting darker by the minute. Getting an overview would become increasingly difficult. Suspecting a Tommy behind every bush, we advanced suitably cautious. I ordered a stop, crawled forward as far as possible and examined the terrain.

In front of us, in the Bénouville houses to the left, everything was quiet. Straight ahead at the bridge there was one mortar hit after another. Staff Sergeant Tanner was making a good job of it. The British paratroopers were probably cussing our mortars; after all, they had been under their fire the whole day. Waving my hand, I ordered the SPG to the front, positioning the Grenadiers to safeguard both of its flanks. I wanted to prevent any surprise flanking attacks by the paratroopers.

Maybe some British reconnaissance patrol had already entered the park to scout the chateau. I was sure that they had to recognize the building's value as observation point as well. "Well, let the Tommies come if they want. We will give them a hearty welcome!" I thought to myself.

The minute we had taken this position, Braatz appeared with one of his runners. He had finally received information from battalion command. His report was shattering. Advances by our regiments to the west and east of the Orne a few hours ago had been driven back by the enemy. Our Panzer regiment had taken heavy casualties. Our 2nd battalion had retreated to Herouville, north of Caen, and our 8th Company near Bénouville was the only one holding out so far to the front.

Our positions in the west had already been circumvented by the British, who moved up to Bieville, and to the right the Caen Canal did not allow for an evasion. Thus we were in danger of getting encircled. We had to escape this trap. There was no talk of a counterattack anymore. Braatz ordered us to retreat, with our rallying point being the young forest at the road. From there, we were to march towards Blainville and Herouville near Caen. Contritely, I realized that our time here was to end. As a farewell, however, I wanted to fire a few last shells towards the bridge before we went. All of a sudden we could hear the distinctive roaring of a tank engine. We all went silent, gazing into the looming darkness ahead. To the left, between the houses near us, something moved.

Our position was elevated relative to the park's wall right in front of us, with a road and a row of houses being on the other side. On this road, just around 80 meters (90 yds) ahead, a Sherman tank slowly rolled along the houses. Within an instant our nerves were strung to breaking point.

"Did they find us?" I thought. For a second, everyone was waiting for the tank's gun to fire. The tank, however, came to a halt, the top hatch opened, and the commander popped up. He seemed irresolute. Some shapes poured from a house, obviously French, and ran up to the tank.

The British commander climbed down to the civilians, and it looked like he was getting instructed. I ordered to fire, but there was a problem. The distance was so close that we could not lower the barrel far enough. There was no chance of firing up the engines either with all the noise at this close proximity, so we disengaged the gear and, with all our strength, slowly pushed the gun carrier forward. After what seemed like an eternity, we succeeded and the gunner reported target in sight. I ordered to fire at will. The muzzle blast tore through the air, followed by an enormous explosion ahead.

Our shell had scored a direct hit on the Sherman, apparently detonating its ammunition or the fuel tank. A fireball rose up, and the house next to the vehicle collapsed. A flaming inferno emerged in front of us. Thinking of the civilians who had been standing near the tank, I was hoping that they had had a chance to escape. But the roaring fire made it impossible to see anything else.

I feared the worst, although I also had to think about the elderly man who had sent the two tanks at Staff Sergeant Tanner in the afternoon. In short order, heavy counter fire broke out. From the bridges and the houses to the left, British machine guns frantically fired tracer rounds blindly into the night. Luckily, their aim was not even close to our well-camouflaged position. Probably they were not expecting us to be this close. As the ammunition of the Sherman tank went up in sparkling explosions, we took the opportunity to fire up the engine and slowly retreat towards the back.

The SPG led the way with me on top. The grenadiers were covering us on both sides. I sent a runner towards the company to inform them of our arrival, but before he could depart, Braatz approached us. He had heard the explosions and the British gunfire. I briefly reported our kill, and he was very pleased to hear about it. We crossed the dark park without interference, although I expected to meet machine gun and anti-tank fire at every moment.

After reaching the rallying point in the forest behind the chateau park, we continued our departure. At this time I was told that our unit had suffered the first men killed under tragic circumstances. One of Staff Sergeant Tanner's heavy mortar carriers had its barrel burst just when he was standing right next to it. The explosion had destroyed the vehicle, killed four men, and wounded the petty officers as well as several grenadiers. The wounded had been carried off by an ammunition carrier. Unteroffizier (Petty Officer) Jelinek, a man from Vienna, had taken up command of the mortars.

Our breakout movement was scheduled one hour before midnight. My orders were to lead the column with my SPGs. Like a rubber ball I was bouncing from one gun to the other, relaying the orders and coordinating the separation movements towards the south. All the climbing up and down vehicles as well as running between them left me gasping for air. Thanks to the fires around us illuminating the area, you were at least able to see where you were going.

Just when we were done and I wanted to report this, a runner came up to me. Enemy tanks had been spotted in an open area to the west. I hurried to the vehicle safeguarding in that direction, pulled myself up the board wall, and shouted, "12 o' clock, short distance, tank, open fire!"

The vehicle's gunner, Private Wicek, was in the middle of spreading butter on a slice of bread, looking at me wide-eyed when I popped up the board wall and pointed into the darkness. In an instant he was pinched to his optics and the gun commander let his men load a shell. I ordered them to wait until the target was in clear sight. The runner had alarmed the rest of the company as well, so all were frozen in place, tensely waiting for what was about to happen.

With the pitch-black forest behind us, we were hard to spot. By now we could clearly hear tank tracks grinding toward us, the noise growing louder and harder to bear every second. When we were strung to breaking point, Wicek suddenly reported, "Sherman. Target acquired!"

"Fire," the gun commander responded aridly. The blast tore through the night, the gun jolted backwards from the recoil, an explosion arose ahead, and a gust of flame burst into the dark sky.

"A hit!" I cheered, amazed at the how close the enemy tank had been to our position.

The knocked out and burning tank's silhouette was now clearly visible over the open area ahead. It was just under 30 meters (33 yds) away. I scanned the terrain in front of us; there was no sign of any other enemy tanks. Apparently we had caught the outermost vehicle of a line formation, with the other members having retreated immediately after the hit. Just to be sure, a few HE shells were fired, and we raked the open area with machine gun fire, wanting to prevent any accompanying British infantry sneaking up on us.

But now it was time to cut and run. The burning wreck was visible from an uncomfortably large distance and falling prey to the well-coordinated British artillery was to be avoided. Braatz hurried towards me. He gave me a pat on the shoulder and ordered us to march off. All engines were fired up and we commenced our movement southward.

One SPG was covered by the other two, one on each side of the road, while it drove 50 meters (55 yds) ahead. In the rear, the rest of the company pressed after our tank hunter platoon. The anti-air platoon secured the retreat as our rearguard. Like a giant caterpillar we were cautiously crawling through the night. Above our heads a large number of planes zoomed through the darkness, and we were expecting one of them crashing on our position at any time. It was clear to everyone that none of these planes were ours. After a short while Blainville emerged from the darkness ahead – a small locality consisting of a few houses in a dip next to the Caen Canal. We reached the buildings half an hour before midnight. Our retreat from Bénouville had been successful, but we had also lost a man in the process. What had happened?

As we counted the men, we realized that a runner of the company command squad was missing. The last time he had been seen on his way to the rearguard. The hitherto dependable man might have been captured by a British reconnaissance squad. From the battle noise we deduced that the British were on our heels. A runner's job was not without danger – I knew that first-hand from my own missions in Africa. Before you know you are out of luck and end up on the wrong side.

Braatz decided to continue towards Herouville with the rest of the company under the screen of night. Upon establishing communications with battalion command, Braatz intended on pulling back my platoon, putting us into new positions. He also took our wounded to the back in order to treat them, and I had the opportunity to wish Staff Sergeant Tanner all the best. Looking quite haggard, he still gave me a firm handshake.

We departed from Blainville, and I took up the position behind the ridge towards the north, along the road towards Blainville. Here, roughly one kilometer (1100 yds) away from the village, you had a good view of the blazing fires raging between us and the coast. Meanwhile, the rest of the company continued their march. Between trees and bushes we made ourselves at home on both sides of the road, looking towards the Caen Canal.

I ordered the vehicles to be concealed extensively even in the darkness, expecting Allied fighter-bombers preying on us from the first light of dawn. After having arrived here, I was finally able to marshal my thoughts for the first time, taking stock of everything. We had made it through the first day of the landings alive. My disappointment with all our actions so far, however, waiting fervently for a meaningful mission and thus being powerless in the face of the events, was limitless.

But just like time and again in the past, my optimism prevailed, dismissing these – in my opinion – tactical mistakes as tiny negative dots in the big picture of what was happening. Encouraged by our mortar shelling of the British paratroopers and the three tank kills we were thinking that tomorrow or the day after would see the situation completely reversed. All we had to do was advancing towards the coast with massive force.

CHAPTER 13

BATTLE FOR CAEN

I n the early morning hours of June 7, 1944, I was already assembling my non-commissioned officers to give a few short orders. Nobody had slept. Ahead of us, to the north and west, the night had been lit up by the fighting continuing in the landing sectors. Multiple large fires were raging in the directions of Blainville and Bénouville. Now, at dawn, I was shocked to realize that carrying out the withdrawal movement southwards planned by First Lieutenant Braatz would not be so easy.

Me and my platoon were situated in a well-covered position on the backslope of a ridge southwards of Blainville. To our rear, an open area reached towards the town of Hérouville, roughly one kilometer (1100 yds) to the south. A road coming from Blainville crossed the ridge, leading towards Hérouville as well as Caen. From our position near Blainville, we had a good view on this road, so having dug in at the backslope proved to be a wise course of action.

On the way towards Hérouville, however, the road was also completely exposed – how were we to ever reach that town unscathed? Moving southwards during the day would lead to us getting spotted immediately, falling prey to Allied fighter-bombers or even long-range naval artillery. During the day, we were trapped. Dawn had already set in, so we had to find a solution quickly. I decided to improve our vehicles' camouflage between the trees and bushes while guarding towards Blainville for the time being. I would look for a way out myself during the day. We prepared for an all-round defense, and I ordered everyone to keep their heads down in order to avoid attention of Allied fighter-bombers. Now we were waiting anxiously for the coming day.

My judgment had been correct. With broad daylight also came the Allied airplanes. Flying at low altitude, they zoomed over the ridge, looking for valuable targets. It would have been easy to down one of them by concentrating our heavy machine gun fire, but this would have led to our end. All those fighter-bombers would have descended upon us like raptors, bombing us and our vehicles into oblivion. We could see the pilots take long turns in their search for worthwhile targets. The Allies had total air supremacy.

Time and again we could make out fighter-bombers in the distance plunging towards the ground with engines roaring, followed by the boom of their cannons or explosions of detonating air-to-surface missiles. Such targeted airstrikes by American Mustang, Lightning or Thunderbolt, or British Tempest or Typhoon fighter-bombers, could wreak havoc on any ground formation.

As such, we had to wait and hope that the British would not commence their push further south for the time being. I had posted two of my men up on the ridge as forward observers. They reported that right ahead of us, on the southern outskirts of Blainville, the first British had shown themselves. As soon as the opportunity arose, I reconnoitered the surroundings with my two runners. After sighting the terrain, we found a good location. Between the road over the ridge, along the Caen Canal, there was a narrow stretch of woodland. To enter this area, only a stone wall needed to be overcome – apparently the perimeter of a castle garden similar to the one at Bénouville. We quickly found a solution.

First we blew a hole in the wall with a *Panzerfaust*. In this small opening we placed a tank mine. Detonating this mine produced a hole as big as a barn door, through which our vehicles could enter the forested garden. In the garden we could, in the evening or after nightfall, march southwards to the company along the Caen Canal virtually undetected. I was glad to have found an escape route and now hoped that Braatz' order to withdraw would soon come in.

After we had established this escape route, I returned to my gun crews and briefed them. They happily acknowledged the possible retreat path we had created. We had only been talking for a short time when we heard the sound of approaching shells. A moment later, they impacted on the ridge directly in front of us, with small mushroom clouds rising from the ground. We quickly went for cover. The bombardment faded out after some time, but after that, shells were striking our area in an almost constant rhythm. Perhaps 105 mm shells, as we competently determined. It became obvious that this bombardment would continue through the night. Just as we had come to expect, the British intended to soften up the ridge with their artillery before daring to attack.

They had probably brought forward the necessary artillery pieces, and after some more time a series of tremendously large impacts showed they were also employing naval artillery for their preliminary bombardment.

For the next couple hours, the British kept up their artillery fire on the ridge before us, but thankfully there was no large-scale attack from Blainville towards our position. Such an attack would have spelled certain doom for us. It was apparent, however, that the British were further developing their beachhead and bringing up additional forces. It also seemed to us that they were only feeling ahead with recon units for the time being, especially to our left in the direction of Biéville, where we could hear intense combat noise. I had no contact to my side whatsoever and thus feared becoming surrounded.

Finally, one of the company's runners arrived. He let me know that I was to report to battalion command, but not take my unit with me. They were still busy establishing a line of defense in our rear at Hérouville, which meant that my anti-tank platoon was, in its current forward position, protecting them from unpleasant surprises. I checked my platoon's fields of fire one more time before assembling my runners and setting off to the rear with a heavy heart.

Before leaving I assured each of my gun crews that I was making sure they were to follow me soon. I could see fear of the unknown in my men's faces; realizing their fear gave me feelings of protectiveness and care towards them which overshadowed my own insecurity. I had already experienced this back in Tunisia. There just like here, caring for my men made me forget my own concerns and doubts. We got into our *Kübelwagen*. Slowly and cautiously me and my runners went along the route we had laid out for our withdrawal. It still seemed like a good plan. Shortly after crossing the hole in the wall we arrived at a small chateau situated directly north of Hérouville, embedded in a small park with lots of hedges and tall trees.

During the ride Allied fighter aircraft had crossed the sky time and again and each time we heard the hum of an engine we all looked up, hoping that we would not have to find out that one of the fighter-bombers had spotted us. Just like in Africa I had employed my second runner as dedicated air observer. Here in Normandy, however, the threat was much more palpable than back in the desert.

Left: That's how close enemy fighter planes buzzed over our heads. Right: Me on the eve of June 7, 1944, the first day after the Allied landings.

Once in Hérouville, I reported to the battalion command post, where Major Zippe was holding an initial briefing. It was here that I would, for the first time, get a detailed idea of our actual situation; I also heard that our 21st Panzer Division was, on this second day of the landings, no longer operating as a cohesive body. Our II Battalion, 192nd Panzergrenadier Regiment had been put on alert at 02:00, June 6, 1944, and detached by our regimental commander, Lieutenant Colonel Rauch, falling under the command of Colonel Krug, 736th Infantry Regiment, at 02:45 already. From 716th Infantry Division, the battalion had additionally received the remains of 1st Company, 716th Anti-Tank Detachment – whose company commander had been killed during the first reconnaissance in force near Bénouville – as well as 2nd Battery, 989th Heavy Artillery Detachment.

Our battalion's orders had been to assemble this *Kampfgruppe* (battle group) in order to recapture the bridges around Bénouville and subsequently advance towards Ranville. As such, Major Zippe had sent us towards Bénouville for the initial attack. After that, however, there had been no further movements of the battalion, as I had unfortunately witnessed first-hand. Now I found out why this opportunity had not been seized. Battalion command had not been able to coordinate the advance as Colonel Krug had been encircled in his command post by enemy paratroopers at the very beginning of the invasion. His position on Hill 61, codename "Hillman," had been one of the first targets of the landing force. Advancing without such coordination was – justifiably – judged too risky by Major Zippe.

In addition, soon afterwards the first British forces had been sighted by the other companies of our battalion in the Beuville area. Eventually the order came for our II Battalion to "… secure the attack of battle group Rauch at the right flank at Lebisey and Hérouville." The rest was known to us. Our own advance on June 6, beginning at 03:00 towards Bénouville, had been the only counterattack by our battle group. And it still fell short of really hitting the British.

Late in the morning of June 6, parts of 200th Assault Gun Detachment were even sent towards us as support. They however were caught in an intense air raid at Caen, and once they had escaped the attack they received new orders and immediately headed back east; this time to support 125th Panzergrenadier Regiment east of the Orne. Furthermore, the Luftwaffe attempted to attack our bridges near Bénouville with Junkers Ju 88 bombers. One of their 50 kg (110 lbs.) bombs even struck the bridge directly but failed to detonate. So all in all, we had spent the whole day of the landings waiting while our Battalion commander tried desperately to get clear instructions from Colonel Krug or arrive at an overview of the general situation.

At 06:45, June 7, 1944, Colonel Krug and his men eventually surrendered to the British. He, along with three other officers and 70 men of lower ranks, became POWs. During their capture of "Hillman," the British had to suffer a high number of casualties. After that, however, our regiment was all that was standing between them and Caen.

In the morning of June 7, there still was no absolutely clear situation report on anyone's desk. All we knew was that the British had already bypassed us west of Bénouville, standing in Biéville and, presumably, Blainville. I realized that from now on we would go on nothing but fire runs. There was no overarching coordination of our division's units to be expected; instead, we would attempt to extinguish one fire after the other in our immediate surroundings. Until we ran out of water. Of a determined attack by 21st Panzer Division towards the coast there was not a single word anymore. I came to the sobering conclusion: "The Allies have gained a foothold in France, and we were unable to prevent it."

Our own II Battalion now was in a defensive position northwest of Caen stretching from Hérouville to the Orne bank near Colombelles. First Lieutenant Braatz had already occupied his part of this line with our 8th Company. I was now to take my anti-tank platoon out of its backslope position and join the battalion's ranks. At the end of the briefing there was a surprise for us. Major Zippe got handed two small boxes by his adjutant before becoming quite formal, ordering us to stand to attention.

Then, Braatz and me were awarded the Iron Cross First Class for our actions at Bénouville. The Major pulled out award certificates and quickly read out their texts before fixing the medals to our chests. The black cross with silver edges was worn on the left chest, and while Major Zippe put them there, he commended our judicious conduct and leadership of our "battlegroup" into Bénouville and back out again without suffering any losses.

Getting awarded this medal came as a total surprise to me. Neither Braatz nor I had expected such a thing. The next tier of medal was the Knight's Cross of the Iron Cross or the German Cross in Gold. Such decorations were the last thing on my mind at the time, however. My thoughts were somewhere entirely different. For me and my men, the fighting was far from over.

Upon return, I immediately started relaying the new orders to my men. Thus, in the evening hours of June 7, 1944, we commenced our breakout movement towards Hérouville. We passed the hole in the wall without any problems, marching on in a spread-out line below the ridge, leaning towards the Caen Canal. Our vehicles were well-camouflaged, such that it looked like a row of hedges was moving through the area. Individual vehicles could only be made out when looking closely during their maneuvers. Our withdrawal from the backslope position came just in time: shortly before our departure it became apparent that the first British units were indeed reconnoitering the ridge from Blainville.

Once we arrived at the outskirts of Hérouville, Braatz welcomed us with a happy face and briefed us on our new positions. The open road between Blainville and Caen lay parallel to the Caen Canal only up to the ridge, after which it bent away, gradually leading into Hérouville. At the edge of the latter, it crossed another road leading east from Hérouville, at right angles; this road went across the Orne river and canal over two bridges before entering the village of Colombelles east of the Orne. These two bridges, along with the ones at Bénouville, were the only crossings over the Orne and its canal between Caen and the sea.

It was these bridges that our 22nd Panzer Regiment surprisingly did *not* use to shift into the area north of Caen from the east – whether due to an assumption that they had been destroyed or because of cautiousness, I would never find out. Battalion command expected a British assault over the ridge to commence soon. My anti-tank platoon dug in west of the Caen Canal at the northern edge of Hérouville, close to the village church and a cemetery.

Right of the canal, in the direction of Colombelles, the anti-air platoon had already taken up its positions, with the grenade launchers sitting further back at a factory site. These two units were next to our right-hand neighbor unit, II Battalion, 125th Panzergrenadier Regiment, which was under the command of Lieutenant Colonel von Luck. Its II Battalion's positions stretched from the east bank of the Orne over the northern edge of Colombelles up to Cuverville. To our left, another company of our own battalion lay westwards near Lebisey, behind which I Battalion, 125th Panzergrenadier Regiment was positioned. The latter had participated in 21st Panzer Division's drive towards the coast on June 6, until it came to a halt here, along with parts of 22nd Panzer Regiment. On this line we waited for the coming dawn.

We expected the British to attack any moment, but such an assault did not materialize. All they did was relentlessly bombarding the ridge; it seemed as if the British were unsure whether to dare an assault or not. This gave us valuable time to fortify our positions.

After dawn we took a closer look at the terrain ahead of us, mostly the area around the Caen Canal's western bank. The road, which was well-paved, stretched from Hérouville towards the ridge in a gentle arc. To its east a smaller, tree-lined road ran north into the chateau park, which we had withdrawn through the evening before. Between the bridges in the east, meaning between the Orne and Caen Canal, there was open ground. This area became wider in the north, since the distance between both waterways increased somewhat before they passed Blainville. Most of our attention was directed at the roads ahead, as we expected the British to either open fire once they captured the ridge or advance along the roads with their armor, respectively. Considering that, our positions were chosen prudently: backslope, a good distance away from the ridge, with the buildings of Hérouville in our rear.

There was noticeable activity left on the ridge ahead of Lebisey as well as to our right around Colombelles. At our left-hand neighbors, I Battalion, the enemy attempted to break through with armored support in the morning hours of June 7. It was only with the help of 22nd Panzer

Regiment, which had remained there since the failed drive towards the coast, that the British assault could be repulsed.

Part of our defensive line was an antitank ditch that had been dug right at the edge of Hérouville. To keep our left flank secure, Braatz ordered a few grenadiers to reconnoiter the area along this ditch and towards the ridge in the midmorning. After a surprisingly short time, however, these grenadiers triumphantly returned, accompanied by a British soldier who they had captured after finding him inside the ditch. As it quickly turned out, he had been part of a British scouting party. Apart from the distinctive saucer-shaped steel helmet, he had only had his rifle with him. His comrades had certainly managed to withdraw in time. All of this indicated the British were already standing on the ridge ahead of our positions.

Since the British obviously felt uneasy about the terrain ahead of them, they had resolved to feeling their way forward with such reconnaissance parties. Braatz and me tried to get more information out of our new prisoner, a sergeant. He turned out to be somewhat talkative. Enthusiastically he told us about the enormous efforts that were undertaken for the landings, and that the Allied air fleet would dominate the skies. He spoke with obvious pride, and I had to admit to myself that he was right with the latter point, considering that I had seen not much of our Luftwaffe to speak of. He went on further to declare his conviction that this war of ours would be over by Christmas, with us Germans on the losing side.

In this regard, I begged to differ. While I had a very different opinion, I was certainly impressed by the confidence with which he had stated his. After the conversation was over, Braatz ordered the captive be brought to the battalion command post.

In that moment we received a message that left us shocked. The life of Major Zippe, our battalion commander, had ended a few hours before. Nobody had expected this to happen. During a field briefing with our regiment's commander, Lieutenant Colonel Rauch, the two had observed the area from the top of a small water tower. A naval gun shell had impacted near the tower, with a piece of shrapnel killing Major

Zippe. We were dismayed at these news. The Major had always been quite caring towards us and the men and as such had been very popular with the soldiers. On orders of Lieutenant Colonel Rauch, Captain Rusche was appointed his successor in the morning of June 8, 1944.

Amidst all this sorrow, however, there was also good news. Our sergeant major, Master Sergeant Guse, reported with us after an adventurous journey from Cairon to Hérouville. He brought something with him that we had longed for just as much as sleep: plenty of rations. After I had visited every single position of my platoon and checked communications to our left and right neighbors, I ordered half the men to rest while the other half would keep on securing the line. I also tried to get some sleep myself, as I had been wide awake for almost 48 hours by that point.

Over the course of June 7, our right-hand neighbor at Colombelles, II Battalion, 125th Panzergrenadier Regiment, had attempted an assault on the British paratroopers holding Ranville, who successfully defended their positions and in turn brought forward additional reinforcements. In the northeast, a simultaneous attack by parts of the German 711th and 346th Infantry Divisions had been somewhat more successful, even taking back the coastal battery at Merville which had been lost earlier. These German attacks had occupied the British in the Sword sector on June 7, which led to us having a relatively calm day. Army group B command now declared the river Orne to be the dividing line between 7th and 15th Army.

This meant that 125th Panzergrenadier Regiment, our right-hand neighbor, now suddenly belonged to LXXXI Army Corps and was no longer part of 21st Panzer Division. As such, the confusing developments around command and control continued.

From June 8, 1944 onward the British, to our surprise, shifted their main line of attack. Once it turned out that German counterattacks on June 6 and 7, which the Allies had expected, did not materialize, while British advances towards Caen from the north had been repulsed, they chose another area to go on the offensive. On June 8th, field marshal Montgomery set foot on French soil. Since the British frontal assaults around Lebisey had not yielded any visible results, he resolved to order a concentrated and energetic envelopment maneuver by his armor. This attack, christened operation Perch, was to achieve a breakthrough of British forces. Originally, this operation had been prepared for the area southeast of Caen, but 125th Panzergrenadier Regiment's attacks near Colombelles had defeated that plan; instead, the British offensive was to commence west of Caen. What followed was a series of fierce and hard-fought battles lasting from June 9 to June 14, 1944.

During that fighting, our 21st Panzer Division held the line north of the town. The area ahead of us saw a multitude of raids over the course of these days. Both sides attempted to find weak spots in the other's line. Our vehicles were covered as well as possible and camouflaged against aerial detection. In addition, we concealed the infantry positions to also prevent them being detected from above. The ridge ahead left us under the impression that the British were able to observe us; from their position, it was easy to designate targets for indirect fire. And indeed, the bridges over the Orne and Caen Canal to our right became subject to naval bombardment by the British battleships' heavy guns. Allied fighter-bombers showed up time and again, dropping bombs on the bridges and the village of Hérouville. The British were right to assume that we were using the bridges to shift forces between the east and the west. We would spend almost four weeks here at Hérouville.

After June 8 and 9 had passed without enemy attacks, I decided to lead a reconnaissance party on June 10. I wanted to take a closer look at the chateau and the park ahead. We had crossed this park during our withdrawal from Blainville, and I knew that it was well-suited to cover the approach of a British scouting force.

The distance between the ridge and the edge of Hérouville was almost 1,000 meters (1100 yds), but the park and its bushes were only half that distance from our positions around the bridge. This was a matter of concern to me, such that I wanted to get some clarity regarding the terrain ahead. I assembled my NCOs and briefed them on my plan. There was not much need to assign men to accompany me, as some of them volunteered without hesitation. In spite of the difficult days we did have to endure, everyone wanted to do their part and was eager to actively engage in helping defend against the British.

Five of us carefully approached the chateau and its park along the road leading out of Hérouville. Trees and bushes next to the road provided cover, and after some time we had come far enough to see the chateau building. I looked through my binoculars. The small chateau appeared to be deserted. No movements. Perhaps its inhabitants, like most civilians in the area, had fled to Caen or even further south. Covering each other, we slowly came closer to this neat little mansion.

As always, my runner, Atteneder, was by my side, with the other members of the squad covering the building's front side from the tree line. Suddenly, in the middle of our approach, I froze. The chateau windows were wide open. I could hear muffled voices coming from the upper floor. These were British, no doubt. I could not understand what they were saying, but they sounded extremely agitated. I looked at Atteneder, who had also noticed the British, gesturing towards the tree line to inform the other three men of the threat.

All of a sudden, there was a blood-curdling scream, which at first came from the ground floor and then spread into the upper floor. For a brief moment I felt reminded of the maternity home at Bénouville and thus expected to again run into nurses, but this time there were none. It seemed like the British had gone crazy. Before we knew it, the front door between me and Atteneder swung open. We could only watch in amazement as around a dozen soldiers stormed out of the house like wasps out of their nest and, just moments later, disappeared in the bushes. Even though we had all yanked up our weapons, not a single shot was fired. I lowered my submachine gun and Atteneder his carbine. We looked at each other too puzzled to say anything. My men in the bushes stood up and also lowered their rifles. It would have been easy to hit a few of the British, but the surprising effect of their helplessness as well as our own cool-headedness meant that we kept our fingers away from the trigger.

We searched the building and found that they had left nothing behind. After that we withdrew back to Hérouville. After our return, the tension quickly subsided and with a laughing face we shared the tale of our little adventure. We convinced ourselves that the British had spotted us on our approach and became so afraid that they judged the only way to save themselves to be running out the front door with a panicked scream. Surrendering had apparently not been an option for them.

Well, the results spoke for themselves: They had utterly surprised us and managed to escape, which they had perhaps not even expected themselves. This incident was talked about even weeks later. The chateau was a good location for a forward base, but we were too few to be able to hold it. Posting observers there would only end in them getting captured sooner or later, and so, we gave up on any plan to occupy it. Thus we remained in position at the northern edge of Hérouville. Here, between the buildings and along a thick stone wall, we were safe from air attacks. The open fields ahead offered a great field of fire.

The enemy stuck to their guns. They had realized that the park was not in our possession. Already on the next day, they sent a whole infantry platoon to feel its way forward through the park and along its approaching road. Only in the last moment, when they were already a few hundred yards from our positions, did our men spot them and open fire. I was in the middle of my breakfast when I heard the first characteristic bangs of our carbines. Immediately I gave the alarm and ordered all men to their positions. Bullets whizzed above our heads as the British returned some unaimed fire. We were in the better position, however, and I could see through my binoculars how they hastily retreated into the park. I let our MGs fire controlled bursts into the tree line and the park for a few minutes before giving the order to cease fire.

I took a few men and went forward to see if there were any casualties. And indeed, we found a young lieutenant, who had been struck by one of our MG salvos. His uniform shirt was torn to pieces, with his chest beneath showing multiple gun wounds. He must have died on the spot. I was surprised by how young he looked to be. I took his body out of its twisted pose and lay him on the back. His face had delicately chiseled features. I closed his eyelids. I wondered to myself whether I also looked this young. Perhaps not. The last couple days had made me considerably older. I assembled my men and returned back to our line.

The following days were relatively quiet, which gave me some time to look around Hérouville. Most houses were completely empty. In the south I could see the town of Caen burning from unending Allied bomber attacks. Only rarely could I see French civilians crouching in their house's doorways, risking a look at the street outside. I refrained from talking to them. What could I even have said? That, thanks to us, they had to wait a little longer for their long-hoped liberation? I felt compassion for them, and I hoped that as few French as possible had to die in the inferno of Caen. On the eastern bank of the Caen Canal, we discovered a small harbor with a station of the German *Kriegsmarine*. To our surprise we were greeted there by a female uniformed German auxiliary. Once she saw us approaching, she ran up to us, reported with her name and rank and asked to hand over the navy station to us. We soon found out that this *German* auxiliary was in fact a Russian who had been pressed into service.

I was astounded. Apparently this small harbor was the base of operations for the patrol boats that we had seen in the fighting around Bénouville on June 6. The auxiliary, a quite pretty young woman who spoke four languages, introduced herself as the *officer on duty*, and only after we agreed to take over the station for defense purposes, she stated that she was now no longer responsible for the station.

After some brief conversation we eventually brought her back to the regimental command post. We were quite impressed by this woman's dedication and bewildered by the fact that she had obviously been left behind. She would perhaps have stayed on her post until the British capture of the station and, in the worst case, even attempted to defend it. At least she seemed resolute enough to do it. Another incident that I regard as one of the almost unbelievable experiences of this war.

21st Panzer Division was now regrouping north of Caen. As such our left neighbor, I Battalion, 125th Panzergrenadier Regiment, was redeployed at Epron, and our own II Battalion took over the Lebisey area. The companies of 22nd Panzer Regiment positioned their Panzer IVs in between. After only a few days, however, I battalion was withdrawn in full and deployed in the area east of the river Orne, where Battlegroup von Luck was under intense pressure by British airborne troops, having lost almost half its men already. Our own II Battalion was now also covering the positions at Epron. By now, our battalion's four companies were holding the entire area northwest of Caen – a line stretching from Hérouville to Epron with a length of almost five kilometers (3 miles).

During daytime, Allied fighter-bombers had almost complete supremacy over the skies above, and there were regular bombardments by far-reaching naval guns to harass us. The two bridges over the Caen Canal and the Orne were the main target of these air attacks and naval bombardments. Their bombs and shells tore holes in the ground large enough to build a small house in them. The terrain around the bridges increasingly turned into a cratered landscape. My anti-tank platoon was lucky to be somewhat protected by the houses of Hérouville, but between the waterways and Colombelles, where our company command post as well as our anti-air and grenade launcher platoon were located, casualties mounted up.

Eventually Braatz ordered everyone without exception to dig their own foxhole with a minimum distance between each dugout. In this way he wanted to minimize losses within the company. Up to that point I had shared a foxhole with my runner, Atteneder, but now each of us dug his own.

My hole was around 200 meters (220 yds) west of the Canal bridge, in an orchard next to a distinctive stone wall on the northern edge of the village. There was a small house nearby that I used as my command post. From here, I had a good view of the chateau and its park, the area which required the most of our attention. Atteneder also decided to dig his foxhole right next to the thick stone wall. From there, we could see and hear each other quite well.

Then my platoon was struck as well. In the afternoon of June 16, a fire attack hit our positions directly. We would feel the naval guns' wrath ourselves now. At first a characteristic hum signaled that shells were incoming, and this time we knew that we were right in the target area. The ground itself roared as impacting and detonating projectiles tore it up, sending fountains of earth up as high as a multi-storied building.

I was near one of my self-propelled guns and thus too far away from my foxhole in the orchard. So I dropped prone right where I was, clawing into the soil with both hands. I could clearly feel the shock waves of detonating shells. As they swept across my body, they pressed the air out of my lungs.

When one projectile hit close by, I thought my end had come. Desperately I tried to be as small as possible, wishing I could dig down into the dirt. Holding on to the ground, I pressed my body down as well as I could. Rocks and patches of soil as big as my fist hailed down on my steel helmet and my back. Detonations left me breathless, my ears hurt, and soon I was practically stunned. Dirt flew into my eyes and mouth, which I kept open due to the enormous pressure waves. After a few minutes, the horror ended just like that. Now an eerie silence set in. Clouds of dust and smoke passed by. Covered in soil and dust, I stood up, my whole body shaking, and ran towards my foxhole. But a quick look made me realize there had been a direct hit right there.

A shell had struck right next to the stone wall behind which my runner and I had dug in. The shell, probably from a British battleship's 13.5-inch main battery, had first penetrated a two feet thick tree, which lay nearby, before detonating in front of the roughly ten feet high wall. The wall had been toppled over from the blast, with its rocks burying our foxholes. I stood before the rubble, aghast and speechless.

Atteneder, who normally would immediately rush to my side ready to relay my orders, was nowhere to be seen. I heard that he had been in front of the wall and preparing his meal, which meant the shell had detonated right next to him. A few moments later we found him, that is to say, we found what the explosion had left behind of him.

The blast had torn off his limbs. The bloody remains of his body were splattered around us, covered in dust and soil. I refrained from looking for his head. My second runner was also still missing, which meant he had to be in his foxhole. The other men had already arrived, and together we started moving the rocks by hand. The rubble piled up to almost seven feet, and we dug through it like crazy with shovels and our bare hands. But it was too late. We eventually found my second runner. Dead, suffocated under the debris of the wall. I was appalled. When my soldiers slowly freed the dead body from the last rocks, I had to sit down. These two men had been by my side through thick and thin, and now, here, death had come to both of them. We collected the remains of Atteneder and wrapped them as well as the other body in shelter-halves. A few of my men dug two field graves on the nearby cemetery, and we buried our fallen there. For the first time, our luck had run out. Depressed I went on my way to Braatz in the evening to report our two losses. It was now his sorrowful duty to write letters to their close relatives informing them of their loved ones' demise. A responsibility for which I did not envy him. I knew that, if I was to survive for long enough, I would soon command a company of my own. It would then be my responsibility to write letters informing my soldier's relatives of their death. But what could one write? That their son, their husband and father, miserably suffocated in the rubble, or was blown to pieces by a shell, their limbs torn off?

I decided that once I was at that point, I would describe their death as painless as possible. It would have been a lie, but maybe it made it easier.

Over the next days and weeks we were subject to multiple such fire attacks, but by some miracle the two bridges were not hit even once. This meant that they remained a constant target for British artillery – much to our sorrow.

On June 18, 1944, I received the order to detach one of my guns to provide cover for a reconnaissance mission of our right-hand neighbor battalion of 125th Panzergrenadier Regiment. Lieutenant Colonel von Luck, the regiment's commander, had ordered his battalion to dare a stronger, more forceful advance in order to capture a forward position of British airborne troops south of Ranville.

Once we arrived at Colombelles, I reported to the battalion commander, a captain. My arrival had been awaited. This battalion had no support weapons of their own. The lieutenant tasked with leading the advance was well-prepared, with the plan being that we launch a surprise attack in the early evening hours. To this end, the lieutenant had ten to fifteen grenadiers and a small truck at his disposal as well as my gun to provide fire support. We crossed Colombelles, left the last positions on our side behind and occupied an initial observation post further north. We remained undetected, and during some closer reconnaissance we could clearly make out the enemy trench line south of Longueval through our binoculars.

We agreed that my self-propelled gun was to cover the advance, but only fire explosive ammunition upon acquiring a target or to cover their retreat. I found a good position and made my gun take it. Shortly before dusk set in, the lieutenant and his men went forward. I wished them good luck as they passed by. We watched the soldiers slowly work their way up to the British lines. Then, once they were close enough for hand grenades, we could see small dark dots emerging from them, arcing through the air, and disappearing in the British positions.

With a dull thunder, the grenades exploded. Before the grenadiers could manage to penetrate the line, however, they were caught in a raging defensive fire. I could make out at least a dozen muzzle flashes. Quickly realizing that our assault had failed, I looked over to my gun and rose my arm. Swinging it down again, I yelled "Fire!"

Shell after shell left our gun barrel. I observed how we were scoring accurate hits among the enemy positions right from the start. Our soldiers now began their withdrawal; while they ran back to us, we kept on firing. I could see that they had suffered casualties. The Lieutenant had been grievously wounded by enemy MG fire. He lay in a shelter-half dragged by three men and kept on passing in and out of consciousness. Two other soldiers had suffered grazing wounds and were bleeding heavily. By now, the first enemy shells were impacting around us. A few British anti-tank guns had spotted my position and began ranging in. Now it was time to act.

I quickly assembled the soldiers, assumed command, and ordered a withdrawal back to Colombelles. Back at battalion command post I gave my report. It seemed obvious that the British airborne positions had already been massively reinforced. Enemy armor and AT guns made it impossible to break through. Offensive action into the north could succeed only after appropriate use of artillery and with heavy Panzer support – both of which we did not have in this sector.

The captain realized that we could not have accomplished anything. I saw how the badly wounded lieutenant was dragged on the shelter-half to the medic station. His feet limply stuck out of the fabric, like those of an inanimate puppet. Thinking of the possibility of dying this way made me shudder.

On our march back towards the bridges at Hérouville, when darkness had already set in, we suddenly came under intense fire from the west. Small-caliber explosive projectiles hit the terrain around and the road itself. The fire seemed to originate from the hill at Lebisey, where I battalion of 125th Panzergrenadier Regiment, my unit's left-hand neighbor, was stationed. It was fire by heavy automatic weaponry, most probably anti-air guns.

"Those have to be our own!" I thought. Perhaps our short engagement at Colombelles had been noticed, leading to the conclusion that the British had broken through our own lines; now their 20 mm flak guns had opened fire on us. I grabbed my flare gun and fired a green signal. Firing was ceased immediately. Without any further incidents, we reached the Caen Canal's western bank an entered Hérouville. There I dropped off into deep, but uneasy sleep.

On the next day I got a visit from one of our converted half-tracks equipped with multiple rocket launchers. Similar to the famous Russian *Katyusha* or, as we called them, *Stalin's Organ*, these vehicles were French-built half-tracks with multiple frames for launching rockets mounted onto them. This allowed firing salvos of up to 24 rockets at once. One of these vehicles assumed a firing position directly behind us after dark before firing multiple salvos in the direction of the British line. The rockets zipped off northwards with a loud howl, long tails of fire behind them. The powerful howl of these rockets along with the glowing night sky gave the experience a haunting atmosphere. After two or three salvos, the vehicle went back again. This procedure would repeat several times over the coming weeks.

We were not all too happy about these visitors, since we feared that they might draw the attention of Allied fighter-bombers. And indeed they would often appear in the sky the morning after. The rocket launchers were already gone by that point, however, and while we hid away deep in the bushes, the aircraft menacingly drew their circles above. Much to our luck, we remained unseen, and so the attack planes would end up dropping their bombs on the bridges every time, graciously missing them as usual. It seemed as if the bridges simply refused to be destroyed despite all the Allies' efforts.

In a firefight north of Colombelles. Our mission was to provide cover for a reconnaissance in force. After firing just a few shells ourselves, we were already targeted by British anti-tank guns' counter-fire.

Watching the Allies waste uncountable numbers of bombs and shells without making any progress was truly exasperating. During a typical artillery bombardment, the British fired up to one hundred shells per gun barrel. Right before a ground attack, this could go up as high as four hundred shells. On June 20, I received new orders. I was to march into the area around Cambes-en-Plaine, a few miles north of Caen. There, not far from the line between our 21st Panzer Division and 12th SS Panzer Division *Hitlerjugend* (Hitler Youth), there had been heavy fighting over the last fourteen days, leaving one of our companies entirely without officers.

On June 13, the positions of 125th Panzergrenadier Regiment there had been taken over by our own II Battalion. The battalion commander transferred command of a whole company to me until further notice. I was told that, thanks to my experience up to that point, I was the right man for this task. I bade farewell to my soldiers and marched to Cambes-en-Plaine by foot. Going by *Kübelwagen* was inconceivable due to enemy air supremacy, and on top of that I had lost both of my runners, who had also been my drivers. I decided to get a motorcycle as soon as the opportunity presented.

At Cambes-en-Plaine I was welcomed and directed towards the company in question. In this area, the 5th and 7th Companies of our II Battalion, 192nd Panzergrenadier Regiment had been stationed for a few days, with a few Panzers of 6th Company, II detachment, 22nd Panzer Regiment in between them. 7th Company was located between Cambes-en-Plaine and La Londe, while 5th Company was further west.

Between the two and further back, at La Bijude, the Panzers were securing their line. When I arrived at the command post, the NCOs were already waiting for me. A master sergeant gave me a situation report. Starting June 10, there had been intense attacks in the sector. On June 13, our companies had taken over the line. Opposite our grenadiers were the British soldiers of I Battalion, South Lancashire Regiment, 8th Infantry Brigade. A few days ago, the British attacks had abruptly subsided, but the next attack appeared to be imminent, and the men were awaiting my orders for the upcoming defense.

I got a rough overview of the situation. The grenadier company had only around 50% of its original strength, but among its positions several Panzer IVs had also dug in. These were the line's backbone. I ran down the individual positions, ordered a few foxholes be improved or relocated here and there, and attempted to direct the heavy weapons such that their expected effectiveness was maximized. I also encountered members of the Waffen-SS for the first time.

What I saw left me astonished. This 12th SS Panzer Division "Hitler Youth" truly lived up to its name. The soldiers I met could not have been older than seventeen or eighteen years. But the morosity I could spot in their young faces told me that they had lived through a lot already. They were fiercely battling the British west of us, at Carpiquet airfield.

Late in the evening, beat and exhausted as I was, I returned to the company command post, a provisionally barricaded basement room, trying to get some sleep on the bed, which consisted of a few crates and boards with a rough blanket. I was called up early in the morning, and before I had really gotten up, we were already deep in an intense firefight. The attackers had closed in before the morning shift had taken over, which meant that not all of our positions were manned yet.

My guards had been attentive and detected the Tommies on their approach, however. The British were feeling their way forward with multiple squads, firing on our positions with their light machine guns. It seemed that they just wanted to test our strength, since apart from their rifle and MG fire there was no further action against us. Here and there a hand grenade flew across, which exploded with a dull bang shortly after. Nevertheless, my heart was pounding wildly in light of this unexpected morning visit.

Shortly before noon, I received notice of powerful British scouting parties ahead. Now, several platoon-strength elements of the enemy attempted to find a gap in our line. But my soldiers bravely repulsed each of these assaults. Hand grenades were flying back and forth, and time and again I saw how several of my men were rising out of their foxholes to target the throwers even while they were winding up. And as soon as they had fired their carbines, MG bullets whipped up small fountains of dirt around their position. One of them could not get down fast enough and was promptly shot through the upper arm. In the end, the British did not manage to break through anywhere. I was glad to have checked all our positions the night before.

I ran from one platoon to the next, making sure that the situation was under their control. Bullets whizzed past me. The characteristic fast rattle of our MG 42s and that of British Brens with their lower rate of fire filled the air, now and then suddenly broken by a dry sharp bang when one of our dug-in Panzers fired its main gun. I could even hear the yells of British officers on the other side, urging their men to advance further.

But their opportunity had passed. We had taken away their attack's momentum. Not in a small part thanks to the effect which our Panzers' explosive shells had had. The British in turn showed their gratitude by raining down intense artillery fire on our line. Ducking in our foxholes, we endured the bombardment.

Some of my soldiers got wounded by artillery shrapnel, and shouts for a medic were heard. Jumping from one foxhole to the next, they worked their way forward. A task which I did not envy them for. Eventually, after many long hours, this day also came to an end. After the last salvo had ended, I could see the maltreated soil around giving off warm vapor, and billows of smoke crept through our foxholes. Picking myself up first, I rushed to our forward positions. The soldiers I met had their eyes wide open and strained nerves but were overly cheerful thanks to having survived the fighting. In this phase of the battle, the men who went through all this unscathed openly showed their feelings of relief.

I made sure the wounded were taken care of, ordered the positions fortified again as well as ammunition getting distributed. I wanted to be prepared in case the British decided to return in the night; what followed, however, was an uneventful yet restless night trying to sleep on crates and boards.

On the next day, the drama's second act commenced. The British attacked again, albeit not as fiercely as before. They kept on sending smaller scouting parties that felt their way forward, remaining undetected for as long as they could. It was apparent that they tried to find a gap in our defense. For the time being, however, it seemed like we had put them off attacking us outright. My soldiers recognized this, much to their relief. Up in the air, British bombers were conducting heavy attacks on Caen, and in the night there was an intense artillery bombardment on our grenadiers' positions at La Londe. A British attack would soon follow. And indeed, in the early morning hours there were fierce attacks on our positions. The grenadiers at La Londe were forced to retreat, but their positions were taken again in the counterattack, during which over 60 British soldiers were captured. In the morning of June 22, a new officer arrived; a young first lieutenant, barely older than me. He was to lead the company from now on. His clean, barely worn uniform made it clear that it was his first time at the front. Instead of a steel helmet, he dashingly wore his officer cap. He was the son of a high-ranking SA official – the *Sturmabteilung*, literally meaning "Assault Detachment." He had been deployed to Normandy only shortly ago and was now burning to take on the enemy. Acknowledging that without comment, I gave him a brief situation report, showed him the area from which most attacks had been coming, and then signed off.

I marched back to Hérouville on foot. On the way I realized that I had lived through the last couple days as if they were a bad dream. The whole situation felt grotesque to me. I had simply walked from one part of the front line to another like a hiker. The soldiers I met on the way all looked crestfallen. Their blank eyes seemed to be deep behind their pale faces. There were barely any heavy weapons in our line. The uninterrupted fighting slowly wearing us down. As I was later told by First Lieutenant Braatz, my successor back at the grenadier company survived for exactly three days before dying in the intense British artillery fire.

CHAPTER 14

CAUGHT IN THE MEAT GRINDER

Once at Hérouville, I received a hearty welcome and first checked my platoon's positions. My men had been anything but lazy during my absence. They had worked on camouflaging our vehicles and digging their foxholes deeper. In the last couple days, there had been no enemy ground attacks in this sector; still, I could make out new bomb craters around the bridge, and the houses of Hérouville had to suffer a lot.

Slowly but steadily, our surroundings transformed into a continuous crater landscape. Enemy artillery fire intensified day by day. They must have brought additional light and heavy batteries into position in the meantime. This, along with their cruisers' and battleships' main guns, gave them overwhelming firepower. While I was on my round, the first intense bombardment happened already. Judging by the different kinds of detonations I could hear, the British were using several different calibers against us. Funnel-shaped geysers of soil and smoke shot up in the air, leaving behind huge craters all around. Eventually, I returned to the command post.

A surprise was waiting for me there. Braatz, together with some soldiers I did not know, had arrived. These men introduced themselves as German *Kampfschwimmer* – frogmen.

Frogmen? I thought. I had expected anything but this kind of reinforcement. Up to that point I had not even known that such a unit existed within our ranks. Braatz and I briefed these men on the situation around the bridges between Hérouville and Colombelles. Just like me, they had been present during the latest artillery strike, and were visibly harried by the experience. The reason for their presence, as they explained, were the bridges over the Orne and Caen Canal. On June 6, 1944, attempts to defend or recapture the bridges at Bénouville had failed, and multiple Luftwaffe sorties to destroy them had also been unsuccessful.

This meant that from the first day of the invasion, a steady stream of Allied supplies could cross the waterways. In addition, the British had begun construction of pontoon bridges over the Orne and Caen Canal, which would allow for even more supplies, large guns and, most of all, tanks to reinforce the British airborne east of the river. Our frogmen were now tasked with putting an end to these machinations. Pegasus Bridge and the nearby Orne bridge were the largest and thus most important; they were to be destroyed in a commando operation. They had arrived with two trucks carrying torpedo-like explosive devices to blow up these bridges.

Their plan was to form two groups of three men each, who would dive into the Canal and the river at night, swimming past us and towards the bridges with their explosive charges. Once there, the charges were to be planted under the bridges. This risky endeavor was to be carried out tonight already, between June 22 and 23. The bomb timers were set to detonate in the early morning. Right after our briefing, the frogmen headed out and left our sector. I was awestruck. Such an operation had been the last thing I had expected. Nevertheless I admired these men for their bravery. I ordered my men to wake me at 05:00 in the morning before sinking into a deep sleep, completely exhausted.

In the morning of June 23, we waited eagerly to hear anything about the detonations. Much as usual, we lay in our positions in the early hours, watching the terrain ahead. All of a sudden, a loud detonation tore through the silence and behind us, at the nearby bridge, a huge pillar of water rose from the Caen Canal. Utterly surprised, we watched from our dugouts as the bridge behind our line collapsed with a loud crash. Then the water came back down, spraying the riverbanks. Baffled, we looked at each other wondering. There had been no sign of aircraft or incoming shells. Had the frogmen ended up attacking the wrong bridge? We went to the site and looked at the result. The bridge was completely destroyed, and we were cut off from the rest of our company.

Many years after the war, I found out what actually happened. The six German frogmen of *Marineeinsatzkommando 65* (65th Naval Special Operations Group) had entered the waters at night just as they had planned. Each of the two groups carried one of the explosive charges. The first problems arose when these heavy, torpedo-like devices, which were built for use in salt water, did turn out to have little buoyancy in the river water and thus sank to the bottom. As such, the charges had to be arduously balanced with empty gas canisters strapped onto them.

After this had been achieved, the frogmen began their approach around midnight. The first group soon had more problems when a few of the gas canisters were lost, leading to the bomb sinking again. Eventually they were forced to have one man carry it on his shoulders while crawling through the mud at the river bottom – an extremely tedious process, as the men had to surface regularly to breathe. In the end, this group still managed to plant its charge and swim back.

The other group also had enough challenges of its own. One of the three men lost his nerves and returned to land, leaving the other two to continue the mission on their own. But they too managed to plant their charge under the bridge. When the river's current proved to be too strong to swim back, they were forced to wait for the entire day before climbing out of the water in the evening, running west and entering the Caen Canal. There, against the slower current, they swam back towards Caen.

Both explosive charges detonated at 05:30, as planned. It was not the bridges at Bénouville and Ranville, however, which were destroyed, but our bridges at Hérouville and Colombelles. The two bridges that were still in German hands. What the largest British naval guns and countless bomber sorties had been unable to accomplish in weeks, the German Wehrmacht had achieved itself in a single night. When the cause for this was investigated, it turned out that the frogmen had been given outdated maps. In order to succeed, they had needed to pass two other bridges before planting their explosives on the third. Due to these incomplete maps, however, both groups had only passed one bridge before blowing up the ones they had come across next – which were of course those still in our possession.

There had been no casualties except one. The frogman who had lost his nerves earlier had grown worried about his comrades, entering the water again in hopes of finding them on their return. After some time he had been spotted by British guards, coming under fire and getting wounded. He had managed to leave the water but died of his wounds shortly thereafter. The *successful* destruction of the Normandy bridges was the first German frogmen mission of World War II.

After almost four weeks of continuous front-line duty, it was decided that 21st Panzer Division was to be withdrawn from the area north of Caen. Casualties had amassed up to a point where some of its companies were down to no more than 25 men – less than what a platoon of that same company should have. The main battle line north of Caen was severely undermanned. Time and again units were regrouped, with individual battalions being brought forward in alternation. Our own II Battalion, now completely deployed at Hérouville and Colombelles, had shrunk to around half its original strength. By early July, 22nd Panzer Regiment had 52 Panzer IVs and seven Panzer IIIs remaining. The support units of artillery and combat engineers were in a similar state. Up to that point, almost 3,000 men of 21st Panzer Division had been wounded or killed. Consequently, from June 29 onwards, our division was relieved by 16th *Luftwaffen-Felddivision* (Luftwaffe Field Division). In the process, we also received a new battalion commander: Major Leopold Lenz.

On July 7, another enemy frontal attack on Caen was attempted from the north. This time, the preliminary bombardment was carried out in large parts by strategic bomber wings; German soldiers of 16th Luftwaffe Field Division were soon forced to retreat, but all the rubble in the northern part of the town hindered any further advance. British and Canadian tanks could not hope to overcome the mountains of debris towering before them. Over the course of July 8, only one kilometer (1,100 yds) of ground was gained. By July 10 eventually, the town center and Orne river were reached. Here, the attackers halted again; they had managed to capture the northern and western parts of Caen, while the town's east, as well as the Colombelles area, remained in our hands.

At first, we did not hear much about the events unfolding. Our company marched towards Mondeville in the night between July 6 and 7, where the battalion was to receive replacements. Our own 8th Company was quite banged up, having suffered heavy casualties from the unrelenting artillery strikes of the week before. It was down to roughly 75 % of its original strength. Me and my men had been among the luckiest; our anti-tank platoon still had all its vehicles, and no more than two of my men were killed by artillery.

Due to the constant threat of low-level air attacks, I had requisitioned a motorcycle for myself. Driving this smaller vehicle made me feel much safer compared to riding in the bulkier *Kübelwagen*. Back in Africa, I had raced around in a sidecar motorcycle for months; as such I was more comfortable with this vehicle, a heavy BMW. In the evening of July 7, I was on my way to a briefing at the company command post. All of a sudden I felt a massive shockwave passing by my head. A fountain of rocks and soil shot up in the middle of the road around a hundred feet ahead. Half benumbed by the blast, I swerved with my bike into the roadside ditch, lying down with my heart pounding wildly. As a matter of fact, an artillery shell had passed by my head to the right and impacted right in front of me. If the shell had come in just a few inches further left, I would have kept going on the road without a head for a moment. I listened for additional detonations but could hear none. I looked at the road. On the other side, around 130 feet down the road, there was a steep hillside in which I could make out a few holes.

These were hideouts of French civilians similar to ones I had already seen near Hérouville. Behind them, it was possible to get a view all the way to the ridge north of Hérouville. Had I been spotted from there, leading to an attempt to score a lucky hit on me? I could not know; in any case, I had been lucky. I pulled my motorcycle out of the ditch and kept going, trying not to think about having cheated death yet again.

When the situation north of Caen became dire on July 8, the alarm was given for us as well. Our 192nd Panzergrenadier Regiment was to assemble in the Hérouville area in preparation for a counterattack into the northwest.

There, the 16th Luftwaffe had already suffered 75 % casualties. Several companies from both battalions of the 192nd, including our 8th Company, along with several Panzers of 22nd Panzer Regiment, were sent to Hérouville. Fortunately, there were dense clouds and soft rain that day, which meant that we were not harassed by ground attack aircraft. Under difficult conditions, we crossed the Orne river over a railroad bridge and then the Caen Canal over a road bridge northwest of Mondeville. Then, we established a temporary beachhead. The attack was to commence in the earliest hours of July 9, shortly after midnight. There, heavy fighting already took place between the British and units of 16th Luftwaffe Field Division, as we could clearly hear by the noise of battle ahead. The situation became less and less clear, however, leading to the attack being suspended. For the time being, all we could do was wait. During reconnaissance of the near area I found an orphaned 75 mm Pak 40 gun, which I immediately let hook up on one of my self-propelled guns. It used the same ammunition as my guns, and you could never know – maybe we might need it in the future.

At 08:00 in the morning of July 9 the order came for "all to move back behind the Orne!" So we marched back again. In bright daylight and without clouds in the sky, this truly was a parforce run. All kept looking up, but nothing happened. Not a single fighter-bomber showed up. We took up a position in the town center of Caen, at the Orne river's southern bank. I was appalled to see the state that the town was in already. All of it had been turned to rubble. Moving through the streets was almost impossible. We waited in our concealed positions, and in the afternoon of July 9 our company attempted another advance further into Caen. The enemy had already occupied the town center, however, and after an intense meeting engagement, we withdrew. The bridges we had crossed earlier were blown up by combat engineers.

With that, the northern and central parts of Caen were now in Allied hands once and for all. After another night in the old positions, we took up new ones to the south of the – now destroyed – railroad bridge northwest of Mondeville on July 10. There, we remained for the time being, hidden in the debris, damned to immobility thanks to the threat posed by Allied aircraft. To our left, at Caen, the 272nd German Infantry Division went into position over the following days, and our 21st Panzer Division occupied the area from Mondeville over Colombelles up to Demouville further in the rear. To the east, around Cuverville and Touffreville, 16th Luftwaffe took up new positions.

On July 18, 1944, the brief calm was over for us. The British now commenced their decisive attack – operation Goodwood. It began with a bombardment the likes of which we had never witnessed before. Such was its intensity that those who would survive it would never be able to forget it. We lay in our holes at Mondeville during the usual morning shift, when shortly before 06:00, a buzzing sound heralded the approach of bomber aircraft. The next thing we heard was the howling of bombs plummeting to the ground before they detonated with a loud crash. Gigantic mushroom clouds rose up and started floating over the terrain ahead. Everyone tried to get as much cover as possible. The air was filled with unbelievable thunder and banging. It seemed as if the world was coming to an end. We had no choice but to endure the entire bombardment in impotent helplessness. Time passed by, but the hellish spectacle continued unabated. All of that, and we were not even in the epicenter of this bombardment. Its main focus lay on a long sector stretching from Colombelles over Cuverville up to Toufreville in the north and Cagny in the south. We at Mondeville were at the edge of the target zone. We could watch as the British lead bombers dropped flares and wave after wave of following aircraft unloaded their bombs.

Impact after impact, the bombardment slowly rolled from north to south. Houses disappeared in flashing explosions, and trees were hurled into the sky. An impenetrable wall of smoke, dust, and detonations formed. When the bombs detonated as close as roughly 100 yards ahead of our line, we thought that our end had come, but then the inferno suddenly stopped; only to make room for the next firestorm.

Starting at 07:30, a barrage of countless artillery pieces of varying calibers came in. It first hit around our most forward positions and slowly crept into the rear. Again the gruesome spectacle happened right before us, and in terror we thought about our comrades that were swallowed by the wall of destruction. It seemed utterly impossible to me that those parts of our 21st Panzer and 16th Luftwaffe Field Division that were in this area had any chance of surviving this hell. Such a display of Allied superiority I had never seen before. Frozen in shock, we endured this attack as well. In our sector, the bombardment lasted for almost an hour.

After the bombs and artillery had gone silent, we looked around in our positions. Once again we had been lucky. My platoon was unharmed. The company as a whole had lost one vehicle – a self-propelled anti-aircraft gun had been destroyed by a close bomb hit. The vehicle, which had been dug in almost five feet into the ground, had been hurled up by the blast along with its crew. Roughly seventy feet away from its original position, it had come down again, now lying on its back. We grew bitter. We wanted to fight our enemy face to face, but before we got a chance we were shattered by his bombs and shells. Ahead of us, in the direction of Colombelles, we could already hear intense battle noise. Braatz and I decided to work our way towards the edge of Mondeville in order to inspect the area around the Colombelles industrial grounds. Just as we had arrived, we spotted British tanks east of us, going southwards in a widely spread formation. We watched some of them getting hit and explode. At the industrial grounds ahead, where most of the companies of our II Battalion were positioned, there was fierce fighting. We could hear bursts of British submachine gun fire.

Braatz and I returned to our command post and resolved to employ my anti-tank platoon at Giberville, advancing in the direction of Cuverville. We intended for this move to create a flanking position that prevented the enemy tanks from encircling us. I gave the according orders to my men, and with the three self-propelled guns we slowly felt our way forward. On the way ahead, the terrain soon became more open, so I let the vehicles take turns in driving forward one by one. All the time artillery shells kept whistling by, and far to the east we could see multiple columns of smoke indicating a raging battle. One of my guns drew forward over open ground. They were only around 200 yards ahead. Suddenly the impacts around the vehicle dramatically increased in number.

"We have been spotted!" flashed through my mind. But the gun's commander did not recognize the danger. I loudly cursed the missing radio equipment. My runner recognized the danger just as I had. And before I knew it, he jumped off the vehicle and hurried towards the gun in the open. All watched him tensely. It seemed as if he would reach it. Only a few steps separated him from the vehicle. All of a sudden it got a direct hit. The gun, its crew and the runner all vanished in an explosion. Debris flew in all directions, and bright red flames emerged, followed by thick, oily smoke.

Now everything happened fast. More impacts splashed up soil around us. "Artillery or, worse, enemy AT!"

I ordered to reverse, the engine was revved up, and we moved back into the cover of some bushes. There was no going forward here. The wreck was smoldering on the open field ahead. In the blink of an eye, I had lost six soldiers. All of them burned up in the explosion. Their faces flashed through my mind. I was shocked by this sudden and unexpected loss.

We turned back. Braatz, a few grenadiers and I attempted to scout northwards on foot. It was afternoon by now, and we received a message from battalion command stating that the enemy had begun crossing the Orne at Caen. Now our position was a risky one. We worked our way forward towards Cuverville. The terrain was filled with huge craters making it difficult to cross. We eventually reached the Colombelles industrial grounds and took cover next to one of the workshops. We knew that our battalion was fighting here but saw none of our soldiers. Just as we raised our heads a bit to see further, the wall behind us started spitting. Chunks of cement sprinkled down as MG bullets hit the building. Directly ahead, in the ruins roughly 220 feet away, I could spot the typical bowl helmets of our enemy.

We had to cut and run. Covering each other, we hurried back.

Alternately leaping and crawling, we crossed an open area and found ourselves back in Giberville. We looked at our watches. Late afternoon. Our situation was completely incalculable. I hurried to my remaining two guns and withdrew them back to the edge of Mondeville. We received a radio call by the battalion commander ordering to withdraw to Mondeville; the positions at Colombelles had become untenable. Canadian infantry began crossing the Orne with assault boats, and strong enemy forces were on the advance southwards out of Colombelles, meaning they were headed directly towards us. To our east bustled the British tanks. The situation seemed hopeless. Finally, in the evening, we heard the desperate radio call from our Major, to regimental command: "II Battalion encircled at Mondeville. We fight to the last! Long live the Führer! *Sieg Heil!*"

Braatz and I were shocked. That radio call took away our breath, and it seemed as if a heavy burden was now put on our shoulders. I could sense a feeling of trepidation taking hold of me. "Is this how it ends?" I thought desperately. The radio operator looked at us eyes wide open. I refused to accept this. I did not fancy entering captivity here or even dying *for the Führer*. There had to be a way out. There always was. I adjured Braatz to let us attempt a breakout. On our own account, if necessary. I was determined that we could make it. We both had seen that to our southeast multiple British tanks had been taken out. Which meant that there had to be one of our units nearby. So I proposed that we should attempt to break out to the southeast. Me and my two self-propelled guns would form the vanguard. If we were to carefully work our way southward after nightfall, it could succeed. During that time the British artillery observers would be practically blind. I could see our men tensely listening to our conversation. They knew it was do or die now. Breakout, captivity, or death. All or nothing.

So, I scouted ahead with my two self-propelled guns along the railroad from Giberville to Grentheville and from there onward towards Frenouville. After several hundred yards of advancing alternately, my gunner spotted an armored vehicle in a railroad underpass, roughly 300 yards straight ahead; apparently a British Cromwell tank. We had a shaped charge shell in the breech, and so I immediately ordered to open fire. The first shot scored a direct hit. A cloud of smoke rose from the tank. With my binoculars I intently examined the area; I found nothing else. I gave the order to keep advancing slowly. The tension was at its maximum, but the danger of getting encircled made us throw all caution to the wind. After some time we had closed in on the tank and to our relief we discovered that it had already been destroyed. The crew had escaped the vehicle, but not made it. Smoke was still rising from the burnt corpses lying around the wreck.

When we slowly went on, we spotted two more British tanks, this time Shermans. They were burnt up as well. By now, we had covered quite some distance and had a free view towards Cagny. It looked as if the armored assault had indeed been defeated. We quickly returned to Mondeville, and I reported our findings to Braatz. He radioed our battalion commander who, with audible desperation in his voice, decided to risk a breakout attempt. The Canadians and British were drawing closer by the minute, and to Major Lenz this was the only possibility to contribute anything to the rescue of his battalion. Contrary to his earlier message, he seemed to gather courage again.

Dusk had already set in, and after some short regrouping we commenced the breakout. I was at the tip, followed by the rest of our company and finally the battalion after it. In a long, stretched column and staggered to the side, we drove southeast. Time and again I ordered to halt and scanned the terrain ahead. The area was brightly lit by a multitude of fires. Wrecks of British tanks appeared in the distance. We expected to run into massive enemy tank or anti-tank fire at any moment. My nerves were strained to breaking point. If I was to lead our battalion into an ambush, it would be our end. A surprising opening of fire would mean our demise. Now, in the middle of the night, it would be a bitter fight to the last, and we would certainly be the ones to lose it. After several miles of driving through the night, we suddenly came across a single soldier directly ahead, raising his hand. I rose mine as well, and much to my relief I recognized the shape of his helmet, signifying that it was one from our side. We had established contact with our regiment.

When the rest of our battalion started arriving bit by bit, there was much surprise. After the last radio call, they had not expected to see us again. Lieutenant Colonel Rauch, appeared and congratulated us on our successful breakout. Major Lenz praised my initiative, and Rauch acknowledged it appreciatively. The regiment was now united again, albeit rumpled by the fighting. Rauch informed us about the defensive victory that our troops had achieved over the course of the day. To our relief we realized that the line could be held for the time being. The entirety of our 21st Panzer Division was now to be pulled back and shifted east to Troarn that same night. The positions in this area would be taken over by 12th SS Panzer Division "Hitler Youth." We had arrived in the middle of the preparations for this takeover. We came just at the right time.

We lined up with the regiment and immediately went on the march southeast. After roughly four miles, having passed Vimont and heading towards Argences, we made halt in a small village. We covered up our vehicles and camouflaged them. This was, after all these long weeks, the first opportunity for us to knock ourselves in shape a bit. In one of the houses we found a bathtub and some water, which we used to get some thorough cleaning. Further orders would come in only by next morning. I took stock of my platoon. My anti-tank platoon had two self-propelled guns remaining, along with a French truck and my *Kübelwagen*. Of my originally 21 men, thirteen were still alive. So, together with me, my platoon consisted of 14 men. This meant that I had lost around a third of my unit. Eight of my soldiers had fallen. I had two full gun crews of five men and three men for the truck, one of which I now assigned my new runner. Not a desirable position since, apart from the gun crew which had been killed by the artillery hit, all other losses, including Atteneder, had been my runners. I also took one soldier from one of the gun crews to drive my *Kübelwagen*. As for me, I decided to directly ride along with one of the SPGs. Riding on the gun carrier would give me a better overview of any situation we could find ourselves in.

In the morning of July 19, I tried to find out where we had ended up. We were roughly two and a half miles south of Troarn, in the village of Le Fresne. We had orders to take up defensive positions between St. Pair and Troarn within the next couple hours. To our left was 125th Panzergrenadier

Regiment, to our right 346th Infantry Division. In the west, there were a large number of British tank wrecks strewn across a large open area. Those I wanted to take a closer look at. Perhaps one of them was still serviceable and, with some luck, could reinforce my platoon to full strength.

I told my men about this plan, who acknowledged it with more or less enthusiasm. They knew me well and I had gained a reputation for my zest of action. Since this had paid off for them a few times already, they tended not to complain and most of the time joined me on my exploits. This time, however, I decided to make the first trip alone. I checked in with the men on guard duty and went on my way, scurrying from one bush to the next. Only a short time later I arrived at one of the British tanks, an American-made M4 Sherman. The vehicle had received a direct hit and burned up. The armor was blackened and still radiating warmth. The tracks' rubber blocks were molten from the heat. I decided to have a look into the turret. I climbed up the hull and looked into the inside through one of the hatches. The unfortunate crew was still there. Unrecognizably burnt up, the contorted bodies lay wedged into each other in the turret. Their heads and limbs were charred, their flesh burnt black and some of the bones were visible. An intense stench of burnt flesh filled the air.

As I was standing on that tank and staring at the horror below, shells already started whistling in. Just as I had processed the sound, the first shell struck straight ahead of me. I immediately dropped down from the tank onto the ground and dug my fingers into the soil next to the tracks. The earth was shaking and chunks of it rained down on me. A British artillery observer had probably spotted me, as now shell after shell was coming down around me. Cursing my adventurousness, I endured the spectacle. Most obviously, the British had more than enough artillery ammunition and did not have to economize it like us. After a few minutes, the show was eventually over, and I slowly crawled back towards our positions on all fours.

When I judged myself to be out of sight, I jumped up and zigzagged the last hundred paces. Out of breath and with a pale face I was welcomed at our line. The whole thing had been watched from a distance and as such I was asked no further questions. In any case I decided to put my plan to capture a tank on hold for the foreseeable future. On the next day, July 20, 1944, I would celebrate my 23rd birthday. And I wanted to live to see it.

On my birthday I treated myself to a simple, but long breakfast. Who knew when I would have time for something like that again. Late in the afternoon we received news that left us all in surprise: an assassination of Adolf Hitler had been attempted. Varied rumors quickly spread around, none of which seemed reasonable enough to believe it. What was clear, however, was that the attack had to have been carried out by one of our side, since no one else would have had access to Hitler's closer surroundings. Hitler had survived the attack, albeit not without injury. I could not help but think, "The war must indeed have turned in our opponents' favor if there are now attempts to attack Hitler from within our own ranks!"

Shortly before our departure towards Troarn. Only one hour after that, we would find ourselves in a chaotic display of bloodshed and destruction.

In the middle of this whole situation, we received a new movement order. The British were again on the attack around Troarn. It seemed like they were starting to break through. Our company was now to reinforce the weakened defenders there. In short order, the whole company had mounted up and was heading towards St. Pair, south of Troarn.

Braatz went ahead in a *Kübelwagen* with two runners. One of these messengers had orders to meet us shortly before our arrival to relay a situation report. The weather was bad, with light rain and darkness setting in. After a short drive we halted at Pont de La Ramée bridge. Here, as had been planned, the runner was standing, ready to brief us on the situation. Our vehicles were spaced tightly, and their drivers tried their best to get them into cover on the roadside as well as under the bridge. There was little room and we also had to keep moving, and so all stayed close together. In the dark of night, the tension was palpable. The assassination attempt was on everybody's minds. "Will all this soon be over? How would the end look for us? Like the end of the last Great War? Would the Allies, assassination or not, be willing to negotiate at all, or keep insisting on unconditional surrender?"

Judging by how fierce the Allies were fighting, I thought the latter option to be more realistic: their demand for unconditional surrender. The word "unconditional", however, made us resent this option. It would mean that all our sacrifices would have been in vain and that we could expect another catastrophic peace treaty like after the last World War. All of this went through my mind as I disembarked from my gun carrier. The runner greeted me, and we went to a small house next to the bridge. Only inside did he light up his pocket lamp in order to not risk us getting spotted from afar while he showed me the way on a map. We had just closed the door when all of a sudden everything was covered in blazing light, and the door was jolted open again.

Almost the same instant there was a shockwave and the hard bang of an explosion. Both of us instinctively dropped prone near the wall. After a short minute, the artillery strike was over. We kept on lying on the floor for a few seconds, practically paralyzed. The door had been torn from its hinges and lay in the middle of the room. Smoke and dust crept in from the outside. I recognized the flaring of fires and the first sounds reaching our ears did bode ill. Medics were called for. Ammunition was exploding. I stood up and ran out. What I saw was a chaos of burning vehicles, smoldering debris, and screaming men beyond description. The artillery had struck right in our midst. Soldiers were crawling out from under the vehicles, their faces blackened. Others were nothing more than twisted husks of smoldering flesh and scraps of uniform. I hurried towards my self-propelled gun.

Right before it I found one of my NCOs, his name was Haering, lying on the ground. One of his legs was hanging on his thigh only by a few muscle strands, and his blood was spreading around him in a large pool. The man, however, was surprisingly collected. Bracing himself on an arm, he yelled commands towards the crew. Just as I knelt down next to him, a medic arrived, who immediately tied off the upper leg and turned the lower one, which was protruding at an unnatural angle, to align with the other one. As if rearranging this gruesome picture would make things better. Only when the NCO saw this, he became aware of his situation. His face abruptly turned white, and he sank down on his back.

I grasped his hand tightly and supported his shoulders. The medic nodded at me, and I stood up again to look for the others. When I wanted to let go of his hand, the NCO squeezed it one more time. I hesitated for a moment, but then bowed down to him again. The words, "Too bad, Lieutenant" softly escaped his lips. He let go and slowly sank down with a groan.

I said: "Everything is going to be all right! Hold on!" before forcing myself to turn around. It was no good, my leadership was needed. I tried to bring some order in the chaos. I sent men from here to there, patted all of them on the shoulder and gave each a task. At the very first we dragged the dead and wounded out from under the vehicles and made sure that the medics could do their job. Over time we found ourselves again. It was obvious, however, that we had to get away as quickly as possible.

After a few seemingly endless minutes, the situation was under control again. I counted four dead and six wounded, some of them severely. Ten casualties; considering our already reduced numbers, this was quite a lot.

Sadly, the NCO had not been the only wounded of my anti-tank platoon. Another of my soldiers had been gravely wounded. But our company was still lucky under these circumstances. The self-propelled guns remained undamaged and only a few trucks had been destroyed. I ordered all to mount up and, led by the runner, we went ahead to St. Pair with our dead and wounded, the survivors heavily battered.

Deploying our company at Troarn was now out of the question for the time being. But we immediately started regrouping the gun crews. Our dead and wounded were picked up in the same night already by ambulances that carried them to the next field hospital. What eventually became of our wounded, we were not told. This was how July 20, 1944, the day of the assassination attempt on the Führer, ended for us. Because of the events surrounding the artillery strike, this attempt completely faded into the background. Only days later would we come to grapple with it. One realization became more and more clear to me: "If you want to leave this war alive, you need more than pure luck!".

Even today, many years later, I have had not a single birthday on which I do not have to think about this nightly slaughter at Pont de La Ramée.

The British attack on Troarn on July 20 was repulsed without us, but only under heaviest losses on our side. Slowly, but steadily, a fatalistic mood set in everywhere. The enemy's material superiority was utterly ineffable. The weather had worsened over the course of July 20, however, with the beginning of a long period of rain, which soon turned the loamy plains east of the Orne into a vast field of mud, preventing any further armored advance. The following hours were characterized by artillery duels. As both sides did not want to give each other too much peace, they resolved to throwing shells at each other. For each and every one of our artillery shells, however, we got twenty back from the "Tommies." Then we received more bad tidings. A salvo of our own artillery had come too short and hit right in our main battle line. Four soldiers could only be recovered dead. Not only could we barely return fire, but once we were actually firing, we also hit our own positions. Our men acknowledged this in silent resignation. Upon looking in their eyes, however, I could clearly see how much resentment they were trying to hide.

Within these pauses in the direct combat, there were also signs of humanity. On the next day we witnessed a ceasefire being spontaneously agreed on by both sides. Fighting around Troarn and St. Pair had been so fierce there had been barely any time to recover the wounded. By now they were lying on the battlefield, unprotected, for hours or even days. In the night, we could often hear their screams of lament coming from no man's land. Only when it ceased we knew that it was over for the poor devil. Many only succumbed to their grievous wounds after days of agony. Their calling was almost too much to bear at night. No man who once hears it will ever forget it. At once, ambulances were driving up on the opposing lines, their sides marked with large red cross flags. Trusting our sense of fairness, they slowly closed in on our positions. Not a single shot was fired. Now, for a few hours, the guns were silent and both sides recovered their dead and wounded in the pouring rain. The medics were helping each other wherever they could. Everyone was recovered, whether friend or foe.

After this time, the British and their ambulances went off again. In one of them, an English officer was standing bold upright. Upon passing by, he saluted us. Later I was told by one of our medics that the man was a British physician who, in summer 1939, right before the war, had been studying at Heidelberg, Germany.

In the evening of July 21, the horror caught up with us again. We were lying in the garden of Château St. Pair, where we had installed our command post. Battalion command had put us into reserve due to our earlier losses. At the time we were coordinating our possible uses at the front lines when we were once again hit by an enemy artillery strike. The first shells whistled in and before we knew it, we were already in the middle of a bombardment. Like a hunted hare, I ran through the exploding landscape up to the chateau and into its cellar. I had not been the only one to come up with that idea, and together with other soldiers we hurriedly funneled down the stairs. Once we were down there, we could listen to the roaring of British artillery shells striking all around the building. The chateau basement was only half below the surface, and once the high cellar windows were smashed open, dust blown up by impacting projectiles was creeping in. The noise was deafening and almost unbearable.

When the pressure of a detonation coming through the cellar window staggered me, I spread my arms to find something to hold on. Trying to regain my balance, I reached left and right and suddenly my fingers encountered resistance by a sticky, warm something. Shocked, I looked to the side and saw how the soldier next to me fell down on his knees. A piece of shrapnel had whizzed through the window, cleanly splitting his head in two from the forehead upwards. My hand had grasped the inside of his head. I recoiled and stared eyes wide open on the twitching body that slowly vanished before me under a blanket of stirred up dust and dirt. It seemed as if time was standing still for a blink of an eye. I threw myself into a corner and tried to be as flat as possible. After a few minutes, this bombardment came to an end as well. Almost trance-like I stumbled towards the stairs. By now I had seen quite a lot, but this had been nothing but pure horror. I tried to not look at the soldiers who had been fatally hit and climbed up the steps on all fours. The chateau and its garden had been badly hit. Half of the building's roof was gone, with the upper floor being almost completely exposed.

Scraps of paper were falling down to the ground. I bent down and picked up a postcard. It depicted the chateau in its undestroyed state. What an irony of fate. Without giving it a second thought, I put the card into my pocket.

In total, we suffered almost ten men killed. This was a shock. My guardian angel, as by now I was quite certain that I had to have one, had protected me from the worst once again. In contrast to the artillery strike at the bridge, my platoon did not suffer any casualties during this bombardment. At the bridge I had lost two men to shrapnel, but this time we had enjoyed good cover. Only I had almost gotten it. In the meantime, I had received two new soldiers from Braatz. My anti-tank platoon was his strongest asset, and he did not want it to remain weakened. Thus I could reinforce my gun crews and was now back to having fourteen men under my command.

The remainder of my anti-tank platoon after over one month of deployment in Normandy. The platoon, initially 22 men strong, had shrunk to twelve men. First Lieutenant Braatz stands in the center; I stand third from the right.

These recent surprise fire attacks left us entirely convinced that the French Résistance was keeping their eyes glued on us. How else could it be that we had been hit in such a targeted manner? We were not directly at the front line, camouflaged well in flat wooded terrain, and the rainy weather did not allow for enemy aerial reconnaissance. Then, where did these targeted artillery strikes come from? We all were full of anger at the unknown enemy. The effects of this resentment would not be long in coming.

After the bombardment I stood together with my soldiers to assign them as gun crews when I saw an NCO of the company command squad approaching. Before him walked a French civilian, visibly scared to death. The sergeant had drawn his pistol and shoved the Frenchman, who must have been around 35 years old, in front of him. The man wore nothing but trousers and a shirt and had no papers with him. The two of them headed straight towards me. Dismissing my soldiers, I waited for the sergeant to come closer.

The NCO was visibly agitated. Without letting me say anything, he panted out, "Lieutenant, sir, we just apprehended this man. I was ordered to shoot him as a spy … Lieutenant, sir, I can't do this … I am sorry, but I simply can't do it."

I had thought long about a situation like that. I went closer to the sergeant, pulled him to the side and sternly told him, "Listen to me. You will take this man now, go to the edge of the village, and after the last house you look around and find out if anyone can still see you. Then you send the man away. Make him understand that he is free to go. Once he is away, you return to me and report the execution. Understood?".

With wide eyes, the NCO stared at me, dumbfounded but also delighted. He confirmed my order with the words "Yes, Lieutenant, sir!", turned around, and went off with his prisoner.

I took a deep breath and waited. After some minutes, the sergeant returned, somewhat insecurely reporting, "Order carried out", before disappearing again. Much relieved, I called for my soldiers again. However, one might think about this situation, I am convinced to this day to have done the right thing. Even if the civilian had been a Résistance member, how could it have been proven? I think that my men knew all too well what I had said to the NCO, but none of them ever brought it up. And perhaps, deep inside, they approved of how "their" lieutenant had handled that situation. Any of them could have reported my actions just like that, but no one did. They stuck with me.

Who had ordered the sergeant to shoot the man, I do not know to this day. It could not have been First Lieutenant Braatz. I had always witnessed him to be very correct. Those two artillery strikes and the resulting high losses had been too much for all of us, however. The nerves of everyone were strained. Maybe there had been actual evidence regarding the Frenchman. I do not know, and I will never find out. In times of war, the line between personal guilt and innocence is only a thin one.

CHAPTER 15

A FINAL ATTACK

Our 8th Company was spared from the heavy fighting that 21st Panzer Division was going through at the end of July 1944. Because of recent losses, battalion command did not judge us ready for action. As such, the by now less than forty soldiers of our company first marched east in early August before joining up with the rest of the battalion in the Lassy area, in the morning of August 5.

On the march back I saw some of our own fighter planes fly towards the enemy. At first, we suspected them to be Allied attack aircraft and immediately drove our vehicles off the road, but then identified them as German Messerschmitt Bf 109 fighters. Flying low, they zoomed over the French fields. Our men cheered and waved at their pilots. Under the planes' fuselages we thought to have seen bombs, but when they returned sometime later with the same "bombs" still affixed, we realized that these had to be external fuel tanks.

"Well, in that case we have to make do with our own hand grenades," one of my men remarked contritely. I knew nothing to say in reply.

When we arrived at the regiment, we were appalled by the state we found our fellow soldiers in. All of them were at the end of their ropes. The unrelenting and constant fighting had worn all of them down. The Americans had broken out of their beachhead at Avranches and were standing close to Le Mans in the south, deep in our left flank. It seemed that nobody was stopping them. Our front line essentially ran over multiple hills north and south of Lassy. The highest peak at 1,200 ft, Mont Pinçon northeast of Lassy, had been one of the targets of the British's latest offense. A few days prior, they had begun an energetic push southward. This meant that their offensive line ran in parallel to our positions, making it perfectly obvious that their attack was to support the American advance.

At the time we were situated very close to Mont Pinçon, which itself was defended by units of 276th Infantry Division. Beginning on August 5, the British attempted to capture the hill. In addition, most likely to keep our 21st Panzer Division from rushing to the embattled 276th Division's aid, our own positions were also fiercely attacked by British and Canadian troops. Taking or holding the vital peaks was the main objective of both sides. "He who has the height, has the depths" is what we had been told back at Wünsdorf Panzer Forces Academy, and it universally applied to all forces in this conflict.

Immediately after our arrival in the Lassy area, I was asked to report to the regiment's commander. Upon entering his office I was quite surprised to find our division commander, Major General Feuchtinger, standing before me. I saluted, which the general acknowledged with a nod before gesturing towards my regimental commander with a smile. Lieutenant Colonel Rauch nodded as well and informed me that we had suffered high casualties among the commanding personnel up to that point. He now needed every officer available to lead his subordinate units. Officers like me, who were relatively senior, now had to take extraordinary efforts. After all, I had been in action since the very first day of the invasion. Over the course of these harsh weeks of privation, I had gained a good reputation and consequently I was now to take command of one of the Panzergrenadier companies that had become leaderless. On top of that, I was informed that a counterattack by our division on the enemy positions at Mont Pinçon as well as further west at Origny was planned for the next day, August 6, 1944. This "battlegroup" of mine was also to be supported by several of our armored vehicles.

Once the Colonel finished, Major General Feuchtinger began to speak. "Well, Lieutenant, I was informed that you are a capable man. So

I want you to execute this attack with all of your vigor. Do not waste any time, bring your battlegroup forward and beat back the enemy. I want your attack to be successful! Do you understand?" he said insistently.

I replied, "Yes, General, sir!", to which he nodded affirmingly.

"Good, Hoeller, then you are hereby dismissed!" he finished. I signed off and was shown the way to the soldiers of my new Panzergrenadier company.

On the way I had to think about the general's speech. On the one hand I felt honored, but on the other I could feel the pressure that was now resting on me. Leading a battlegroup was quite a lot of responsibility for a mere lieutenant. Today I know that Major General Feuchtinger was hard-pressed himself at that time. There was even the possibility that he could have been relieved of command. His absence on the first day of the landings had not been overlooked among his superiors. Although he had been just promoted to major general on August 1, this perhaps had been done in order to convey that impressive results were expected in return. Today I cannot help but believe that the general was dealing with me personally only because he was in dire need of some success to point to. In this, he probably did not care in the slightest who and how many were sent to the slaughter.

My Panzergrenadier company in essence comprised around 60 soldiers, who were all obviously more than battle-weary. When I assembled the company's NCOs to introduce myself and explain next day's mission to them, I could see in their faces how they were anything but enthusiastic about the prospect. Nevertheless, they listened attentively; after all, all of our lives were at stake. As had been promised, a mixed platoon of Panzer IV and Panzer V Panther tanks of 22nd Panzer Regiment showed up in the evening hours. I briefly conferred with the tank platoon commander, a young sergeant, before lying down with a queasy feeling at midnight to try and get a few hours of sleep. I could not catch any, however; too many memories of my first assault in Tunisia came to my mind. "What will tomorrow bring?" I kept asking myself. If things were to go down like in Tunisia, we would have to walk through hell.

Back then I had commanded a platoon of almost 40 men, now it was a company, but with its 60 soldiers it was barely larger than my old platoon. Around 02:00 in the night, we marched to our staging area, which we arrived at without any incidents. Shortly before our attack was planned to commence, things suddenly came thick and fast. Battle noise emerged ahead of us, and after a few minutes a runner came rushing in. The British had preempted our attack, going on the offense from the west and north towards Mont Pinçon and the surrounding hills.

We were now ordered to immediately advance towards the enemy. We went on the march towards Origny. Our staging area was located in an open forest southeast of the town, which ran up a hill slope. The crest was covered in trees and bushes, with some boulders visible between them. Through the binoculars we spotted soldiers up there breaking branches off the trees. We could not clearly identify them, but since good camouflage had by now become necessary for our survival, we assumed them to be German troops. We passed by Origny without further incidents and eventually ended up west of the hill. I conferred with the tank commander about how we should advance through the terrain ahead. To get a better view, we went up to a nearby road. Suddenly we heard engine noise ahead. Before we knew it, a German Kübelwagen came around the corner and stopped right next to us, in which sat a sergeant and a corporal who identified themselves as members of one of our infantry divisions. With the engine still running, they explained that they were stragglers looking for their home unit. We in turn explained our mission to them and before we knew it, they turned around their car and drove off in the direction they had come from. The tank commander and I looked at each other puzzled.

But just as the Kübelwagen had disappeared behind the corner, a British armored scout car suddenly emerged from it. The green and yellow striped vehicle came to a halt, its engine humming, and turned its turret towards us menacingly. All of this happened so fast that we were completely surprised. The distance to the British Humber scout car was almost 500 ft. Before we could even drop into the roadside ditch, it opened fire on us. Its salvo came up short, however, the heavy machine gun bullets hitting the road before our feet. "Now off we go!" both of us thought as we jumped into the ditch.

But apparently the British were also unpleasantly surprised to have encountered us, as the scout car's engine revved up and it reversed back out of sight. All this had only taken a few seconds. With our hearts pounding we retreated, returning to our soldiers panting, but unharmed. I now ordered the grenadiers to march ahead in a widespread line, followed by the tanks which lumbered forward through the terrain with gunning engines. In case of enemy fire, the tanks had orders to immediately suppress any enemy positions identified.

The morning mist had vanished, and the sun rose up. Everyone kept searching the sky nervously. The woodland ended, we reached open ground with a small house on the edge. Then I gave the order to halt. I was walking roughly in the center of my battlegroup, immediately next to a Panzer IV. The tank had already left the woodland and was now covering the slope before it with its cannon. Just as I wanted to raise my hand, I heard the characteristic hum of aircraft engines ahead. Everyone winced, heads quickly turning in all directions. A moment later we spotted the enemy attack aircraft approaching low over the horizon. Jabos (short for Jagdbomber, meaning fighter-bombers), a soldier next to me shouted at the top of his voice, "Full cover!"

All tried to disappear from the scene. Some of the grenadiers around me ran up to the tank and threw themselves under it. I wanted to join them but hesitated for a moment and then sprinted towards the house, where I dropped down next to the wall. A shadow passed over me, followed by a howl and an enormous detonation. As if in slow motion I witnessed a bomb hitting the Panzer IV, tearing it apart in a mighty explosion. In horror I had to think about its crew and the grenadiers who had taken shelter under the tank. All were now expecting another bombing run, but to our surprise, this had been the only attack by these fighter-bombers. For the next couple minutes they devoted themselves to the area in our rear. As we would later find out, regimental command would come under attack and take a hammering.

After we had recovered from the shock, we began advancing again. We left behind the smoking wreckage of the tank, whose turret had been flung several yards away by the force of the blast. The crew of five as well as five grenadiers were left behind dead. We turned to the right again, succeeding in taking the next hill without any further air attacks. We were met by some small arms fire, but managed to force the British Infantry back. From the rear, we then got the order to hold position on the hill until further notice. I made the men prepare for the defense and cover up the tanks in all haste. Now we were safe for the moment. By the end of the day, however, the British had managed to capture Mont Pinçon east of our position; With that, the enemy had the area's highest peak in their hands, their flank was secured, and their objective met.

In other areas, advancing British units had been successfully delayed by efforts of our artillery. In addition to the assault on Mont Pinçon, the British also tried their luck on the point where our 21st Panzer Division was joined to 326th Infantry Division. This time with suitable artillery preparations. But despite the intense bombardment, our troops managed to repulse all British attacks until the evening as well as stabilize the old frontline north of Lassy again. In the night, however, long intense enemy artillery fire resumed. Under the flashing lights of exploding shells, we dug deep into the ground and pressed ourselves down in our foxholes. All around us, shells kept plowing up the landscape. First reports of casualties came in. Luckily, all of them could be treated by the medics for the time being.

During the night I lost contact with the regiment. It became apparent that me and my battlegroup would not be able to hold this position for much longer. My tanks had withdrawn due to the fierce artillery fire, leaving us alone on the hill. Nobody wanted to run around in the bombardment, and so I resolved to take two of my runners and rush back myself, hoping to reestablish communications with the regiment. Again we ended up in the middle of a British artillery barrage, but by jumping from one ditch into the next like hares, we escaped it just as well. Finally we found another runner. The man told me that the regiment's latest attack had failed too, after which our right flank had collapsed. Regimental command had then issued a general order to withdraw. I now tried to hurry back to my company with my two runners. After a short time, one of my NCOs already crossed our way. He had a shrapnel wound in his upper leg which was bleeding profusely. I yelled into his ear to go back. He looked at me, his eyes opened wide, gazing at me bewildered, and kept lurching on towards the rear. We left him behind and kept running forward. The artillery fire ceased, and everything went quiet. We stood at the foot of the hill and looked up. Suddenly we heard combat noise and English shouts ahead. The British were already close by and had commenced their assault. Seconds later, the first bullets whizzed by around us. Everyone took cover wherever they could. I ran across a road and jumped into a field.

Again I heard voices. I squatted down on the ground, as there were obviously British on the road closing in. "My company's positions on the hill must have been overrun already!" I thought. I rolled to the side and entered a small depression which, as it turned out to my dismay, harbored a swampy pond. Within a moment I had sunk into the mud up to my breast. The English-speaking voices grew louder and so I froze in the exact position I had entered the mire. I could feel the swamp water quickly soaking my clothes. Once the British had apparently passed me by, I immediately tried to free myself from this awkward situation. I managed to roll out of the mire; exhausted and covered in mud from head to toe, I crawled into a bush. My gun and camera were left behind in the gargling swamp. Over the sound of my pounding heart, I could hear another British scouting party marching past on the road. Once the British had passed by, I started running in the direction of my company. After some time I found another NCO, who had also been separated from our unit. When he spotted me coming towards him, completely covered in mud, he stopped and looked at me blankly. Only once I told him my name did he recognize me. We first took cover in a ditch. He told me that our company, or rather what was left of it, had retreated on its own after the British assault.

We kept on walking and together managed to find our way back to the regiment. The staff there had already thought us to be missing in action. Until evening, some more additional soldiers trickled in. We spent the whole night trying to find our remaining men. In the morning we finally gave up. I was completely exhausted. I had gone three days without sleep, and my little excursion into the mire had almost been the final straw. With my uniform soiled by dry mud, I must have been a terrible sight to behold. When I eventually assembled the remains of my Panzergrenadier company in the morning of August 8, I counted two NCOs and fourteen other soldiers. No more than sixteen men were left of the almost 60 with whom I had headed out. My company was virtually wiped out.

Together with these soldiers, I reported back at the regimental command post to Lieutenant Colonel Rauch. He was surprised to see me again, but immediately offered friendly greetings. He was quite elated, and I quickly saw why: he had been awarded the Knight's Cross of the Iron Cross for his actions at the Normandy front. Rauch told me that, although our attack did not result in a breakthrough, the front line had been successfully stabilized. His adjutant, First Lieutenant Ackermann, had been killed in the fighting. A fact which I was shocked to hear, since I had only become acquainted to him a few days ago. Ackermann had also embarked on a special mission similar to mine; unlike me, he had joined the long list of lives lost in the merciless fighting.

I also received the news that our division commander, Major General Feuchtinger, had been awarded the Knight's Cross as well. He had received it already on August 6, 1944 – the day of our advance on Mont Pinçon. Apparently his division's attack that we carried out had yielded the desired result, even though this "successful" attack might perhaps not have been the sole reason for Feuchtinger to be awarded his Knight's Cross.

As I was now standing before Lieutenant Colonel Rauch completely exhausted, I realized that the Cross was apparently awarded not only for one's own personal acts of bravery. This was, however, what national socialist propaganda always told us the award was for. Of course I was aware that higher commanders were also awarded the Knight's Cross for their efforts. I have to say, however, that neither Feuchtinger nor Rauch had struck me as energetic military commanders; Feuchtinger in particular was always a controversial figure. Many rumors made the rounds among us officers about "him and the women," and in addition we had not forgotten about his absence during the first hours of the invasion. But he was also known for his close ties to Hitler which traced back all the way to the 1930s Nuremberg Rallies. As for Rauch, on the other hand, I definitely regarded him to be a fair and responsible commander, but most of the time I could only find him with his staff far behind the front line.

To be fair, my views about the whole situation might be a result of my subordinate perspective. It was just that at a time where I had just returned from a difficult and bloody mission, where I had lost almost all of my company, I had a hard time accepting the awards my superiors had received as something they truly deserved. I realized that in wartime, each individual order could be awarded for its own unique reasons – and bravery was just one of them. Lieutenant Colonel Rauch expressed his appreciation for my efforts. "Lieutenant Hoeller, you're going to make it far!" he told me. In the same breath he ordered me to get some rest. On the loss of my company he did not elaborate. What was left of it was integrated into another. I went to clean myself and my uniform as well as I could and looked for a place to sleep. In the very moment I had found a cot and laid down, I was already gone. Almost fifteen hours later I was roused and received orders to report back with our 8th Company. Still weary, I went on my way.

CHAPTER 16

HELL IN THE FALAISE POCKET

I arrived at Lassy in the evening of August 8, where I reported to First Lieutenant Braatz. Our company was to repel the British armored formations advancing southward. We found good positions in and around the village and immediately began shelling the previously reconnoitered British positions, which were roughly two miles west of Lassy, with our grenade launchers. My two self-propelled guns covered the main line of movement westward. They drove into house walls in reverse and nestled into the buildings, thus creating well-concealed defensive positions. Not a very considerate course of action, but in this situation we had to take any measure necessary to improve our chances of survival.

In the early hours, our forward posts had reported advancing tanks, and a moment later everyone was lying in their dugouts. The British tanks only dared to close in on Lassy in a slow and deliberate manner; one of them was too bold, however, going forward directly on the road. My two self-propelled guns were in a favorable position and at a distance of around a hundred yards, the crack of a cannon shot sounded. The British tank immediately came to a halt and started smoking. Luckily for its crew, it did not explode; the British managed to bail out and ran away. We watched the fleeing tankers without opening fire.

Shot up British M4 Sherman tank in the village of Lassy. The tank had dared to move up too far and fell prey to one of my 75 mm anti-tank guns.

After our successful kill, we allowed ourselves some time to inspect the enemy tank. While the vehicle itself was unusable, we were happy to find several crates of British provisions inside. A very welcome surprise which amazed us with its high-quality food. Everyone got a part of this gift, and we delightfully ate up all of it. After this armored advance, the British settled for repeated artillery strikes and infantry scouting parties for some time. During this, I lost a man from my platoon, who was caught in an artillery strike just as he was out to relieve himself. A piece of shrapnel put an end to his young life. We found him lying in a field with his trousers down. Apart from the lethal shrapnel wound he had not a single scratch.

Our division's mission was now to enable the movement eastward of 5th Panzer Army's withdrawing formations. Like a stinger, our unit was the last protruding west into the Allied lines. Over the next couple of days, the British were battering us from three sides. Due to repeated artillery bombardments, we had three more casualties within a short time. All wounds were serious injuries caused by the shrapnel of explosive shells. These could cause horrible wounds, sever whole limbs with one blow or even rupture the lungs through their shockwaves. You were lucky to receive only light wounds. During a reconnaissance patrol of our near surroundings by one of our NCOs leading ten to twelve men, they managed to capture three British soldiers from a scouting party. Interrogation did not result in any intelligence which we did not already possess. Namely that we were once again in danger of becoming surrounded. It was high time to withdraw eastward. Since we had barely any manpower to spare for guarding our prisoners, we decided to send them back to their comrades after a short interrogation. We gave them a white sheet and told them to march westward along the main road. Visibly puzzled, but understandably relieved, they went away with their arms raised.

Soon, enemy pressure on Lassy became too strong. There was a great danger of becoming surrounded. We found ourselves in the same situation we had been in before at Bénouville and Mondeville. This time our battalion commander recognized the looming threat in time. In the following night, between August 11 and 12, our battalion withdrew roughly 1.2 miles eastward to St. Vigor, where we took up a new defensive position. As support we received a Panzergrenadier company from the battalion. It comprised a whopping thirty soldiers. That was not necessarily a staggering battle force. Our two companies formed a small battlegroup, which was tasked with covering our regiment's retreat westward. In the night before August 13, our 21st Panzer Division withdrew onto a line between La Chapelle and La Rocque. Our battalion was now the division's rearguard.

As we were shifting more and more toward the east our front became less and less coherent. German troops were streaming past us. All tried to escape into the east. Together with the leader of the Panzergrenadier company assigned to us, I decided to reconnoiter into the north. The situation around us was quickly becoming more chaotic, and we wanted to find out how far the enemy was away, or whether they had even overtaken us already. My plan was approved and so the two of us drove off in my Kübelwagen. Ahead of us on a hill, there was a large farmstead which could be seen from all directions. We wanted to have a closer look at it as it appeared to be a good spot for looking over the area. We were also painfully aware, however, that this trip could end in our demise if the farmstead was already occupied by the enemy. We decided to not take any unnecessary risks during our reconnaissance. We left the Kübelwagen in the concealment of several bushes next to the road and kept going on foot.

In addition, we left our submachine guns in the car and only took our pistols with us, which we kept holstered. If the British were to encounter us in such an unarmed state, we thought our chances better for them to not open fire on us immediately, but rather call out from a distance in the hopes of capturing us without a fight.

We sneaked our way forward. Our nerves were strung to breaking point. A lone soldier with a submachine gun and loose trigger finger could have led to our demise. We trusted in our obviously displayed inferiority. With utmost tension we reached the farmstead. We spotted a man, apparently the farmer, busying himself with clearing out his cattle's dung. Calm and placid, as if it was blissful peacetime and not August 1944. We slowly went closer to the farmer. When he saw us he paused for a moment before leaning onto his pitchfork and staring at us. In an inquiring tone I said, "Anglais?"

"Non!" he muttered sullenly before resuming his work. It was as clear as day that we were not welcome here. Perhaps he was irritated by still encountering German soldiers and not Allied ones. We tried to get a look from the hill on the surrounding area. There were pillars of smoke rising from burning vehicles and buildings all around. We could also spot enemy aircraft far away. There was no unmistakable sign of advancing enemy forces, however; the situation was still not clear. We decided to go back again, as moving forward even further would have been pointless.

Back at the battlegroup we reported our observations to our superior commanders, but the battalion could not give us any additional information about the situation around us either. Only one thing was clear: there would be no such thing as holding the line anymore. Whenever we caught sight of the "Tommies," we would open fire and then withdraw to the next favorable position. Most of the time it was British armored scout cars rushing over the road before halting for a moment to scan the area with their rotating turrets. One or two high explosive rounds usually sufficed in ending such incautious activities. In one of these actions, one of my guns managed to light a British scout car on fire. The gun was in a good firing position. When the scout car slowly passed behind a wrecked German truck and closed in, it was already done for. A short order to fire and our first shell struck right on target. We watched from a safe distance as a few of the crew members bailed out and the armored car eventually burned up completely.

But these advances by the British were always followed closely by Allied fighter-bombers, which then circled above us like vultures. During these times we were effectively paralyzed and each of us hoped that there were no British tanks following these scout cars. In that case we would have been doomed, as the fighter-bombers would have prevented us from withdrawing in time, and we had nothing to withstand a massed armored attack. Our two self-propelled guns would have only bought the shortest amount of time. Fortune was still on our side, however, and our small battlegroup kept up the slow fighting retreat towards the east.

Some of the German formations around us were disintegrating completely, and time and again we had stragglers come in and join our ranks. Soldiers from the infantry divisions were most often appearing especially distraught. Some of them just sat down and could not be moved to march on with us. The relentless Allied attacks had brought them to the very end of their tether. There was nothing we could do for them.

From August 16, 1944 onward it became apparent that there was a pocket forming around us in the Falaise area. Everyone now attempted to escape into the east. The once orderly retreat turned into chaotic flight. The infantry divisions were supplied almost entirely with horse-drawn vehicles, and so we saw a multitude of carts congesting the roads. Between them walked the wounded and demoralized soldiers. Allied fighter-bomber attacks became more intense by the day, and everything around us descended into chaos, destruction, and death. As for our own unit, we tried to make our withdrawal with leapfrog maneuvers. My SPGs took a position and covered the Grenadier company's movement; then the latter was covering us and we withdrew past its position. Then, one night, we lost communications with each other, and our 8th Company was now completely alone again.

Another victim of my self-propelled guns. On our retreat from Lassy eastwards we managed to take out a British armored scout car. This photograph shows the burning vehicle.

From August 17 to 18, the situation grew increasingly worse. The enemy kept attacking from Falaise in the direction of Trun. This led to German Panzer Divisions standing in the west becoming huddled into each other more and more. For them, the way east was not at all an easy one. They had to cross the river Orne on their retreat, behind which another obstacle awaited them, namely the river Dives. Masses of men and materiel were building up on and around the bridges. Allied aircraft and artillery were bombarding these concentrations constantly, making any form of progress almost completely impossible. Each formation now attempted to break out on its own. Every man was fighting for his immediate comrades and nothing else. Within our company, too, feelings of desperation became more prevalent. Fuel was almost impossible to get, the masses crowded the roads and vehicle after vehicle had to be left behind by ourselves as well. In the end I only had my two self-propelled guns remaining.

In the morning of August 19, we were positioned roughly three miles west of St. Lambert. Runner communications with regimental command had ceased several days before. Judging from what reports we were getting over the course of the day, we concluded that the Allies must have managed to tighten the pocket to a few kilometers already, albeit only loosely. We were in danger of getting cut off completely. Battalion command now tasked me with reestablishing communications with our regimental command post south of Trun. It had to be somewhere a few miles behind us.

To this end I procured a motorcycle, which had been standing in the middle of the street, apparently left behind by its former owner. My men saw to it that its fuel tank was full, and shortly before dark set in, I set out alone. Wanting to avoid the congested roads as much as possible, I went across country at breakneck speed. Time and again I had to stop and orientate myself. What I witnessed was an inferno beyond any description. On the meadows around me were countless groups of soldiers, dozens at a time, either wounded or already dead. Between them lay dead horses, stood carriages, trucks, ambulances, guns, tanks, or armored cars. Many vehicles were ablaze, spewing oily smoke into the air.

Sometime after nightfall, I eventually found our regiment's command post south of Trun. Lieutenant Colonel Rauch appeared to be crestfallen. An advance by the Canadian 4th Armoured Division from Falaise towards Trun had split our division right in the middle. Our regiment stood south and southwest of the Village of Trun and was in danger of being ultimately cut off by the next Canadian push southwards. The battlegroups of 21st Panzer Division now had orders to attempt to break through into the east on their own. Battlegroup von Luck, meaning 125th Panzergrenadier Regiment, had commenced its breakout the day before, and battlegroup Oppeln had followed that day, August 19. Our own 192nd Panzergrenadier Regiment, battlegroup Rauch, was to begin its breakout attempt in the night before August 20.

The regimental command post was now hastily readied for the march. When I reported to Rauch and asked for further orders for his II Battalion, he at first could not believe that I was actually standing before him.

"Hoeller!" he exclaimed, "where in all the world did you come from?" Rauch explained to me that he had already been informed that our battalion had been wiped out. Apparently one company had been mistaken for our whole battalion. Rauch now wanted to withdraw eastwards with the remains of his regiment as per his orders. He ordered me to drive back to my battalion and relay these orders immediately to Major Lenz.

The new rallying point for 192nd Panzergrenadier Regiment was to be St. Lambert. There, the pocket was apparently not closed, and it seemed that breaking through was feasible on the road leading through this village as well as another road through Chambois further southeast. It was also obvious to me that now all of our forces wanted to escape along this route. Only the quickest ones would succeed, however. I jumped back on my motorcycle and drove to the battalion. I had trouble coming through. After a few miles I ran out of gasoline. I kept going on the road on foot for a while.

On an empty stretch where the road had a bend, a German Panzer IV came towards me at high speed. I saw that it was much too fast and had the presence of mind to leap off the street, landing next to the end of a sewer pipe below it. I hurried into the pipe and only moments later, the tank's tracks burrowed into the ditch right where I had just entered it. I crawled out of the pipe through its other end and looked at the Panzer lying in the ditch at a tilt. The tank's commander climbed out of the turret hatch before starting to yell and gesture in the direction of the driver, obviously furious about having effectively lost his vehicle. I turned around and stumbled along on the road.

After some time, I discovered an abandoned Kettenkrad standing on the roadside and drove on with it. I eventually arrived at the battalion. There, all hope had already been abandoned. Major Lenz had assembled all remaining officers around him. I reported to him, which he acknowledged stoically. It was apparent that an orderly retreat was barely possible amidst all this chaos. Nevertheless, he issued commands for all to rally at St. Lambert. We would attempt to initially break out together; in case any unit would get separated from the rest, however, each company commander was to try reaching St. Lambert with his remaining men on his own.

The Major ordered me to take his adjutant, Lieutenant Schulze, and drive ahead on the tracked motorcycle to reconnoiter the way towards St. Lambert. Since I was already familiar with the route, I was to take the lead. Major Lenz ordered the companies to arrange in a marching order. Our 8th Company with my two self-propelled guns was again tasked with forming a rearguard. I bade farewell to First Lieutenant Braatz, we wished each other Godspeed, and together with his runner he returned to our company on a sidecar motorcycle. Like with most men of our company, I would never see him again.

The rest... The last photograph before the escape from the Falaise pocket.

Late in the evening of August 19, 1944, we went on the march to St. Lambert. The roads were completely covered in vehicles standing in two or three columns immediately next to each other. Many of these were burning or already wrecked. Artillery shells were striking continuously, ammunition and fuel was exploding everywhere around. In the midst were streams of soldiers slowly making their way. Tanks were ablaze, horses lay on their back, their legs thrashing about in their death throes. We came across ambulance cars which had burned up while they were full of wounded. Horribly mutilated, their charred corpses lay inside the wrecks and on the ground before it. After just a short time, Lieutenant Schulze and I had already lost contact to our battalion. There was nothing to be done; all around us the chaotic masses pushed onward. Eventually, we arrived at the center of St. Lambert, where we found a command post that was apparently trying to coordinate the breakout. There I saw something unforgettable: two German generals sitting on crates right among all the bustle. We were told that they were commanders of two infantry divisions who had lost contact with their respective units.

Both of the two SS Panzer Divisions' vanguards had already succeeded in breaking through towards Vimountiers, and every man able to do so was following in their tracks. Since Lieutenant Schulze and I had no more contact with our battalion whatsoever, we decided to join up with 10th SS Panzer Division "Frundsberg." Its soldiers seemed to us to be still undeterred, and their vigorous demeanor looked promising when it came to making it out of the pocket. Just like our unit, 10th SS Panzer Division "Frundsberg" had arrived at St. Lambert in the morning hours of August 20. In the afternoon, the breakout attempt was to be made, following the lead of the other two SS Panzer divisions which had gone before.

Within a column of armored vehicles, we went on the march in the afternoon of August 20. Burning wrecks on the road were ruthlessly pushed to the side by the Panzers. Several type V Panther tanks were at the tip, with armored personnel carriers and infantry on foot behind them. I also saw the two generals in the middle of it all.

The streets and ditches were littered with countless dead and wounded. We took with us whoever we could, but the heavy tank tracks mercilessly ran over the dead on the road. A disturbing sight beyond all description which will forever leave a scar on my mind. Some artillery shells struck nearby, everyone ducked for a moment, but the march went on. Our vanguard was caught in a firefight with enemy anti-tank guns further down the road, but these were successfully defeated. Finally, we crossed the Dives and entered the area east of St. Lambert, where we dug in around midnight. Jumping off the APCs, we secured the surrounding terrain. I was impressed by how disciplined the Waffen SS soldiers were conducting themselves. Most of them were still quite young fellows, but something in their faces made them look like old men. What a difference between them and the regular infantry divisions' soldiers.

We stayed until around 02:00 of August 21 before setting off again. Marching on at walking pace, we walked to the left and right of the armored vehicles, ready to immediately react to a possible ambush. Many of the wounded were at the end of their tether, there was too little room to carry them, and as such more than a few were left behind. With the break of dawn, heavy artillery fire started coming in. The pocket behind us had to be the sight of horrible carnage. The realization we had made it out of St. Lambert was truly elating.

After more skirmishes with enemy tanks and anti-tank guns, we eventually arrived at the positions of 2nd and 9th SS Panzer Divisions, II SS Panzer Corps, southwest of Vimoutiers. After their successful breakout, these two divisions had commenced a counteroffensive, which had contributed to our own breakout's success in a considerable way. Thanks to their pressure, the attacks on us had remained limited in scope. Completely exhausted, we now finally had a few hours of rest. It was hard to believe that we had actually managed to escape this hellscape of death and perdition. The tenseness of the days before now started to fade, and everyone, be they a humble soldier or proud general, was glad to have survived and to have made it through.

Destruction in the outskirts of St. Lambert.

CHAPTER 17
RETREAT EAST

After our successful escape, everyone hurried towards the river Seine. Back on August 21, 1944, Army Group B had ordered a general retreat behind this large stream. For the time being, we assembled what was left of our 21st Panzer Division between Bellou and Fervaques. Individual regiments were down to 30 % of their original strength and had barely any heavy weaponry left. Lieutenant Schulze and I asked our way and eventually found the rally point of our 192nd Panzergrenadier Regiment. The regiment had been one of the last formations to escape the pocket and had been weakened the most. Divisional command had thus given provisional orders to rally at St. Germain la Campagne and remain in reserve.

When the Lieutenant and I reported at the rally point, we were welcomed by Colonel Rauch – he had been promoted in the meantime. Visibly glad to see us, Rauch quickly briefed us on the general situation. It did not look all too well. The losses suffered inside the pocket were neither quantifiable nor even conceivable. The next big problem was that now the entirety of Army Group B had to cross the Seine. Our regimental staff had been decimated during the fighting retreat. I was the only lieutenant to have been part of the regiment right from the beginning of the Normandy landings. Some of the other subaltern positions had to be replaced up to seven times.

Colonel Rauch made a surprisingly long time for me. After he had dismissed Schulze, he asked me to sit down for a moment. "Hoeller," he commenced his address in his characteristic, fatherly tone. "I already know you since 1943. I always saw you as a very capable, industrious, and, most of all, courageous officer. So, what would you say if you were to switch from a career as reserve officer to active officer duty?"

I was staggered. I had not expected that. In the time during and shortly after the breakout, I had gotten the chance to think about many things. We had escaped along with the soldiers of the 10th SS Panzer, and I had conversed with them a lot. During these conversations, I would often compare these Waffen SS soldiers to our regular Army men. The fact that our replacements were of lower and lower quality while at the same time the ranks of the Waffen SS seemed to be filled with expertly trained soldiers gave me pause. The levels of training and motivation within our division were only a shadow of what they had been back in 1941 during the Africa campaign. Back then, all soldiers had been confident and capable fighters almost without exception. This kind of vigor could not have been eluded. Even in Tunisia in 1942, everyone had still been full of conviction. Now, in the year 1944, it appeared to me that most of the time, many were only following orders apathetically. I had to admit that this change of mind had not happened within the ranks of the Waffen SS. During the unfathomably chaotic escape out of the Falaise pocket, soldiers of the Waffen SS showed a level of mutual support and camaraderie that left me utterly impressed. Deep inside I even envied them for their proudly displayed will to persevere, their still first-rate discipline and, most of all, their internal solidarity. After all these months of turmoil, it seemed quite enticing. But of what use was this perseverance in the face of the sheer superhuman enemy superiority? I was still convinced to be standing on the right side, but last three months' events had not left me unchanged. Events like the July 20 assassination attempt left me thinking, and for a long time I had been contemplating the rationale behind this world war. However, the demand for unconditional surrender, which the Allies had stated during their 1943 Casablanca conference, had left many of us more determined than before, including myself. Should we surrender ourselves to a return to the infamy that the 1920s and 1930s had been for

Austria and Germany? To me, this was unacceptable. Better to endure all this fighting to the very end than having to suffer the same way as one's parents. But what would this very end be? How would it look like? I could not know. I tried to talk myself into believing that everything that had been accomplished over the last few years could not have been in vain. In what short moments of respite I got, I always found myself conflicted about these issues.

Anyway, when the officers of the 10th SS Panzers asked me to join them, I was indeed tempted to give in to their solicitation. Only after the war would I learn of the war crimes committed by the Waffen SS; not just the general SS and *Totenkopf* (Death's Head) formations, who were responsible for the genocide happening inside the concentration camps, but fighters of the Waffen SS had just as well incurred a great guilt during their combat operations.

Besides, there was another thing, about which I was thinking a lot: During my time with 21st Panzer Division, I had sensed a difference in how I was treated by my superiors. I was under the impression that active-duty officers were given many more opportunities to further their career compared to us reserve officers. While this was certainly not the case in all of the German Army, my personal experience in the hard-fought battles of Normandy had led me to believe it personally. Again and again I was assigned special missions, while active-duty officers, some of whom had higher ranks, were not burdened that much. This left me disillusioned and somewhat resentful, and it actually convinced me to return to civilian life as soon as possible right after the war.

As Colonel Rauch was now sitting before me and making this offer, all of these thoughts went through my head. As a matter of fact, his sincere and honest approach had impressed me, and in any case his offer made me resolve for myself to stay true to my division. I hoped that some of the men under my command had made it out of the Falaise pocket, and I wanted to lead them through the horrors of war as well as I could. I simply owed it to my soldiers.

Near the end of our conversation, Colonel Rauch eventually shook his head and ended by saying, "Well, Hoeller, I understand, but I ask that you don't take too much time to decide this. In any case I see a future career officer in you. I will in the near future see to it that you will be assigned to my staff. As soon as replacements from home reach us, you will come to me. For the time being, you stay with II Battalion. Right now I need every good officer, and as far forward as possible at that. I will also push on with your promotion. If everything goes well, you will be first lieutenant by October 1. Then things will look different again. Also, there's still time after the war to think about your activation."

He then ordered me to report back with my battalion commander, and with that I was dismissed. I signed off, leaving the command post without any further comment.

Major Lenz had indeed managed to escape with the survivors of our II Battalion. I found our unit, or rather what was left of it, without much of a problem. The soldiers were housed very close by. I reported back to Lenz, who was already completely occupied with bringing his unit back into a somewhat battle-ready state. He also looked surprised when he saw me enter. I was tasked by him to assemble and make ready for action a reconnaissance platoon, which was to be held *z.b.V.*, meaning *zur besonderen Verwendung* (for special deployment). Its purpose was to give the battalion the most possible freedom of action and also prevent the few men that were left being lost in an unsuspected attack. Once there were only little forces available, good reconnaissance became increasingly valuable. The Major allowed me to choose my men for myself. I just had to make sure we were ready for action.

To my great joy, I found one of my self-propelled guns along with its crew. There was much cheering as we greeted each other. I was told that our company had been torn apart in the mayhem of the pocket. The second self-propelled gun had received a direct hit by enemy tank fire and burned up along with its crew. None of them had made it. Other soldiers from my platoon had gone missing in the pocket. With that, this vehicle crew was all that had made it out. A whole five soldiers were left of my anti-tank platoon. There was no trace of First Lieutenant Braatz or the other platoons from our 8th Company as well. They were assumed to be either dead or captured. Only sometime later did some men of the grenade launcher and anti-air platoons trickle in. They reported that the First Lieutenant had most probably been captured during the breakout attempt along with his runner. The two had last been seen riding a sidecar motorcycle. I sincerely hoped he had somehow made it, as he had always been a good superior. Over the last couple months, we had grown closer through all the hardships we had to share.

Upon request to Major Lenz, I received two small French Renault personnel carriers as well as seven *Panzergrenadier* soldiers. Together with my remaining self-propelled gun, my reconnaissance platoon was now complete. Commanding the individual vehicles and their crews were three first-rate NCOs. From now on I wanted to ride along with the self-propelled gun again. After I had assembled my soldiers, I reported ready for action to Major Lenz. In the meantime, the latter had already rebuilt two Panzergrenadier companies from those who had escaped the Falaise pocket along with newly arrived soldiers. These companies still had very little combat power, however, and our II Battalion was barely at a strength of 200 men.

In the night before August 23, 1944, we marched further east past Bernay. At the time, the danger of getting overturned by rushing Allied troops was omnipresent, and as such the river Seine appeared to be the only sensible line of defense. In the morning of August 24, new orders reached the division. It was to relocate to the Seine south of the city of Rouen without any delay. The area there was to be held as long as possible.

In addition, our division was tasked with organizing the orderly crossing over the river of any forces there. Around noon on August 24, we arrived at Bourgtheroulde, south of Rouen, where parts of our division were again facing the Allies in battle. Their action was to buy as much time as possible for our own troops to cross the Seine. Also on August 24, 1944, French and American forces of the 1st Army reached Paris. The French capital, along with its Seine bridges, fell into the liberators' hands almost undamaged on the next day. The French Résistance contributed significantly to this, and as such German resistance inside the city itself was very limited.

In the evening of August 24, we finally reached Rouen and the river

Seine. Between here and the sea, there was not a single bridge across the river still intact. All of them had been destroyed by repeated Allied air attacks. The only option left were French civilian ferries, a portion of which were operated by the German *Kriegsmarine*. Around their landing stages, retreating German formations were amassing once more. The Allied menace in the air turned crossing the river into a dangerous endeavor. *Panzerpionierbatallion 220* (220th Armored Engineer Battalion) was now tasked with repairing the damaged railroad bridge in Rouen. Our regiment was ordered not to wait, but immediately cross this bridge. As our II Battalion was at the tip of the regiment, me and my reconnaissance platoon had to scout the area around our crossing. The railroad bridge was indeed in a severely damaged condition. Heavy bombs had brought it to the brink of collapse. Only a single lane was still negotiable, which was already congested by a multitude of Waffen SS vehicles that had begun their crossing a while before.

The crossing over the Seine.

During nightfall, we investigated the bridge on foot. One man stayed behind at the bridge's end to serve as messenger while me and an NCO boarded a Waffen SS APC and went up to the bridge's midpoint. There we dismounted and got an overview of the situation. The middle part of the bridge had been made somewhat drivable by laying wooden posts and boards across the railroad tracks. Crossing with our vehicles would be a difficult task, but still a feasible one. As long as we guided the vehicles very carefully, it could be done.

I sent a man back to report our findings, and as a matter of fact we managed to cross the bridge with the entirety of *Battlegroup Rauch*. First, we queued up among the seemingly endless columns of Waffen SS troops before, long after midnight and several arduous hours of anxiously feeling forward step-by-step later, we finally reached the other side. Luckily for us not a single vehicle got stuck on the bridge, which would have caused a traffic jam and massive delays. Once on the other side, we went eastwards through the streets of Rouen, a city that was by now completely in ruins. Fires were raging everywhere. All these destroyed houses, some of which were utterly ablaze, made for a scene that was as eerie as it was terrifying. We left the city behind us in the black of night and after a few more hours of driving we eventually arrived at Beauvais, roughly 35 miles east of Rouen. There, we set up camp in a bushy patch of terrain outside town before finally falling asleep with much exhaustion. As we would later find out, we had been quite lucky again, as the bridge was ultimately destroyed by an air attack on the very next day. It does not bear contemplating what would have happened if we had been right on the bridge at that moment. Fortune had again favored us.

From Beauvais, our journey went on to Compiègne. Crossing this small town left us all in a contemplative mood. On November 11, 1918, in a railroad car parked in the woods near Compiègne, the armistice which ended World War I had been signed. 22 years later, June 22, 1940, France had signed its formal capitulation to Germany at this very same place – Hitler had arranged it, knowing full well about the location's relevance. Now, four years later, we crossed this important town as an army defeated, and nobody dared to think about how this railroad car might soon be in use again. This time perhaps under the same circumstances as in the fall of 1918. Despite this small village's historic significance, we did not stop or try to look for the railroad car. There was no point in it. We had to get ahead.

On the march east we learned that the Allies in southern France had made rapid progress after their landings. Much like the American and British armies in northern France, they kept on rushing forward. We acknowledged the report with much indifference, as we would not have expected for our own forces to stop this advance. All our thoughts were now fixed on Germany and its border. We were convinced that if we managed to reach it, we could halt the Allies there. Rumors were making the rounds that a massive line of fortifications had been constructed at the old German border, which we would be integrated into. In addition, it would be no later than there that the civilian population would welcome us with open arms again. It occurred to none of us that these people might be just as war weary as we were ourselves.

Major Lenz told us that our depleted *Battlegroup Rauch* was to receive replacements at Reims, roughly 90 miles east of Paris. By August 28, 1944, we had arrived at this area, at all times followed closely by Allied troops. As such, we also did not stay at Reims for long. Allied pressure was simply too much. We were told that our 21st Panzer Division was from now on subject to German Army Group G. A new battlegroup consisting of two Panzergrenadier battalions, a combat engineer battalion as well as an armored artillery detachment, was to immediately transfer via Metz into the Nancy area. The units selected for this mission were I Battalion, 192nd Panzergrenadier Regiment, 200th *Feldersatzbataillon*, 220th *Panzerpionierbataillon*, as well as II detachment of 155th Panzer Artillery Regiment. Me and my reconnaissance platoon were also assigned to this battlegroup, much to the chagrin of my battalion commander, who did not want to lose his reconnaissance capabilities again. But orders were orders. Together with my men I signed off and left II Battalion behind.

So our journey took us from Reims further into the east. While the Americans took the city already on August 28, the last parts of our division only crossed the Seine at Rouen one full day later. We drove by day and night, always spreading out as much as possible. By day we always looked out for enemy aircraft, which scoured in the sky like wasps searching for rotten fruit.

On some occasions we only managed to disappear in the undergrowth mere moments before a plane passed by. We would also see a new type of aircraft which we had not recognized before. American twin-engine twin-boom fighters called P-38 Lightning. These we soon nicknamed "fork-tailed devils." Like the single-engine P-51 Mustang, they had auxiliary fuel tanks enabling them to operate far behind enemy lines on the ground. And this they did with much success, as evidenced by the many burnt-out vehicles we were passing on our route. Many of these wrecks had charred corpses still inside them. No one had the time to bury the dead.

We avoided the main lines of movement, opting for side roads as much as was feasible. Getting enough supply of fuel worked surprisingly well on our march. Only ammunition was short. On August 30, 1944, we passed Verdun and drove further towards Nancy. There we could again see increased activity by the French resistance movement. We learned that there had been multiple attacks on our communication lines over the days before. Most of all, our forces had been raided by the Résistance in the vicinity of Lunéville. After that, Waffen SS units had combed the area, but failed to score any success against the French. We spent the night in a village, and in the morning we found the streets littered with three-pointed forged-metal caltrops.

Colonel Rauch had a discussion with the mayor, and within an hour the caltrops were gone again. It was obvious that the local population feared reprisals from our side. To ward off bad surprises, we kept up full combat readiness on our march. We did not want to risk running into an ambush. By the first September days we stood in the area north of Epinal, a town roughly 90 miles southwest of Strasbourg. This meant that we were not far from Germany, as Strasbourg can be considered a border city. By now, Allied troops had already reached the Belgian capital of Brussels.

Our 21st Panzer Division was in an extremely poor condition. A report issued by the division staff estimated that the division was down to a strength between 6,000 and 8,000 men. More accurate assessments could not be made, as individual units and formations had been forced back on their retreat as far as Aachen. There were no tanks that could still be reported as operational, only one or two *Sturmgeschütze* (assault guns) as well as a few AA guns and artillery pieces. Nothing more than that.

In Alsace-Lorraine, we turned back west again for the first time in a while. Our battlegroup received orders to immediately reconnoiter from Nancy along the Moselles river in the direction of Epinal and determine whether the enemy had already crossed the Moselles. Following that, we were to secure the area and thus create the prerequisites for a planned 5th Panzer Army attack westward. Beginning September 5, 1944, we commenced feeling our way forward from our starting point south of Nancy, going further south. The first few days passed by without enemy contact. In the windows of the villages we passed, however, were at all times scared faces staring at us. Some streets had already been solemnly decorated, obviously in anticipation of the arrival of the Americans. Most French had not expected to now witness German forces driving through their home village again. We ignored the whole situation, passing through with a stony and grim expression.

In the village of Chatel sur Moselle north of Epinal, we halted and made camp. Here, too, the streets were decorated with flower bouquets. As we billeted ourselves in a barn, the locals told us – once being asked and only after some hesitation – that a few hours before an American scouting patrol had entered the village. They had already withdrawn westward again, however. After leaving Chatel sur Moselle the next day, we turned westward ourselves and cautiously drove towards the surmised American spearheads. On September 8, we arrived at Mirecourt, roughly 13 miles west of Chatel sur Moselle. It was here that we would again come into contact with Allied troops.

This contact did not come as a surprise, as we were on the alert. The local civilians' reports about the approaching Americans made us proceed with extraordinary caution. Before entering a new village, we would first observe it from a safe distance. In addition, we always tried to allocate forces to our direct support. This effort would pay off at Mirecourt, as shortly before we would have entered town, we spotted an American M8

Greyhound armored scout car covering a street. Its 37 mm main gun as well as its heavy .50 machine gun posed a serious threat – as such, this threat had to be neutralized as soon as possible.

We slowly drove our self-propelled gun into a favorable shooting position. Everyone's nerves were extremely strained, but still they all did their part with great zeal. Now we finally had a chance to strike back. In a village house's backyard we found a good position to engage at around 1,000 feet. The enemy scout car was well-camouflaged and covered by a small wall up to the height of its turret ring. Hitting it in such a position would be difficult. The American himself, on the other hand, could not get a bead on us. This we could see by how far his gun was elevated. It was a standoff. I now sent one of my runners to one of my trucks, ordering the latter to roll forward on the road slowly and for all to see. When that truck arrived, prudently with only the lone driver inside, my plan came to fruition. The Americans at once took our bait, and as the armored scout car slowly went forward to open fire on the truck, I shouted, "fire!"

With a loud bang our shell left the barrel, striking the armored car at the rear. Smoke emerged. I ordered an explosive shell be loaded and fired at will. The scout car was still able to move under its own power, however, hastily rolling back behind a group of bushes. Our second shot missed. To us, it was now as clear as day: Soon we would come under artillery fire or be hunted by fighter-bombers. Things we did not want to find ourselves in. As such, I gave the order to withdraw, and we leapfrogged back behind the next ridge. We quickly covered several miles until arriving at Charmes, a town at the Moselles river. Here, too, were decorated streets and people looking at us anxiously. The fact that we had engaged the American vanguard without any casualties made us euphoric. Happily waving at the surprised French, we crossed the town at maximum speed. Once arrived at battalion command, I gave my report, which was acknowledged without any further measures taken.

Our side had too few troops available to do anything meaningful; in all likelihood the Moselles crossings would soon fall into American hands. Merely part of our 16th Infantry Division were strewn across multiple bases in the area. Between their positions, however, were none of our forces.

By September 10, 1944, the Allies pushed their troops forward again. To this end, German 112th Panzer Brigade with its Panzer V Panther and Panzer IV tanks were now to conduct a first limited attack into the area west of Epinal. Our battlegroup was also assigned to this unit for the duration of the attack. Since Colonel Rauch had fallen ill, Colonel von Luck, regimental commander of 125th Panzergrenadier Regiment, took over command of the now-called *Battlegroup von Luck*; it was further reinforced by II Battalion of the 125th Panzergrenadiers.

The planned attack west of Epinal ended in catastrophe. When the Americans and French of XV Army Corps identified our staging areas west of Dompaire and Epinal, as well as detecting the beginning advance of 112th Brigade's brand-new German Panzers, they lost no time. On September 13, they destroyed a total of almost seventy German tanks with concentrated air attacks and artillery fire. As a result, 112th Panzer Brigade's attack was already over before it had started at all.

Our battlegroup was now to conduct a limited counterattack to cover the retreat of 112th Panzer Brigade's remains. Thus, we advanced from Epinal in the direction of Dompaire. There was a fierce meeting engagement with the tanks of French 2nd Armored Division, which were themselves advancing from the Darney area.

On September 12 already, the French had crossed the Moselles at Charmes. We were now drawn back towards Epinal. These engagements left us at a total strength of only 600 to 700 men and a few guns. Going in an arc over Rambervillers, we transferred northward towards Lunéville. Now the plan was for German forces to establish a defensive line along the river Meurthe. The Americans were faster, however, taking Lunéville on September 16, 1944, along with its Meurthe crossings. This meant another change of plans for the Wehrmacht. After the catastrophic failure of 112th Panzer Brigade west of Epinal, Army Group G ordered another attack.

This wish was not to be denied. The conditions for this planned offensive just became more and more difficult, however. Again, consolidated elements of our 21st Panzer Division and 112th Brigade, now called *Battlegroup Feuchtinger*, were to advance along with 111th and 113th Panzer Brigades as well as remains of 15th Panzergrenadier Division, from the Baccarat area in the direction of Lunéville.

In the night before September 17, 1944, we readied ourselves for this attack. On the ride to our staging area, I had a rare exhilarating experience for a change. As we went through a village, a cow suddenly ran on the street right in front of our vehicle. I sat in the first of our two Renault trucks when in the blink of an eye this cow came out from behind a bush, standing right in our vehicle's way. My driver could not brake in time, such that we rammed the animal at full tilt. The poor cow was hurled on top of our hood by the impact, from which it slid down again once we had come to a halt, mooing loudly. Without serious injury, the animal trotted off.

We were as startled as we were dumbfounded. I did not want to leave a bad impression. After all I was quite aware that, especially in rural areas like this, losing a single cow could end in a family having to starve. We were somewhat ahead of the others, so me and the driver spontaneously went to the close by farmstead. I was intent on offering the French farmer my apologies for our accident with the cow. In the stead's yard, there was a little girl staring at us with a start, and a moment later the farmer himself came running toward us, gesturing loudly. He was obviously fearing for his child, as he knelt down and embraced the girl tightly, scowling at us. He then slowly pushed the child behind his own body. I now attempted to explain to him that we had possibly hurt one of his cows, but to no avail. My French was obviously bad and after the first few sentences the farmer apparently believed we had come to appropriate his car – when he opened the barn doors and showed us the car without being asked to, we realized that we could not hope to communicate.

We gestured to make him understand that everything was fine, and closing with the words "Pardon, … la vache!" (Apologies, … the cow!") we took to our heels. We left behind a more than confused French farmer, who was probably happy to be still in possession of his vehicle, and who almost certainly had no clue what cow these two Germans had been talking about.

In the morning of September 18, our attack commenced according to plan, and indeed we made swift progress until noon. When we crossed through Baccarat in the direction of Lunéville, however, Allied P-38 Lightning fighters spotted us and swooped down on us. Their attack only took seconds to manifest. We had not heard the aircraft on their approach due to the noise of our own engines, and our air observes could not spot them in time. When they turned to face us and closed in, it was already too late. We saw muzzle flashes below the enemy two-engine crafts' cockpits and a moment later small fountains of dirt were racing towards us. I was still with one of my trucks, whose driver was quick-witted enough to steer the Renault into a small patch of brushwork. We jumped off the vehicle and pressed ourselves into the road ditch. All were now expecting bombs to explode, but none of that happened. The fighters circled us for several more times before flying off again.

I gave the order to mount up again and find out whether there had been casualties. After a few minutes I received a dire report. The chief gunner of my self-propelled gun had fallen victim to one of the enemy fighters' salvos. After spotting the aircraft, the entire crew had reacted correctly, but the Sergeant had been just a moment too slow and jumped right into a burst of fire. He had died on the spot. I despondently acknowledged the news and made the men mount up again. Once more, death had come to haunt us. And, like most times, it had come surprisingly and without a warning.

I secured the right flank with my reconnaissance platoon, and we advanced from Baccarat in a northwestern direction without further incidents. We first crossed the river Meurthe, and by evening we already stood at Xermanénil, south of Lunéville. Here, protected by the village, we halted for the time being. But the pressure exerted by the Americans to our north and the French further west became more and more intense.

In the morning of September 19, 1944, the fortunes of war turned against us. The Allies launched a counterattack. To this end, American units had taken up elevated positions at Lunéville the night before, such that by dawn we found that they had direct sight of our own position. Single American tanks were now firing shell upon shell into the area they could overlook. We were trapped; as soon as one of our vehicles showed itself, it became the target of intense fire.

We attempted identifying the enemy tanks and opening fire ourselves. This worked to some degree, although we could not hope to get out more than three to five inaccurate and hastily fired shells. Nobody wanted to make themselves seen by enemy spotters for too long. We knew all too well that the American tanks' gunners were only waiting for us to show up. Every time our shots were detected immediately and followed by intense counter fire. We rapidly switched to a new position and tried again from there. The same result. Over the course of several hours, shells kept striking around us in irregular intervals. We never had the chance to score an exact hit. One Panzer V Panther tank of 112th Panzer Brigade tried to change position and failed to avoid the area visible to the enemy. When it closed in on a road junction that had come under fire multiple times, each of us expected the tank to be hit directly. All of a sudden a young Panzergrenadier jumped out of the roadside ditch, stood up in the middle of the road and put up his arms right in front of the lumbering vehicle. The tank's driver stepped on the brakes, such that the whole vehicle tilted slightly forward from the abrupt deceleration. A second later, the brave infantryman was already gone again, followed immediately by the staggering detonation of an enemy anti-tank projectile right in the middle of the junction.

The Panther's commander, realizing the impending danger, slowly backed up into the protection of nearby houses. There was no getting forward here. The entire area was visible to our enemy.

Further in the front around Mortagne, Allied pressure became overbearing, and in the evening we eventually received the order to withdraw. To this end, the armored units of 112th Panzer Brigade diverted into the woods south of Lunéville. Driving from cover to cover, we followed them. During our departure, we had yet another lucky moment. The hours before I had spent with my self-propelled gun, to which we had hooked on a small trailer that we used to stow equipment, but also ammunition. We had procured this trailer only a short time earlier. When we turned around a house corner and crossed the road at full speed, an explosion tore apart our trailer right behind our backs. An enemy shell had missed us just by a fraction of a second and hit the trailer. Apart from the hitch, nothing was left of it. We found that, in light of us all surviving this incident, it was an acceptable loss. Finally, during nightfall, we were able to escape over a meadowland.

In the night before September 20, 1944, we withdrew further back. In the dark of night we managed to go back across the river Meurthe by a very narrow margin. While wading through the water, we suddenly sank into a deep hole and ended up with the vehicle's hood under water. In the pitch black we feared for a moment to sink entirely. But much to our luck, we remained half above the waterline and only the engine had stalled. We managed to win over the commander of a Panther tank that was also fording the river. Under water we fixed two steel cables to our self-propelled gun, and after a single hitch we were free again.

The Panther continued towing us until we entered a nearby forest, where we spent the entire rest of the night getting the engine to run again. Finally, as the sun was about to rise, we did it. The engine started. The Panther tank that had took us out of that wet mess had been one of only a few of 112th Brigade's Panzers to successfully cross the Meurthe. Apart from them, the brigade had to leave behind almost its entire remaining vehicle inventory.

We hastily formed a defensive line along the Meurthe between Lunéville and Baccarat. In essence this meant that we initially secured possible river crossings. My two Renault trucks had also made it across the river, and after repairing our self-propelled gun we joined the mass of withdrawing units on the way back to Baccarat. Once again we had suffered losses in battle, and of the almost 700 soldiers of the former *Battlegroup Rauch*, only half of that number was still capable of fighting.

With all that, the counterattack had ultimately failed. The front lines now hardened into a gentle arc from Lunéville over Baccarat to Rambersvillers and Epinal. To our benefit, the Americans and French had to first reorganize their forces and things were somewhat calm for a moment.

Before Colonel Rauch had transferred command to Colonel von Luck, there had been one final conversation between us, in which he had also announced that he was to give up command due to illness. Still, he wanted to stay true to his words and thus told me that, after the conclusion of our attack, I was to be assigned adjutant to the commander of his I Battalion, Captain Werner Raetzer. I was to stay with Raetzer until Rauch's return and a reassignment into the regimental staff envisioned for me. Rauch also let me know he had arranged for me to become an active officer. In case I had any objections against that, I would still be able to change my mind at the end of the war.

Since the failed attacks at Epinal and Lunéville were now over, I reported to I Battalion, 192nd Panzergrenadier Regiment, on September 21. My reconnaissance platoon was disbanded and integrated into the battalion. With that, I had no more direct subordinates to command. One last time I talked to my men, wished them all the best and that they would come home in good health. Taking our farewells really was hard for us all – too long had we been serving close together. Counting myself, only five were still remaining. Not more. The rest were either dead, missing or had been captured. It would only be a matter of time until I would meet such a fate as well.

CHAPTER 18
GUN TO THE HEAD

Since I was now serving as adjutant of the commander of I Battalion, 192nd Panzergrenadier Regiment, I could for the first time truly take stock of and devote some time to only myself. Strained by the week-long reconnaissance missions, I had barely been able to get some rest. Feelings of exertion had become almost permanent, and there had been hardly any chance to sleep. I was worn down both physically and mentally. Several boils had formed on my feet as a consequence of me getting no chance to change clothes for several weeks. All the time since my involuntary excursion into the swamp at Mont Pinçon I had not gotten a single chance to wash myself properly.

Caring for my soldiers had always left me as the last to find any rest. Even if I did not want to acknowledge it – I was, as a matter of fact, completely exhausted. Responses by my soldiers, who knew that I was willing to give everything for them, had helped me persevere and find the strength to go on.

That was now over. All of a sudden, there was no one left for whom I needed to care. An utterly unusual feeling. Time and again I would suddenly startle up in these days of relative calm, thinking that I had to check our positions or go look after my men. I was acquainted to my new battalion commander, Captain Raetzer, already since the rebuilding of our 21st Panzer Division back in 1943. The first time we had met was during the weeks of training at Versailles. Back then he had struck me as a very decent person, and in the time since then I had only heard good of him as well. Raetzer was known for caring for his subordinates with all his energy. And indeed, he now gave me several days to collect myself. I seized the time; after all I did not know what my new adjutant position would require of me. Raetzer also confirmed that Rauch had submitted a request to transfer me to active officer duty as well as promote me to first lieutenant by October 1. Within the next few weeks, a positive response by higher authorities was to be expected.

Around us, all German forces were busy reestablishing a continuous front line. After all it was only a matter of time before a renewed powerful Allied offensive would follow. Considering this expected large-scale attack, defensive measures along the German border were stepped up. Back in the years 1938 to 1940, the so-called *Westwall* had been built from the Netherlands to the Swiss border. Along this 400-mile line stood over 18,000 bunkers, trenches, tank obstacles and other fortifications. On August 24, 1944, Hitler ordered the Westwall be reactivated in light of the rapid Allied advance. Among Allied soldiers, this German defensive line became known as the Siegfried Line.

On October 1, 1944, the Americans and French of Allied XV Army Corps continued their offensive along the entire front line. If they were to capture the heights east of Rambervillers, then the entire Meurthe valley would lie open before them. Army Group G, thus gave the order to resist with utmost tenacity. 21st Panzer Division had to form another battlegroup and go on the attack again. To this end, my former II Battalion of the 192nd Panzergrenadiers, a company of 220th Panzer Engineer Battalion and a few tanks were assembled. These forces were to be readied at St. Barbe, roughly five miles northeast of Rambervillers, to await the order to attack the town. The Americans and French pushed out of Rambervillers into the northeast in the morning of October 1, 1944. Soon the units of our I Battalion there were caught in intense fighting.

It was now of vital importance to direct II Battalion's counter push to the right location. The situation ahead of us was unclear, however, and we had already lost contact to one of our companies south of Menil-sur-Belvitte. Thus I went on my first mission as battalion adjutant on this October 1 of 1944. Together with a driver from the battalion staff, I was to reconnoiter the area in a camouflaged, formerly civilian Opel P4 automobile. Our main objective was to reestablish communications with First Lieutenant Haeffele and his company. When the captain gave me these orders, I was immediately overcome by feelings of disquiet. Having to reconnoiter only with a driver in an enclosed, unarmed vehicle seemed like a suicide mission to me. We would have nothing to put up a fight against the enemy. On an open-topped *Kübelwagen*, there was at least the possibility of mounting a machine gun, but this Opel P4 did not have room for anything like that. But it could not be helped, orders were orders.

At any rate, I resolved to take my MP 40 with me and keep one hand at the door handle for the entire ride; this would at least allow me to disembark quickly and defend myself appropriately in case of an unexpected encounter with the enemy. If we were to drive into the sights of a tank, it would be the end of the story. One hit by a tank gun shell would turn our vehicle into a ball of fire. Needless to say, we would not have the opportunity to disembark in that case.

I signed off, and we left the village of St. Barbe, where II Battalion had made its preparations, heading in the direction of the presumed front line. Without incidents we passed through Ménil-sur-Belvitte, where we encountered the last, most forward of our own forces in the area. These were a few individual soldiers in a handful of foxholes, with no heavy weapons and no anti-tank guns. The soldiers reported to have no communications to the neighboring company further south.

First Lieutenant Haeffele's Panzergrenadier company of almost fifty soldiers was supposed to be in a small patch of woodland directly between Ménil-sur-Belvitte and Rambervillers. We left the village and drove on a road between fields and meadows in a southwestern direction. Then the wide edge of a forest emerged in front of us, with our road leading straight into it. Roughly 1700 feet in front of the forest, some combat engineers had worked to create a barricade. It consisted of several tree logs and had not yet been completely closed. This was a good sign. Slowly and carefully, we passed through the barricade with our car and shortly thereafter we were about to enter the forest. Ahead of us to our right, there was a small dwelling house with a sawmill behind it. To the left was already dense forest. We kept on going on the road until we suddenly, around 300 feet ahead and well-camouflaged, saw several tanks standing at the edge of the forest.

"What? We don't have any Panzers this far forward!" I exclaimed loudly, realizing in the same second that these were enemy tanks. The very next things I perceived were muzzle flashes from multiple machine guns and bullets hitting the road ahead of us. It seemed to me in that moment as if time was standing still. Without giving it any thought, I opened the car door with my right hand and a moment later I was already hitting the road. Luckily for me, the driver had just hit the brakes, whether deliberately or from shock. Due to the remaining, still high velocity of the car, I tumbled around, ending up lying on my stomach before rolling to the side in a flash.

I could not sense any pain and thus concluded that I had not broken any bones and also had not been hit. I turned on my back, looked around and immediately knew that I had no chance. To my right was completely open ground, and the roadside ditch next to me offered no cover to speak of as well. My driver had also escaped the car unharmed, and now we were both lying on the road. We could see that the forest ahead of us was just brimming with soldiers in olive green US Army uniforms. We had driven directly into their guns like absolute beginners. Perhaps they had observed the road barricade from a safe distance.

Some of the soldiers left the forest, running towards us, yelling loudly. I could discern from their calls that they had to be French. Before I knew it and before I could even stand up, the soldiers were next to me. They stopped right in front of us, eyeing us with grim faces and without saying a word. I saw that they were entirely wearing US uniforms. Then, just a moment later, one of them stepped forward, bent over me, lifted his pistol, an American Colt M1911 as I discerned, which he then rammed into the side of my chest. With the muzzle aimed right at the Iron Cross I was wearing on my uniform jacket. He pulled the pistol back and again rammed it into my flank to hurt me. The man was only barely older than me, but I felt that he was full of anger. With fleeting eyes he investigated my uniform, apparently to find out whether I belonged to the *Heer* (regular army) or the Waffen SS. Then I saw how his eyes got stuck on the lapels of my tanker jacket. He had spotted the two skulls fixed there to signify my allegiance to the Panzer forces. His look suddenly turned triumphant; he gripped the pistol more tightly, readied it, and pointed it towards my face slowly and deliberately.

I was stunned, shocked, unable to utter even a single word. This is it, I thought. He is going to shoot me. I could clearly see the intention in his eyes. The soldier thought me to be a Waffen SS member, of that I was sure. The uniforms of *Heer* and Waffen SS were almost identical, with the Heer showing the German eagle on the chest while the Waffen SS had it on the upper sleeve. The skulls on my tanker jacket, however, seemed to be enough evidence for the French soldier that I belonged to the Waffen SS. In that moment I had to think about my brother who, deployed as a tanker in Russia, had mentioned how the skulls on their uniforms had cost the lives of many after their capture. Normally, I would wear the other jacket with braids on it, but today of all days I wore the one with skulls.

It seemed to me as if the world around me was fading away. All I could see were the pistol's muzzle and the French soldier's finger which came to rest on the trigger. Suddenly, it felt like there was a noise coming from somewhere far away, there was a loud yell: "*Halte!*"

My field of view became wider again and I saw how a hand was put on the soldier's arm. His arm was pushed down, and another hand gestured towards my left arm along with the armband attached there, which showed two palm trees with the word "AFRIKA" in big letters between them. Then I saw the person to which the new hands belonged. They came out of the sleeves of a uniform jacket, and judging by their cuffs, it seemed to be an officer's clothing. Perhaps a lieutenant like me. Apparently this young French officer had some objections about his soldier's intentions, talking to him loudly and insistently. Then the officer turned to the side and said something to another soldier, who indicated me to stand up. Once I was standing, the man suddenly spoke in German.

"Did you serve in Africa?" the translator asked.

"Yes!" I said and nodded. The Frenchman wanted to translate it back, but the officer already understood my nodding.

He made his soldier translate another question. "Where have you been deployed?" he asked.

"In Libya, Egypt, and Tunisia ..." I replied quickly without thinking. The French officer raised an eyebrow when I mentioned Tunisia. I continued without a pause, named the Marshal Foch Barracks as well as the towns of Djedeida and Tebourba. "Now it's all about luck," I thought to myself. And once again I was quite lucky. Just like that, the spell was broken. The officer grinned before talking to the other soldiers around, who acknowledged it with either a scowl on their face or no expression at all. Maybe this officer had served in Tunisia himself, perhaps he had joined his comrades who had landed there. Many French soldiers had joined the ranks of General Leclerc's formations on their advance through Tunisia under the command of British 8th Army in 1943. In any case, this young officer had apparently kept the German soldiers and possibly his own action in Tunisia in good memory. It saved my life. The officer finally said something to the soldier with pistol in hand, who upon that stepped back, creasing his face sullenly. Then he suddenly stepped forward again, grabbed my Iron Cross with his hand and tore it from my uniform at one go. The French officer indicated us to follow him, and we walked the few yards to the nearby sawmill.

When we arrived there, I was much surprised to see around 25 German prisoners already standing there. They were standing huddled together in a small shed, which was open to one side. All of them had their hands up and looked into our direction more or less frightened. The small firefight in their immediate vicinity had not left them without an impression.

Upon coming closer, I saw more German soldiers, who had obviously been wounded, lying on the ground. Then I heard English-speaking voices and discovered a few soldiers to whom the American uniforms were better suited. One of them, an American surgeon or medic, tended to a German wounded, while three others were having a conversation.

The French soldier who had pointed his gun at me now started frisking me. This he did not gingerly, simply throwing anything he pulled out of my pockets on the ground. Only the belt with my holster and pistol inside he hung over his own shoulder.

The French officer watched these proceedings attentively, and when the soldier finished his task, he said something else to him. Apparently about my service book and wallet. After some back-and-forth argumentation, the soldier shoved both items towards me with the tip of his boot and a visible cuss on his lips. He indicated me to put them up. I complied without hesitation; after all, my wallet was where I kept important notes and some personal photographs. My driver was then frisked as well, and after we had both been processed this way, we were sent to join the ranks of the other prisoners. Now that I was not in the spotlight anymore, I had some short time to contemplate what had just happened. I was now obviously a prisoner of war in custody of the Allied Free French. "Prisoner of War? This would mean that the war is over for me!" I thought. This thought would not stick in my head, however. I rather wanted to return to my side.

Immediately I started looking for possible escape routes. The next moment I realized that another German officer was standing next to me, his hands raised. I recognized him at first glance. It was First Lieutenant Haeffele. I had seen his face during multiple briefings, and it was just him that I had been ordered to reestablish communications with. He greeted me in as friendly a way as the situation allowed for before explaining how he had been captured. The French had silently snuck up to his positions through the woods from one flank and then, with a surprise assault, had rolled up his entire company from the side. An unknown number had been killed in the short but bloody fight, with the remaining almost thirty men ending up as prisoners.

Resistance to the last would have been futile, and there had been no possibility of retreat. Their positions had lied directly in front of the sawmill, and so they had been brought here after their capture. I now told Haeffele that I had been sent to find him. "Well, Hoeller, at least you have found us!" he said with a sarcastic undertone.

Only in that moment did I also spot a French civilian that had followed us up to the sawmill. This elder man now started wildly cursing at us in front of the gathered French soldiers, repeatedly spitting at Haeffele and me. He shook his fist in a threatening manner and shouted triumphantly in the direction of the French soldiers near the road. The atmosphere around us grew increasingly more hostile. Haeffele whispered to me that he could understand everything – that these were apparently efforts to get us shot. Again I felt an incredibly heavy load on my shoulders. That my comrade was able to speak French, however, now paid its dividends. He shouted in the direction of the French officer and American soldiers, loudly complaining about the hostile sentiments uttered against us. This resulted in the officer hastily coming closer to our band of prisoners.

All of a sudden, the characteristic howling of incoming artillery fire was heard, and moments later the first shell struck the road right in front of us. In an instant, the French were lying on the ground or ducking behind their vehicles. We prisoners wanted to lie down as well on the shed's floor, but the French indicated that we were to stay standing with our hands up. So that was how we witnessed the spectacle that followed. One by one, five or six shells impacted in the middle of the road. Shrapnel whizzed through the air, chunks of soil and rocks rained down on us. The French civilian that had cursed at us had not disappeared into the roadside ditch but remained standing right on the road roughly 25 yards from us, staggered and wide-eyed from shock. In that moment a shell struck right behind him, the man vanished in an explosion, and fractions of a second later his torn-up body was flung far up. A few yards away he came down again, now lying there motionless and mutilated beyond recognition.

The artillery strike lasted for less than half a minute. Perhaps our side had noticed my vehicle being shot at and rightly concluded that the French were already positioned at the sawmill near the forest's edge. As such, the bombardment of the French by our artillery had been ordered. After the last shell had exploded and no others were following, the French rose from the road ditch again. I saw that there were wounded, as some French were bending over their comrades and obviously screaming for a medic.

Some of our soldiers now had quite frayed nerves. I saw some of them shaking violently, and all had pale faces. My heart was beating like crazy, and I was now expecting for the French to enact their vengeance on us. I feared they would open fire on us at any moment. But none of that happened. The French officer broke the silence by vigorously shouting a few orders. Then, around fifteen minutes after I had been captured, we were made to stand on the road in rows of three, and with our hands at the back of the head we marched on the road into the forest. Haeffele, his second in command and I walked at the tip, with the others, including our wounded, following behind. The Americans and the French officer where also following us.

When the French soldiers at the edge of the forest saw us approaching, several of them started cursing loudly at us. As we reached the forest's entry, we saw how a few French soldiers were kicking dead German soldiers into the roadside ditch. It was clear to see that their uniforms had been ransacked and several were even missing their boots. Inside the forest, the road was covered in French military vehicles, which were exclusively of American design. I saw multiple Sherman tanks, M3 half-tracks as well as several medium-sized Dodge trucks. Instead of showing a white star on their hulls as with American vehicles, the Shermans and half-tracks had an outline of France as well as a white cross of Lorraine painted on.

After roughly a kilometer, we left the forest again and entered open terrain. Here, too, were long columns of American and French vehicles. After around a hundred yards of marching, a French soldier suddenly stepped out of the line that was standing at the roadside and threw a punch in my face with all his strength. It struck me completely by surprise, and with enough force that I had a short blackout. I tumbled on the ground and ended up lying on the road. Once again, I expected that we would now come under fire, but all I heard was the voice of First Lieutenant Haeffele, who immediately started protesting in strongest terms in French.

My lip was busted, blood ran from my nose. Our column had halted and two of the other German prisoners helped me get back on my feet. French soldiers encircled us and with loud shouting they apparently demanded that we were handed over or perhaps even shot. Haeffele stood firm, however, talking insistently to the French officer. Eventually the latter managed to put the French soldiers in their place and reorganize our column. In addition, this time a French NCO from our guards came through for us as well with a loud voice, imploring his comrades to let us be. Finally, we resumed marching. Still dazed from the punch, I stumbled along, taking a while to fully regain my senses.

I had not expected to be treated like that as prisoner. I was appalled. I had always done my best to treat my opponents correctly. Every time we had captured someone, they had been treated well. Not a single time had I witnessed any form of mistreatment. But of course, it had also happened on our side. This I would only learn after the war, however.

We saw the town of Rambervillers ahead, towards we kept on walking. After a short march between fields and meadows, we reached the town's outermost houses. There had been intense fighting here, as many of the houses were damaged. There were also signs of fires and several pillars of smoke rising from the town. Every place was full of American soldiers. I was in fact amazed by how many I saw. Military equipment was clustered all around, and it seemed as if in every single alley American soldiers were preparing for their coming attack. For me personally, the war was now over. From that day on I was a prisoner of war.

CHAPTER 19

POOR GERMANY

In Rambervillers we were brought to the command post of an American infantry regiment, which was located in a civilian home. The house had its own yard, which was enclosed by a man-high stone wall. We marched through the driveway and were directed into a corner of the yard. After that, our French guards left, and a few American soldiers took over the watch. Behaving deliberately casual, their helmets not strapped on and slid back to their necks, as well as smoking cigarettes, they commenced their task. We were relieved to find that we were now entirely in custody of the Americans. They had, at least until now, displayed much less resentment and hostility towards us than most French soldiers. And indeed, soon after, several among us were gifted cigarettes.

Once more I found some time to think. I assessed that the reality of my capture had hit me hard and left me disillusioned. I really had not expected it. Time and again I had thought about what getting wounded or maimed might be like, or even finding a gruesome death. Becoming a prisoner was not a fate I had thought about, however, and now it had befallen me.

In the American command post, things were busy. All the time soldiers came and went. American vehicles, mostly Jeeps or Dodge trucks, drove up. Jumping out of these were officers or messengers who then hastily entered the command post. One by one, every one of us was picked by a soldier and taken inside, starting with us officers.

After Haeffele and his second in command, it was my turn as well. I was taken into the house, where the different rooms served as offices for individual sections of the regimental staff. I was brought to an American officer who, as I could discern from his insignia, had the rank of a captain. He began by asking in English for my name and the number on my identification tag. I answered, and while he was writing both down I looked around a bit. I spotted a letter on which I managed to read that we were apparently at the command post of 157th Infantry Regiment, US 45th Infantry Division. I thought that the interrogation would now commence, but nothing happened. The American officer indicated that I could now go. As such, I left the house again with my guard. Outside I asked Haeffele what had happened to him, and he could confirm my observations as well as having had the same experience. Apparently, we were only here to be registered. Next, our wounded were carried off by an ambulance, leaving behind only those with minor injuries or none at all. The following hours we spent sitting in the yard, leaning against the stone wall, and waiting. Nobody was really in the mood to talk. Everyone was absorbed in thought, perhaps thinking about home or the uncertain future that now awaited them. As for myself, I was still contemplating escape. Up to that point I had always made it out, so why not now as well? The longer I kept looking around, however, the more hopeless such an attempt seemed to me. I would probably not have made it far. And even if I had managed to escape the Americans, the French would get me further out. What could happen to me if I was handed over to the Résistance I did not even want to imagine; what behavior the French soldiers had shown towards us had already been more than enough.

In the evening eventually several trucks showed up, we were loaded in and as it became dark we set off in an unknown direction. After some time we arrived at a town, which we identified as Epinal. Here, we halted on a large, open field, where a large number of captured German soldiers was already camped under the open sky. We were dismounted and looked for a place to sleep. Haeffele and I had gotten along well from the first moment, and so we decided to stay together for as long as possible. There were no blankets available, and there was no food to be seen far and wide. Thus I spent my first night in Allied war captivity; freezing and hungry on an open field. From the east we could hear the rumbling of the front, and everyone probably thought about our comrades who were lying there in the attacker's artillery fire. The following day around noon, a young American officer approached, addressing us in fluid German. He demanded to see my service book. I handed it over and he started to flip through, immediately noting that it had a bullet hole. This of course piqued his curiosity, and he asked about it. I responded by telling him about my action in Tunisia and the wounds I had suffered there.

The officer kept on reading the service book, finding my home address. "*Oesterreich?*" (Austria), he said inquiringly. I replied with a short "*Ja*" (Yes), registering how he had used the original name for Austria and not that of *Ostmark*, which was in the book itself.

The officer grinned, handing me back the service book. Then my comrades were briefly questioned as well before the American eventually sorted out five men, us three officers among them, signifying us to follow him. Again we boarded a truck and headed off. This time the ride took longer, and it was already dark when we reached a French town named St. Loup. Here, we were brought to a large villa-like building inside a small park. Finding some orientation in the dark was difficult, but I tried to memorize as many details as possible while entering the house. We were led to the upper floor and assigned individual rooms. Within mine I found a cot, two military blankets and several cans of food, some of them even with meat. The window had been covered up and a single light bulb was hanging from the ceiling. Any other furnishing had been removed; I could still see where pieces of furniture had been standing by their outlines leaving traces on the wallpaper.

Upon looking at the cans, my mouth was already watering, but before I had time to get my teeth into this treasure I was taken out and subjected to another registration procedure. This was carried out by two American officers, both of whom spoke fluent German without any discernible accent. In addition to a simple registration, there were now first questions about my unit, the names of my superiors, our weapon and personnel strength as well as our current mission and area of deployment.

I had expected to be asked such questions and stated that I was not willing to answer them. Politely but firmly, I referred to the Geneva Convention and my rights as prisoner of war. I was under no obligation to share any information which could be used to harm my own comrades.

The Americans seemed to have expected this kind of response as well. Without hesitation they told me that the war was lost for Germany, and that it would only be a matter of time until we were to capitulate. There I butted in, defiantly stating that we would never surrender unconditionally and simply accept the same kind of humiliation as after the end of World War I. Nobody would ever abandon themselves to that. The demand for unconditional surrender was the greatest obstacle to making peace, as it excluded any possibility of a negotiated solution, including an armistice. After that conclusion, I expected a reply or at least another question. But nothing more was said. The discussion was over. The two officers called for a guard, who brought me back to my room. Before I was to enter it, the guard demanded my wristwatch. I was so perplexed that I handed it over without comment. Once inside the room, I felt to be in good heart. I thought myself to have done not too bad. Finally, I had some time to devote to these canned goods. After I had finished eating, I laid down on the cot and fell asleep immediately. But just as I had slipped away, I was ungently woken up again. I squinted at my American guard, which indicated me to follow him once more into the interrogation room, where I was again greeted by the two officers. They instantly started asking questions with the same composure as before. Their questions were also the same: which unit, names of superiors, equipment and strength, current mission, and area of deployment. Furthermore, I was told to report about my participation in the fighting in Normandy, about the Falaise pocket and about our redeployment to Alsace and Lorraine. I replied in the same way as the first time but was still surprised by how accurately targeted these questions were being asked. To substantiate their inquiry, the two Americans had inserted multiple details about the units and formations deployed by our side which, as far as I could tell, had to be correct. It was apparent that the intention was to make me believe that everything was already known and that my information would only serve as final confirmation. I did not want to fall for that trick, however, so I replied not by answering any questions but by elaborately complaining about the way in which I had been captured by the French. I described how we ourselves had treated our prisoners and then questioned whether or not an adequate treatment by the Allied side could be expected.

It seemed to me as if this had, for the first time, broken through the two officers' reserve for a bit. Already a little annoyed, but still unemotional and composed, they let me know that, if I was to not cooperate right now, I could be handed over back to the French at once. And that, unfortunately, there would be no responsibility taken for whatever happened to me there. Perhaps I would even be sent to Africa to do harsh labor in the desert. Defiantly I replied that I had been to Africa twice already and that I would weather my third deployment there just as well. I was not at all willing to endanger the lives of my comrades through my testimony, still invoking the rights granted to me by the Geneva Convention.

According to it, I as a prisoner of war only had to state my full name, date of birth, military rank, and identification number. Nothing else. After that statement, this second interrogation was concluded, and I was brought back to my room. When I returned there, I found that the remaining cans of food were missing. What now followed were several days of repeated interrogations, always following the same pattern. The same questions were being asked time and again, with others being added in. For example, they even wanted to know the name of the local NSDAP leader in my home village of Pottschach. I continued to remain unyielding, which in turn had consequences for me. Although I was still given food in irregular intervals, my room was stripped of what little commodities were left one by one. At first the cot disappeared, then the light remained on at all times. Eventually, I was only left with a single blanket, and when I became tired, the interrogations were conducted in ever shorter intervals. Each time I came back to my room I would quickly fall asleep, was woken up soon after and the whole thing started over. This way I slowly lost my sense of time. My other comrades I would see not even once. After some sessions of questioning, a new method of interrogation was added in. Now I was being told of atrocities committed by German troops during the invasion of Poland, deportations of dissenters by the *Gestapo* (German secret police), and finally the organized hunt for all Jews within Germany and any occupied regions. These reports were completely new to me; they seemed utterly implausible. I thought them to be pure propaganda, smiling pityingly at the Americans, shaking my head and not reacting to them any further. I had absolutely no clue; I dismissed it all as nonsensical talk and continued referring to the Geneva Convention and my rights.

When I think today about what the Americans already knew back at that time and I on the other hand knew not, I have to shake my head in regret. How naive have I and so many others been. Even more, the very atrocities that these two Americans were already confronting me with in October of 1944 still paled in comparison to the horrors that the Allies would discover on their advance into Germany in early 1945. I then, in turn, held Allied bombing attacks against the Americans; the death of women and children who perished in the firestorms caused by incendiary bombs. At that time I was still convinced that we were not the ones to commit atrocities at a grand scale, but rather the Allies. In these hour-long interrogation sessions, during which I remained stubborn and persistent, there was certainly an assessment compiled of me, which described me as obstinate and arrogant, meaning a typically German officer – just like our opponents' conception of a German officer had to be. Tough on himself, unwilling to cooperate, despicable, inveterate, fanatical. An assessment made by these interrogation officers that would be of significance for my future treatment.

After I had been interrogated around a dozen times, this phase ended just as well. As usual, the guard came to take me to the interrogation room. When I arrived at the American officers and they surprisingly gave me back my watch, however, I knew that it was now over. I looked at the face to read the time and date, finding out that it was now October 6, 1944. So I had been continuously interrogated for more than three whole days. All five of us, meaning the men that had been brought here together three days ago, were now assembled in front of the building. We looked each other in the eyes; everyone was tired, their expressions showing little more than exhaustion. After a short while we were put into a truck and taken back to the outdoor camp. On the ride, we talked a few words. Each said that they had been treated the same way I had been, claiming to have remained unwavering during their interrogations. As we were all completely overtired and exhausted, our conversation soon ended; the remaining ride to the outdoor camp we spent sleeping.

Once arrived at the camp, we were split into groups right after leaving the vehicle. Word was that we were to be transported off by rail. From the hundreds of prisoners, columns were formed and one after the other marched to a nearby train station. A long freight train was standing ready, consisting of individual cattle cars. While the lower ranks and non-commissioned officers were loaded into the train cars together, us officers were segregated. A little while later we were around twenty officers of varying ranks. A group of five immediately separated themselves from the rest of us, letting us know that they did not want to have anything to do with us. They demanded of the American guards to be treated separately. At first, I was dumbfounded by their behavior and could not think of any reasons for it, but then the others and I realized that these were men that did not consider themselves to be bound to their oath anymore. They now saw themselves as "allies" of the Americans, with us being their "enemies." I was utterly surprised and shocked. Never before had I witnessed such a behavior. So, this was how fast things could change once you were not among your own anymore. After the shocking capture and the hardships of interrogation, this was the next damper put on me.

In spite of those five officers' complaints, our guards put us into a single shared train car. This, however, was now unacceptable for our own group. Several of us started complaining loudly, not wanting to be locked into a carriage with the "deserters." Among our American guard crew, there were also several black soldiers, some of whom held NCO ranks; they saw the unrest in our group and came closer. One of us quickly explained the situation to them. The American NCOs reacted without hesitation; without any further discussion, our two groups were assigned separate train cars. We were quite surprised that our wish had been granted immediately – and indeed this would not be the last time that black soldiers would display a commendable willingness to help towards me and others. The reason for that may perhaps be found in the racial segregation prevalent in the US at the time. Black Americans, marginalized by the white majority, apparently had a much more compassionate approach to our situation thanks to their own history of oppression. Any black US soldiers we encountered over the course of our entire war captivity would always conduct themselves humanely without exception.

The cargo carriage was completely empty, so we sat down on its floor and leaned against the wooden walls. The doors were slid shut and locked, and the train slowly began moving. Due to the airstream, any warmth left inside was soon blown out, and we were freezing bitterly. There were multiple stops, always after several hours. Buckets of water were then passed up by our guards, but no food. Through the barred windows we could see how the five "cooperative" officers were allowed to stretch their legs during these stops, all the while happily chatting with their guards. During one of these stops our guards, apparently on behalf of the other officers, used white paint to mark our train car in some way. This led to rocks being thrown at our carriage by French civilians on the following stops between St. Loup and Marseilles. We were stunned and confused. In one railroad station, a train with French soldiers inside halted on the neighboring track, and when they readied their weapons and pointed them at us, we felt incredibly uneasy.

After three days inside the train car, with no food and forced to relieve ourselves in the corner, we arrived at the French port city of Marseille. Here, we were told to detrain, and we could finally see what had been painted on our carriage. In huge letters we read the words "GERMAN OFFICERS," written in both German and French. Resentful and outraged, we could only acknowledge it. I could not understand how anyone could behave in such an unworthy manner. At Marseille, we were at first brought to another huge prison camp outside the city. This was again barely more than an empty open field. In the ice-cold night, we were again freezing; I regretted not having worn an overcoat during my capture. I could have made great use of it.

It was obvious that the Americans either had not been prepared for such a large number of prisoners, or that they wanted to let us know that we were the losers of this war. The following three days were marked by privation and cold, but at the least we were given food again. On the third day, we were marched back into the city in groups. Everyone was happy to leave the camp behind.

On October 12, 1944, we were loaded on an American Liberty cargo ship in the port of Marseille. Our group of officers went on board with several hundred other prisoners of war. Inside, we were briefed by one of the ship's officers on the rules of conduct during the journey. A translator put them into German words. In case we broke these rules, we were threatened with harsh and draconian punishments, including being put under arrest in the ships' lower decks. In that case there would have been no chance to get out during a submarine attack. An audible murmur went through the crowd as we heard that. Apart from these rules, we were allowed to roam the ship freely, albeit always under the watchful eyes of our guards. For the nights, we were assigned quarters with hammocks, and there was sufficient food prepared at a fixed schedule.

On October 13 we left port, and after three days on the Mediterranean Sea, we arrived at the port of Oran, Algeria, on the North African coast. Once again I found myself in Africa, albeit under entirely different circumstances. We were not allowed to leave ship but could still move freely on deck. As such, we assessed that there was a large convoy being assembled here to cross the Atlantic and reach America. When this assumption was later confirmed to be correct, I was depressed. Up to that point I had not had any opportunity to send my loved ones any message, and the distance between us and Europe was only increasing. I was sure that back at home everyone was in great distress – if they even knew anything about what had happened to me. After five days in the port of Oran, we left harbor on October 21, 1944 early in the morning, going on a course towards the Atlantic. So I was indeed going to America. The very country whose entry into the war had proven so fatal for us. On our passage through the Strait of Gibraltar I was amazed by how long the coast could be seen from the ship; it remained clearly visible from early in the morning until late afternoon, long after we had crossed.

After passing the strait, our convoy was joined by additional vessels, until the sea around us was eventually littered with a variety of ships. Standing at the railing, we all were smitten with amazement. Within sight from our ship alone, I counted over thirty cargo vessels of varying types, with more individual destroyer escorts strewn in between them.

Our group of officers had stayed together after the train ride, and the five officers that had separated themselves in the beginning had also come aboard with us. Now, during the first few days of the Atlantic crossing, they repeatedly tried to make conversation with the American ship officers. The latter were somewhat astounded by these attempts, not necessarily accepting them in a favorable way. The atmosphere had been quite tense after the Americans had given their harsh instructions. They could see that the German prisoners of war were not feeling at ease. Something was in the air. So it was time for the Americans to act. They did not contact the five other officers, however; instead, they came to us. The ship's captain assembled our group and openly asked what the deal with these five officers was. According to the captain, they had come to him with the notion that we were causing problems and fomenting unrest among the prisoners. We were outraged and explained the details of how our current group composition had come to be to the Americans. The captain, who hailed from Alsace-Lorraine and spoke German, made us understand that a split into opposing groups would not be tolerated, and that discipline aboard had to be upheld at any cost. Our highest-ranking officer, a major, now proposed making us prisoners responsible for order and discipline among ourselves. Nevertheless, the five other officers were to be segregated, and the rules of the Geneva Convention were to be upheld. The Americans agreed, and as such we prisoners of war took command of ourselves.

The Major saw to it that our agreement was announced to all prisoners aboard. Among the German NCOs and lower ranks were some very talented artisans, and our very next measure was to organize several improvised theater plays. For these, we used a large empty cargo bay in the ship's belly, which the Americans placed at our disposal. There were vocal performances, shows of magic tricks and even acrobatic interludes. All were quite delighted by these shows, as there was now something to do

– even if it was just watching something. Thanks to these performances, we managed to keep boredom at bay for all the weeks of crossing the Atlantic. Even some of the American crew were watching our shows, and the captain expressed his appreciation for organizing them. The Americans had achieved their goal, and the five other officers could not be seen for the entire rest of our voyage. That was only fair to us, and we soon forgot about them.

After a few days on the Atlantic we encountered one of the October storms typical for this season, which eventually grew into a hurricane. Most of us were "landlubbers" like me, and we thought that the world was coming to an end. We could not go on deck, and upon looking out of a porthole I sometimes could not tell where up and down was. Fortunately, I did not become seasick, but our mood worsened to a new low. Like a piece of cork our ship tumbled between gigantic waves. Then, from one day to the next, the hurricane was gone. We crowded on deck and enjoyed the fresh air. Standing at the railing, we spotted another convoy slowly coming into sight. We counted over a hundred ships that passed us heading for Europe. "O, poor Germany!" I exclaimed, saying aloud what perhaps all of us were thinking at the sight of this display of overwhelming superiority.

The fact that we were coming closer to the American mainland was becoming noticeable by the crew starting to throw boxes full of supplies overboard. When we asked why they were doing this, they replied that the ship was to be resupplied in full after its arrival. As such, any old supplies left would not be needed anymore. We were puzzled. None of us had expected something like that. Once again we were confronted by the abundance in which the Americans lived their lives. What a contrast to what we had to live through. I became more and more aware of what enormous amounts of resources of the Allies, and most of all the Americans, had to have available. How could a war be won against such an economic powerhouse? "O, poor Germany," I again whispered lost in thoughts.

CHAPTER 20

PRISONER OF WAR

On November 6, 1944, we reached America's east coast and entered the harbor of New York. On that same day, western Allied troops in the Netherlands stood east of the town of Nijmegen, and with Aachen the first major German city had been captured. Further east in the huge woodlands west of the Ruhr river, however, November 6 saw most intense fighting. The battle for Hürtgen forest there would grow into the largest ground battle for American forces on German soil. On the eastern front, the Red Army was preparing for the assault on Warsaw and Budapest in early November.

Of all this struggle along Europe's front lines we did not learn anything, however. We all stood at the railing of our ship, gazing at the Statue of Liberty and the Manhattan skyline. The former, which just seemed gigantic to us, left an especially deep impression. When some American seamen noticed our amazement, they laughed and remarked that there would not be much liberty for us POWs in the foreseeable future. We had to contritely acknowledge that they were quite right. Now we had to hand over everything we had treasured up from supply and food crates during our journey. All we were left with was our uniforms, a duffle bag with a blanket and additional clothing, as well as any personal items we were carrying on ourselves. The ship docked at a harbor mole, and we went ashore over the gangway.

As we walked out, we were greeted by a crowd of curious American civilians. With much interest they watched us falling in lines and being counted. Suddenly a man from the crowd shouted at us in German. "How are the Panthers doing? How are the Tigers doing?" We had to smirk but remained silent and waved at him in a friendly manner. We were marched into a great hall, where we had to take off our clothes and take a shower. Then we were examined by a doctor and received new clothes. Black trousers, light-colored shirt, with the old uniform getting shoved into the duffle bag. After that, we were again registered and divided into new groups right after. Us officers were also reorganized, but this time we were separated immediately; our group of around fifteen men and the clique of five "renegade" officers. From now on, each of the different groups of POWs was to be relocated separately.

Our group of officers, along with some guards, marched right through the middle of busy New York City to a public subway station. Everything was new to us, and with much astonishment we looked at our surroundings, which to us were unusual and, most of all, colorful. The inhabitants of New York registered our presence more or less casually, mostly occupied with their daily business and hurrying past us. At the station we boarded a subway train that took us across the Hudson river. I would have never imagined to one day be riding the New York subway. We kept going under Manhattan until we arrived at a railway station from where trains were departing westwards. Here, we were loaded into large Pullman carriages and sent off into the west. What now followed was a multiple day long train ride over a distance of almost 1,550 miles.

Inside the train, we learned from our guards that our destination was Alva, Oklahoma. If the United States were to have a central point, it would be around there. The town of Alva was around 90 miles northwest of Oklahoma city, the state's capital. And we were told something else: we were to stay in a "Nazi camp." I was puzzled. "We are to be sent to a Nazi camp?" I thought exasperatedly. Back at home, and especially at the frontlines, I had never bothered with politics. Today, this could be the grounds for accusations against me. Back then, however, I viewed myself to be a soldier first and officer second, and as such I had a duty to serve our people. With that, any questions regarding politics were answered from my point of view. I bore the responsibility for the lives of all soldiers under my command and was thus obligated to facilitate their survival. After each casualty that we had suffered, I puzzled my head over how it could have been avoided. The result was that I oftentimes came to the depressing realization that pure luck alone decided between life and death.

When First Lieutenant Braatz and I had been writing letters to a fallen soldier's loved ones, we always tried to depict their death without any pathos. But we also avoided asking questions about the meaning of death. Our understanding of duty would not even let such questions come to pass. This was the world of thought that we were living in. But calling us "Nazi" based on that would never have occurred to me. Quite the opposite; already back in the Hitler Youth, I felt deeply repulsed by those party barons strutting around like cocks in their brown uniforms. Apparently, our restive behavior during the days of interrogation at St. Loup, but also the animosities with our own "renegade" officers, had brought us this assignment to Alva. Once again I felt bitterness. How could it be that only because someone invokes the rules of the Geneva Convention, they are immediately branded as fanatics? Did being in captivity warrant that I give up all sense of honor? This was absolutely repugnant to me. I would rather stay true to my principles, just as I had been taught. To immediately throw in the towel now that I was in the victor's hands seemed vile to me, as if I would betray my loved ones back at home. To the reader, these words may appear stubborn, but many others had sentiments just like mine. And in the long conversations we had on the ship or now on the train, we only found our convictions strengthened. The war was not over yet, and of the inhumane atrocities that had been committed in Hitler's name, at least most of us still had not the slightest knowledge.

As such, we proudly viewed ourselves as German officers that, albeit having been captured, had not been stripped of their pride and dignity. "What would people think of us back at home?" we kept asking ourselves. On the long train ride to Oklahoma we had much time to think. The unusually flat American landscape was passing by, and each time we would stop at a station, there were new things to discover; among those were huge spherical water towers that created the pressure necessary to run water lines in these pancake-flat regions. Our train was not marked in any way, and thus we were often waved at by American girls during our short stops, who certainly thought us to be US soldiers. We would then happily wave back. At the railroad station of a town called Emporia, we even had the chance to chat with an American girl that spoke perfect German. Our military police guards were deliberately lax and did not intervene.

At night, we often passed through towns that were lit as bright as day. This was a most unusual sight for us, as back at home we had to keep everything dark to avoid air attacks. Here, however, work in the factories could continue through day and night. To us, America seemed truly humongous. Hitler had not gotten about much. That much became clear to me as we went through the vast stretches of the American lands. On November 9, at 02:00 in the night, we arrived at Alva. In the earliest morning hours we were brought to the camp. To us it appeared like a small city that was lit by electrical lamps as bright as day. We were assigned quarters. Haeffele, who had been by my side since the day of my capture, moved into a room together with me. It had two beds, two lockers, a table and two chairs. After a short night of sleep, we went to breakfast at 07:00 AM, which was handed out in a huge mess hall. To my great surprise, there was a lectern at one end of the hall, decorated with a swastika flag. Behind it hung an imperial eagle with a wingspan of almost seven feet. On the long tables, the meal was already waiting. We sat down and were immediately engaged in conversation.

Then we were asked for attention and, I could not believe my own ears, an actual speech of the *Führer* was read aloud. I started to understand why this camp was called "the Nazi camp" by the Americans. Later I would learn that American soldiers also called it "Devil's Island." On the way back to our barrack, I talked with Haeffele about what had happened. Like me, he was no NSDAP party member and also had not too much sympathy for our supreme party barons. In his opinion, his duty as German officer bound him to his people, not the party. We resolved to maintaining a low profile and keep waiting. This way we found out that many of the prisoners here, just like us, had insisted on being treated correctly and according to the Geneva Convention during their capture and interrogation. Nevertheless, there was also a core of irreversibly convinced national socialists, who were quite anxious to let us know which supreme commander we were still serving. To most of us, however, all this was by now completely irrelevant. They had come to terms with life in this American camp, hoping to be able to return to their loved ones at home as soon as possible. We decided for ourselves that we did not want to deal with politics or group formations, and we stayed true to that decision.

On the day of my arrival, there were around 1,500 German officers of varying ranks in the camp. A large number of those had been captured in 1943 through the capitulation in Africa or later during the fighting in Italy. Prisoners were organized into companies of around 200 men each. Roughly fifty men were housed in each individual barrack. The higher the rank, the more space was given to any individual prisoner. In addition to the housing barracks, there was the mess hall with kitchen, washing and restroom buildings, a sick bay, the commandant's office as well as varied smaller barracks and storehouses. The camp occupied an area of roughly 550 by 550 yards and was girded by manned guard towers and barbed wire. In order to quickly detect possible escapees, we were additionally counted every morning and evening.

There had indeed been several escape attempts already, and they had all failed within a few days. This was no surprise to us. After all, where was an escapee to head from a camp right in the middle of the United States? The prospect was simply too hopeless to really plan an escape.

Climate in the heart of America was similar to the dry conditions that I had already had to deal with in the North African desert. From time to time there were even sandstorms in or near the camp. In contrast to Africa, however, we could now take shelter in our barracks, which were made well enough to barely let any dust creep in as well. As such, we sat in our quarters and watched the storm rage outside through our windows. Most of the time we wore our old uniforms, and especially those we had left from Africa proved useful on days like these. It was also allowed to wear rank insignia and even medals; I found not a small number of Iron Cross bearers among us inmates. Still as proud as before, I obtained another Iron Cross first class to replace the one which the French soldier had torn off my jacket during my capture.

POW in Alva, Oklahoma. My comrade August Haeffele to the left.

Some of the prisoners had built a short-wave radio transmitter, and as such the Wehrmacht's press reports were read on a regular basis. The Americans obviously had no objections to this, as by now it was no secret that German armies were retreating on all fronts. Those with true allegiance to the Nazi regime had a hard time accepting this, however, and they tried to rekindle our faith regarding *Volk*, *Reich* and *Führer* with their best efforts at persuasion and stirring rhetoric.

Still, most of us were realizing that we had lost the war. This admission as well as realizing what disaster we had brought over the world put an ever-growing weight on our conscience. You tried to not be alone but talk about all kinds of things for hours. If you were alone, you started sinking into thought, which inevitably ended in worrying about your loved ones at home. There was also the possibility to send postcards via the Red Cross. Many of us were happy to do this, and I was of course one of them, even though there was never an answer coming back from home. We could not know whether our letters even reached them. But hope dies last, and so we all kept writing eagerly.

Since the day that the first German POWs had arrived at Alva camp in the summer of 1943, things had changed considerably. By now the camp had its own academy, including a library and a reading room. Many of the captured German officers had worked at universities in their private life, and now they were giving lessons in the camp as well. I decided to make use of my time and began studying mechanical engineering. Thanks to this, the following weeks went by quickly for me, as they were filled with studying, sports, playing skat and having hour-long conversations about everything under the sun. Naturally, these conversations also included how the war was developing; in late December of 1944, we learned of the German Ardennes offensive, which aimed at pushing back the western Allies one more time. For a few days, many of us thought that the Wehrmacht could make progress again, but it soon became clear that this offensive by three German armies had not resulted in a breakthrough. Meanwhile, the number of German POWs streaming into America kept on increasing.

Even though one day was exactly like the other, we did our best to not lose our sense of what a week was. To this end, there were often shows organized by prisoner artist groups on Saturday evenings. Some of the artists were really talented, and there were many musicians. Since I was a capable yodeler, and since I had met a first lieutenant from Hall, Tyrol named Franz Posch who could yodel as well, the two of us became the stars of some nights. Christmas of 1944 was celebrated in such a manner as well; this did a lot to alleviate homesickness. But nevertheless, at some point you always ended up being alone with your thoughts. I still had no idea whether my loved ones had received any sign of life from me. This uncertainty could drive you crazy.

In late February 1945, a new rumor made the rounds. All officers were to be transferred to another camp. And indeed, on March 1 we boarded a train that went via Arkansas City towards Dermott. The town of Dermott was in Arkansas, the state neighboring Oklahoma, not far from Mississippi river. Here I was to spend the remaining seven months of my imprisonment. Climate at Dermott was completely different from that at Alva, that much we realized the moment that we left the train. Here at the Mississippi, the weather was quite damp and muggy. The camp at Dermott was considerably larger than that at Alva. Originally it had been built as "Jerome Relocation Center," an internment camp for Japanese and American citizens of Japanese descent. Its maximum capacity was almost 10,000 men. At the day of my arrival, there had to be around 7,000 German prisoners there, who were housed in roughly forty blocks. The Americans used Dermott exclusively for housing officers.

Haeffele and I once again moved to a shared room in one of the barracks. As it was a three-bed room this time, we were "reinforced" by Lieutenant Ernst Hahn. A veteran of the Russian campaign, he had been wounded five times in total; the last time in Normandy, where he had eventually been captured. The three of us got along well right from the start, and we would stay together until the very end of our imprisonment through thick and thin.

Dermott had all kinds of facilities to offer, including a camp academy like the one at Alva. This allowed me to continue my engineering studies – my days were busy again. I would study and engage in sports, most of all handball. Once again there were shows performed by various artist groups. Under leadership of Lieutenant Kurt Woess, an Austrian orchestra conductor who would later make a name for himself, a respectable camp orchestra had formed, which gave concerts on a regular basis. In addition, there were even cinema shows. Like before at Alva, we received twenty Dollar-stamps each month, which we could use to shop at the camp cafeteria. There was writing paper, pencils, books, fruit, cigarettes and even jewelry. Cigarettes were an especially valuable barter good for this and that. Some of these Dollar stamps I managed to save up, and later in Austria I could even change them into Austrian currency – ten Schilling per Dollar.

As before at Alva, there were those officers in our ranks that were still certain that the German Reich would be the victor, even though the whole world was by now at war with us. They spoke of *Wunderwaffen* (wonder weapons) that would turn the tides of war. By the end of March 1945, however, the western Allies had already crossed the Rhine and stood before Frankfurt in western Germany. And in the east, the Red Army stood at the Oder river before Berlin as well as crossing the border between Hungary and Austria on March 28, 1945. The "thousand-year long empire" that Nazi Germany had proclaimed itself to be, was in its very last days. I remained true to my resolution and kept out of any political conversations. After all, it proved to be quite difficult to explain to an officer captured in Africa in 1943 what masses of troops the Allies had landed in Normandy in 1944. Whenever I recounted my encounters with the overpowering foe in Normandy, my accounts were often dismissed as exaggerated.

At some point I gave up trying. Only those who had also fought in Normandy knew it better. Attempts to form our own Austrian group failed miserably, however; too great were the differences in opinion and personal experiences among my compatriots. The three of us resolved to keeping out of everything, and so I kept living under a shared roof with a man from Saxony and one from Baden-Wuerttemberg. We had gone into this war together, and now we had to make it to its end together as well.

What was bound to happen eventually happened. We learned that Adolf Hitler had committed suicide on April 30, and finally on May 9,

1945, we received news of the German capitulation. Even though we had been expecting it, actually hearing the news still took our breath away. Now it was certain once and for all. We had lost the Second World War. Words can hardly describe what was going on inside us that moment. We became horribly aware of the fact that we had sacrificed the best years of our lives in vain. That our home was in ruins. Indeed, that in our name almost all of Europe had been badly affected. I felt infinitesimally small. The burdens of the coming future seemed impossible to bear for me. Then came the atomic bombings and the Japanese capitulation. With that, World War II came to an end. What did not end that day, however, was the suffering of all the peoples that had fought it. Many human lives would still be lost in the immediate painful aftermath of the war, many would take years to find a new home, and many would never be able to return to a peaceful life.

We were in the middle of a hot, sweaty summer, and another unpleasant circumstance came upon us as well. The way we were treated by the Americans worsened rapidly. We could not help but think that they had hitherto only treated us so well because they had feared for their own captured soldiers in Germany. Now there was no need for that anymore, and they made us feel it. Food became markedly worse in quality. I got problems with my kidneys; when I could not bear the pain anymore and went to sickbay, I was diagnosed with kidney stones. It would take quite some time to get rid of them. Problems with my kidneys would stay with me for years to come, however; a lasting souvenir from the dry and poorly hydrated times in Africa.

At the end of August 1945, a new rumor suddenly emerged. We were to be put to work outside camp. That was something entirely new. According to the Geneva Convention, forcing captured officers to work was prohibited; a right which we had always invoked up to that point. Well, as it spread around the camp, it quickly stirred up unrest. The military order and discipline that us prisoners had kept up until the end of the war was now mostly gone. Faith in the possibility of a victory had been the grounds for a certain kind of solidarity among many. After the German capitulation, this hope was now gone for good, and many were now struggling within their own interest groups, while others were completely on their own.

The Americans were smart in how they veiled their announcement of our coming use as forced laborers. To those that would be willing to work, they promised a timely return home. Now two large factions formed among us imprisoned officers: on one side, there were those who wanted to work in order to come home as soon as possible; on the other side were those saying that they insisted on their rights and did not feel obligated to work. Tensions between the groups became unbearable. Eventually the Americans handed out forms with which we could enlist ourselves for work. The emotional stress was extreme. As a prisoner of war, you were at the mercy of your enemy; you could only make decisions based on vague assumptions, but never on the grounds of actual certainty.

August Haeffele, Ernst Hahn and I conferred, and we came to the decision that we would not sign. After we had decided on this, we felt somewhat relieved, being able to observe the arguments and often even physical fights among the other officers with some aloofness. Many claimed to not have signed their form, but indeed did so in secret, hoping to return home sooner. After the Americans were finished with these dealings, the next measure was taken. Now we were repeatedly ordered to participate in film screenings. The pictures that we were forced to see were truly unbelievable. Recordings made by American troops during the liberation of German concentration camps. The images we saw were so nightmarish that we could not believe that they were actually real.

Indeed, we did not *want* to believe it, because if these atrocities were real, then the guilt we had brought upon us would be of a magnitude that was almost impossible to bear. We tried to convince each other that this had to be mere propaganda, but deep inside we slowly started to realize that behind our front lines, in our homeland and in the occupied territories, something so inhumane had happened that no words could ever hope to describe it. During lunch, we sat in silence and, due to the heat, dripping with sweat over our thin soup, racking our brains about what we had been shown. Time and again I did my best to remember whether I had heard the term "concentration camp" before. Time and again I had to give myself a no as an answer. All this wore me out, and over the following weeks I lost over eleven pounds in body weight. I suppressed what I had seen, burying myself in my textbooks and studying like mad. I got back to my childhood dream of becoming an engineer – a profession that would be much needed in the future. It seemed like a sensible goal to strive for to me. But the images I had seen, the sounds I had heard, they forced themselves into my mind again and again.

For more than five years I had, as a young German officer, fought for a better life and a well-respected Germany full of idealism. Now, however, it became painfully aware that I was being made responsible for the political atrocities that had been committed far in the background.

September of 1945 passed by, and October 1 drew closer. On this day, the Americans wanted to separate those willing to work from those unwilling. This happened more in secret: those willing to work had received the order to leave camp from the Americans the day before, and now, in the morning hours, they began "skulking off." Many of them had become our good friends over the course of the last few months, and now they left without goodbyes.

At first, Haeffele, Hahn and I did not notice it at all. Then we realized that we were all of a sudden almost alone in the camp. At noon, the remaining prisoners were assembled by our American guards. Around 1,200 officers were still left. All other POWs had been moved from the camp for good. This was another day of disillusionment for me, and it showed how even the best camaraderie and closest friendship had their limits. With that being said, I understand that many men simply wanted nothing more than to return home. The officers that were left, were now concentrated in their own area in the camp's center. The three of us moved into a new barracks there. Over the days that followed, we were anxious to find out what would come next. To our surprise, however, nothing happened at all. The Americans even started treating us more accommodatingly than before, and the food became noticeably better. None of us had any real explanation for this, but we were all visibly relieved that things had turned out well for us. Peace and order as well as a regulated daily routine returned to the camp, and the Americans even refrained from showing us more films.

Curiously, most of those who had been especially faithful to the Nazi party were also those to sign the form in secret. Now they were gone, and we did not miss them in the slightest. In late December of 1945, meaning only two months later, we learned that we were to be brought back to Europe already in January of 1946. We were delighted. Those were fantastic news. Christmas of 1945 was spent with all of us in very high spirits. On January 20, 1946, we were loaded into railroad carriages, and on a multiple day ride we were transferred to Camp Shanks at Orangeburg, north of New York City. Right until the very last moment, we still had been doubtful, but when the train slowly started moving, we knew that we would actually get to go home.

On each stop on the way, we would wave at American civilians radiant with joy, such was our euphoria. In New York, we once again boarded an American Liberty Ship that was to carry us home. In conversations we had directly before going aboard, we heard that many German officers that were now doing labor had not been told when they would return home yet. We could not know if this was true since it sounded hard to believe.

Apparently, the Americans could not make any use of us who were unwilling to work. All we did was costing them money and manpower. Would it in the end have actually paid off for us to have stayed true to our principles? In any way, the important thing was that we were going home. In an almost exuberant mood we went aboard. There, we were first instructed on the rules yet again; once more by an American naval officer, but this time a German naval officer was present as well. The latter would also serve as spokesman for all prisoners of war. He was an Austrian, and as I would later find out, he hailed from Carinthia.

Crossing the Atlantic ocean took ten days, and our destination was the port of Le Havre at the French Channel coast. We were allowed to move freely on the ship, and food was good as well. During the journey, we were questioned by American officers. We had to state where we wanted to go in our home countries. This had something to do with the fact that Germany and Austria had both been divided into different occupation zones, with the Soviets controlling one in each country. I had already heard of this and so I stated my home address to be in Admont, Styria; this was further west from my actual hometown, well outside the Soviet zone. When it was pointed out that the record listed Pottschach as my hometown, I claimed that my parents had fled from the advancing Russians into the region of Styria. This was acknowledged with some raised eyebrows, but still the new address was registered without discussion. I was told that I would be transferred from France towards Germany via multiple transit camps, until I would eventually be released in a special discharge camp. At least this was the intention of our American guards at that moment.

Shortly before arriving at Le Havre, we were assembled one more time. An American officer announced that we would be handed to the French after our arrival, who would then bring us to a first transit camp, and from there we could then finally travel home. Lastly, he made us understand that the French were not well-disposed towards us, warning us officers that we could possibly become subject to rough treatment. We were advised to remove any rank insignia and medals from our uniforms. As soon as we were in French hands, there would be no responsibility taken for how us prisoners would be treated. In addition, the American officer mentioned that we should hide our personal belongings as well as possible, since we would certainly be searched. An audible moan went through the crowd.

This announcement definitely lowered our spirits. However, as we had come this far, we decided to keep our chins up and stay together for as long as possible. We felt stronger as a group. At the port we were disembarked and immediately loaded onto American trucks. In the first minutes on European soil already, we were shown that we were not welcome here. French harbor workers looked at us hostilely, reviling us as we passed by. The trucks carried us to a camp near the town of Bolbec, roughly 15 miles east of Le Havre. To me, this name of Bolbec had no meaning at the time, but years later I would learn that many German soldiers had met their end here due to inhumane treatment by the French. In the completely open terrain and without any sustenance, thousands had met a miserable death after their capture. Once we were at Bolbec, we instantly felt thrown back to the time of our own capture. We were greeted by gaunt and exhausted German prisoners staring at us with weary eyes. All this almost a year after the war had ended. We got out of the trucks and were taken in by French soldiers, who at first made us 1,200 men assemble in lines. Then followed a long discussion between our spokesman, the Carinthian naval officer, and one of the French officers. Our spokesman managed to negotiate that we would be housed together in one part of the camp. Once there, we realized that the times of good treatment were now truly over. All we found were barracks that had their interior littered with straw, and nothing else. Thus, we spent our first night there, which in this time of year was extremely cold.

The next day, our spokesman demanded to be able to speak to an officer, which was granted. A small delegation of French officers and a civilian working for the Red Cross appeared and listened to our concerns. Our man requested better accommodation as well as treatment according to the Geneva Convention. He also handed a letter to the Red Cross worker. The French listened to all that without saying a word, then they went off again. After another ice-cold night, they returned the next day. This time a Red Cross representative from Frankfurt was with them, who listened to the objections of our spokesman, promising to forward them. But things went differently.

Nothing happened for a few more days, but after around two weeks a large force of French soldiers came in, split us into small groups and put them into separate trucks, which then headed for different parts of the camp. August Haeffele, Ernst Hahn and I knew that we would be separated now; thus it was time to say goodbye to my trusty friends. We quickly exchanged addresses, promising to contact each other as soon as possible. Each of us wished the others well and, most of all, good luck in finding back to their loved ones. Then we were finally separated and brought away.

After perhaps another fourteen days, I was again put into a truck as part of a new group and transferred to another camp. On our arrival there, we had to endure the first searching. I had been preparing for this and thus was able to keep all my personal belongings, including a necklace with a small golden cross I had bought for Helena in the Dermott cafeteria. We spent several more days in this camp before embarking on a multiple-week odyssey that would bring us to two more French prison camps, the names and locations of which remained unknown to us. Each time we were searched on arrival. Much to our resentment, German prisoners were employed to do this, who had apparently pandered to their French captors, now doing this ignoble work for them. Food and shelter in these French camps was always bad, but there was something that still gave us hope: slowly, but steadily, we were being transferred further and further east. It was also a time of trepidation, however, as time and again prisoners were being weeded out and relocated. We never learned where they went.

Many rumors made the rounds, and we often heard that many were assigned to forced labor. There were destroyed French cities to rebuild and having German prisoners of war to work for you seemed convenient. Many that had come from America to France full of hope would disappear in French labor camps for months or even years, and they were even forced to clear minefields. In these camps or minefields, your life was not worth a lot. Many suffered irreversible damage to their health and not a few lost their life.

Then, after several weeks, Germans and Austrians were separated from each other. At first I was alone for a few days, but I made friends with Lieutenant Heimo Schoberl. He had been a *Fallschirmjäger* (paratrooper) officer and hailed from Leoben in the Austrian region of Styria. When he learned of my dilemma – that my loved ones were in the Soviet occupation zone and that I had stated Admont, Styria to be my home address, he offered to help. I got the address of his parents, who lived in Leoben, and he promised that I could find shelter there after my possible discharge. I thankfully accepted his offer.

In late March 1946, I boarded a train in eastern France together with a large group of Austrians, and we set off towards Germany. Heimo Schoberl had not come with us, but I staunchly remembered to take his offer. At Karlsruhe, we crossed the French-German border, from where we swiftly went on via Stuttgart and Munich all the way to Salzburg, Austria.

The lands drawing past us were bleak. We crossed through devastated cities, their railroad stations little more than heaps of debris, their people housing in bombed-out ruins. We were devastated by the enormous scope of destruction that the Allied bombings had caused. How long would it take to build all this back? Our mood was at an all-time low, but nevertheless, as we crossed the German-Austrian border at Salzburg, we knew we had made it, we were back at our home. We embraced each other beaming with joy, and many a man had tears in their eyes. We were home again.

CHAPTER 21

COMING HOME

When I set foot on Austrian soil after long years of combat action and war captivity, I returned to a home that had been destroyed and occupied. I knew absolutely nothing of my loved ones. All I could do was hope they had stayed in our home region, which was not the Soviet occupation zone, and had survived unscathed. Visiting the Russian zone, however, was impossible to think of. Many advised against it, as there was a real danger of the Soviets cashing you in on the spot and send you off to Siberia. My friend Ernst Hahn would meet this fate. He returned to east Germany, was arrested by the Soviets right at the demarcation line and had to spend two years of harsh work in a Soviet prison camp. He would never fully recover from this time.

The train carried us from Salzburg on to Villach, where we entered a British discharge camp. Here, we were already allowed to move somewhat freely. I now needed a notice of discharge, however, for which it was required to show a home address. So I requested being allowed to go to Leoben to visit my family there. This was granted to me as POW, and so I followed up on the promise made by Heimo Schoberl, appearing in front of his parents' door. The latter were delighted to receive a sign of life from their son through me, pledging to support me. Mister Schoberl got me a job in a workshop, and together we went to the local authority to apply for a residence permit. This was also granted at once. The very next thing I did was sending two telegrams: one to my beloved Helena and another to my parents. They had to know that I had come home. Thus, endowed with the necessary documents, I took the train back to Villach. Back in the discharge camp, I presented them and was handed a notice of discharge without any further complications. Now, in early April of 1946, I left the British camp as a free man and civilian.

Without hesitation I boarded a train and went back to Leoben, where I moved into a room at the Schoberl family. A couple of days later, I managed to contact my own parents via telephone. My telegram had not reached them, but Helena had received hers and had already announced my coming return, brimming with joy. This had indeed been the first message they had gotten from me. I had been reported missing since October 1944, one and a half years ago. Not a single one of the many postcards and letters I had sent through the Red Cross had come through.

Over the weeks that followed I made plans for a first journey home. This was not that simple, as I had to cross from the British into the Soviet occupation zone. Eventually the British gave me a permit to leave their zone; it was a pass limited to three days. With that in hand, I put my plan into practice. I boarded a train and went to Pottschach. At Semmering pass, where the border between the zones was back then, there was a short moment of fear when Soviet soldiers checked my papers. But thankfully, after having a critical look at the pass, they let me be. To me, this was a delicate situation, as it was the first time I had anything to do with Soviet soldiers – after all, I had not met a single one during the war. When I arrived at Pottschach in mid-April 1946, the first thing I could do at the train stop was embrace my beloved Helena. Our first way was to my parents' house. Walking home from the train stop only took about fifteen minutes. Everything looked just the way it had always been. When I stepped through the front door, my parents were already waiting for me.

A moment later we were already in a tight embrace. The next walk was to the town hall where I intended to register as resident. Once there, I realized that things in Pottschach had, in fact, changed after all. Although I was not greeted by those who had joined the Nazi party in the past, but many of those who had full-throatily called for the *Anschluss* to Germany back in 1938 were apparently living a good life after the war's end as well. I came to the sobering conclusion that there were some people who always managed to end up on the winning side. Many former Austrian communists had been instated by the Soviets in communities and police stations. Where the old regime would have persecuted them, they were now the favored of our Soviet occupiers. This would now have consequences for me: as I arrived at the police station, I was given a document confirming my discharge from war imprisonment. It also stated that I had been *Oberkameradschaftsführer* (companionship leader first class) of the Hitler Youth, which at the same time made me a former Nazi party candidate. The transfer from Hitler Youth to party candidate had in fact been made automatically; back then, in 1940, there had been no reason for me to object to that. In the years that followed, however, there had been no relation whatsoever between me and the party or its politics. The only mentions of it between me and my comrades had been when we cussed the party barons up there.

I acknowledged the documentation and was told that I furthermore had to report for labor duty already on the next day. I presented my British pass and stated that I was to return to their occupation zone. In addition, I let them know that I had not been forced to work during my imprisonment and that it would stay that way; this principle would hold just as well for the new rulers of Pottschach. The policemen took note of it without comment.

My trip to Pottschach had been a short one, but it helped clearing the uncertainty that had overshadowed Helena's and my future. Despite the completely unforeseeable conditions, I proposed to her, and she said yes with great joy. We agreed on my next birthday, July 20, 1946, to be the date of our marriage. This would also be the occasion for my next visit at Pottschach. Even though there was barely anything edible to find anywhere, my parents and parents-in-law had done their best to make us comfortable as best as they could. To this very day I am most grateful to them, and without exaggeration I can say that this was the single best day of my life. I was brimming with joy to have made it home, and the fact that my brother Otto had also returned in good health was a source of great joy for us all.

I had made it through unharmed, and my loved ones had also survived the chaos of the war unscathed. Thus we had something that millions upon millions of human beings had not been granted. This fact I perceived with conscious humility and deep humbleness. So many of Europe's people were dead, had suffered lasting injury, had lost their dear loved ones to mindless violence or outright murder, had been subject to unfathomable suffering, had been displaced and made without a home, not knowing what even the next day would bring for them.

My two visits to Pottschach had only been short ones, and it would eventually take a long time for me to be able to return for good. The months that followed were marked by difficulty and harsh setbacks. I spent the next year in Vienna, where an acquaintance had helped me get a job. My participation in the Hitler Youth and the fact that I had been an officer would haunt me for a long time. The first setback I had at the Vienna University of Technology, where I had intended to finish my mechanical engineering degree; first, however, I had to appear before a committee that decided whether I was "inculpated" through my past dealings with the Nazi party, such that I could not be allowed to enroll. When I arrived and presented my papers, I was told that I had been a party candidate due to my leadership position within the HJ, and that as a consequence having me enroll could not be tolerated. Much less so since I had also been a Wehrmacht officer. I was asked politely, but firmly, to leave.

My nose had been so thoroughly put out of joint that I was too perplexed to say anything in return. In that moment I felt the resentment rise up inside me that had shown itself for the first time in American war captivity; back when we had been shown the terrifying images from the concentration camps. And even though we had thought them to be mere propaganda, they still had caused something deep inside us to change. A nagging doubt that had finally grown into resentment. It would take months for me to wash myself clean of my stigma and I would, against all odds, be allowed to finally work as the engineer that I had aspired to become.

Little by little, I would also learn more about the final months of the war. Near the end of 1944, our 21st Panzer Division had been withdrawn from the western front to recuperate in the hinterland, from where it was deployed to the eastern front at the beginning of 1945. There, it fought against the advancing Red Army forces until the end of the war – at last in the Halbe pocket, where tens of thousands of German and Russian soldiers would meet their end. The few survivors of our 21st Panzer Division became prisoners of war to the Russians. Some would only return years later, many others never again. Hans von Luck, commander of our neighboring regiment, would return only after five years of imprisonment. In this time he had witnessed much horror, but also learned to understand the Russian people. It had truly been a difficult time for him, as he would only barely escape death more than once, as well as having his gold teeth violently ripped out of his mouth.

But there were not only stories about the military resolution of the war and the fate of men that had waged it, or the formations that had played it out. Things got worse. I learned that in the last year of the war, there had been more destruction, and even more lives lost, than in the years before. In retrospect, I could now mount a wild case against the crimes committed by our "German" side. I could compare them with the atrocities that Allied troops had committed. But that would be utterly pointless, a means with no end. I can only come to the conclusion that this catastrophe of the twentieth century had its roots in the year of 1919 with the inhumane peace treaties of Versailles and St. Germain. That fateful day was the cause for resentment that would ferment over the course of the 1920s and 1930s to inhumane and degrading excesses beyond all description.

Without the treaties of Versailles and St. Germain, there would have been much less impoverishment in Germany and Austria, no communist threat and thus perhaps no Adolf Hitler as an answer to the imperialist and exploitative power politics of the victors of the Great War. With a just, honorable peace serving to facilitate international understanding after World War I, there would not have been a World War II. Some of those in power had realized this back in 1919, but their voices were not heard. Thus, the vicious cycle continued. As for me, my entire worldview collapsed at the end of World War II. I entered a new life and tried to live it as well as I could. And after years of resentment, I began to grapple with the time of the war again. Visited the places where I had fought. Walked through the Eucalyptus orchard at Djedeida, along the road to Pegasus Bridge at Bénouville, through the fields and meadows of Falaise.

Each time I was seized with gratitude for having survived and having found the strength to emerge from the turmoil, to become a refined person and to be able to start anew. Many others, however, who had not survived, who had never been given the chance to think about it all, who indeed could not have acted differently, still lie there to this day. They all, be they friend or foe, have my own and all our greatest respect. May their death be an eternal reminder for us and our children.

EPILOGUE

After publishing this book in German and having received much positive feedback, The publishers (Markus and Andreas) and I decided to travel to Normandy together in the Summer of 2014. Markus and Andreas were eager to visit the places of which I had told, and as for myself, I was curious to see in what form the sacrifices of both sides were being remembered today. Commemorations of the 70th anniversary of the Allied Normandy landings presented us with a fitting occasion. After arriving at Paris, we rented a car and went straight towards the French coast of Normandy. In the Caen area, we met a young Frenchman, who had contacted us earlier out of interest in what I had experienced. He offered to be a helpful tour guide, and indeed he would not be the last French to stand by our side and offer a helping hand. After taking up quarters in a hotel near Benouville, he took us on a drive to visit a restaurant in Quistreham.

Naturally, we talked about my past during dinner as well as about our travel plans, and to our surprise an elderly man from the next table approached us within a short time. He introduced himself to be an Englishman who was the current head of the British paratrooper veteran association. As such, he invited us to a joint commemoration ceremony on the grounds of the former Merville coastal battery – an invitation which we were of course happy to accept. The next day, we visited Benouville early in the morning. We had planned to first look around the chateau, but we were turned away, being told that the premises were currently a restricted area. As a consequence, we first went to Pegasus Bridge. Here, we had the chance to attend a small ceremony with British paratrooper veterans.

The British were quick to recognize me as a former opponent and welcomed me without any resentment. Another result was an interview with a BBC reporter and a chance to take a picture with British soldiers. Eventually we also managed to take a short detour into the chateau. We were marching along the Caen Canal from the bridge towards the chateau grounds. After a short time, Markus had "reconnoitered" two young men who were apparently responsible for the building's external security. Although they were dressed in plain clothes, their behavior was unmistakable. So Markus spontaneously approached them. The two were quite surprised, but willing to let us enter the premises. Walking past dumbfounded uniformed French police officers who had turned us away earlier, we marched into the chateau garden. Here, we also learned why there was so much security staff present. On June 6, there was to be a meeting between French president Francois Hollande, Russian president Vladimir Putin, Ukrainian prime minister Petro Poroschenko and German chancellor Angela Merkel held here. Under the watchful eyes of members from all kinds of security services, the four of us went for a walk through the chateau garden.

It would indeed not take long for us to find that some of the bullet holes and other battle damage on the castle's outside were still there. We could clearly distinguish between hits from 20 mm cannons and machine guns. The fact that these scars of war could still be found after all these years was a surprise, even to me. We then went to the place from where I had shot at the first British tank.

Markus and Andreas were amazed by the extremely short distance over which the engagement had happened. The terrain, in fact, allowed for firing right over the park's wall. At the spot where the tank had been hit and exploded, there was a large gap in the row of village houses. Apparently, there had been another house here before. When we took a closer look at the spot, a young family walked up to us, who Markus also talked to; it turned out that they were the owners of that plot. They could confirm that their ancestors had owned a house here that had been destroyed, and – much to my relief – they assured us that all their relatives had survived the building's collapse.

When I told them about my experiences, they were more than surprised, asking questions and showing great interest. I could not find any sign of them thinking negatively of me. Quite the opposite, they thanked us for talking to them, as their family history was now enriched by another notable facet. And I was myself delighted to have heard their story.

The days that followed would play out in a similar fashion. Wherever we went, we were welcomed most jovially. In Merville, I had the honor to be allowed to join British veterans in laying a wreath in commemoration of those who had been killed in action. On this occasion, we were introduced to a commanding general of the British paratroopers, who we presented with a book. We visited Hill 61, took a look at the British landing sector in the Quistreham area as well as the hills around Lebisey and the D-Day museum in Caen. Everything had clearly been arrayed for the anniversary celebrations. On top of that, the streets were populated by tourists and young men, but also women, who went around in historical uniforms and with restored vehicles. We also went to Omaha and looked around the American landing sector there.

We all, especially myself, were surprised by the long distance between the beach shore and the heights behind it. The American soldiers had to have suffered horrendously here. I was deeply moved during our visit to the La Cambe war cemetery near Bayeux. Here lie more than 21,000 German soldiers. Among them my messenger, Atteneder, our Sergeant Major Guse and my battalion commander, Major Zippe. Upon visiting each of their graves, I tried to recall my memories of them. Most of all, it was Atteneder who I remember well to this day. At the cemetery, we were approached as well, this time by a French family who showed us much respect, declaring that they had come voluntarily to honor the fallen. They assessed that it could only be right to honor the victims on both sides on this occasion. I could not have agreed more.

Over the days that followed, I experienced several more moments of similar intensity, especially when we visited Chateau St. Pair, or when we walked on the meadows of the former Falaise pocket. Each time I shuddered at the thought of what gruesome scenes had taken place there, be it the artillery strike in the cellar of St. Pair or the all-consuming death, destruction, and chaos of Falaise. The area around St. Lambert bloomed in vibrant green, nature was flourishing everywhere, and amid it all the small French villages nestled into the astounding landscape. My memories of these lands were entirely different. Dark and frightening, the stench of burning and death filling my nose. How beautiful it was to see that the war had barely left any trace.

Like a way of the cross, one can move through the landscape of the Falaise area today, and only the depressing photographs shown at individual stations can give an impression of what had happened. On Mont Ormel, we looked around the museum there, which presented a rather objective perspective as well, serving collective memory. As a grim reminder, a makeshift red cross flag had been draped on the wall. This flag had been made from a bed sheet on which a red cross had been painted in extreme distress, presumably with human blood. The flag had been found only a few years prior in an old farmhouse. Inevitably it caught the eye in an admonitory way, silently reminding of the horrors of days long gone.

After little less than a week, we went home again. What I took home with me was the certainty that the victims of war were being commemorated honorably, with no differentiation between victors and defeated. I had found new friends. British and German veterans, elderly men like me, and we all knew too well that we had been the luckiest ones. I had also gotten to know young French. Their approach to this past shows me that the idea of Europe of today shall lead us into the future. Never again shall our children and grandchildren face each other in the trenches. This time has to remain in the past alone. I wish for a world in which we are allowed to maintain the memorials of war in reverence, without ever having to build new ones.

Visiting the grave of my runner Atteneder at La Cambe cemetery, Normandy in 2014. Here, he rests along more than 21,000 other German soldiers.

The End

APPENDIX

IM NAMEN DES FÜHRERS
UND OBERSTEN BEFEHLSHABERS
DER WEHRMACHT
VERLEIHE ICH
DEM

Leutnant H ö l l e r
3./ Btl. T IV

DAS
EISERNE KREUZ
2. KLASSE

Div.Gef.St. , 31. 12. 19 42

(DIENSTSIEGEL)

Generaleutnant u. Div. Kommandeur
(DIENSTGRAD UND DIENSTSTELLUNG)

IM NAMEN DES FÜHRERS
UND OBERSTEN BEFEHLSHABERS
DER WEHRMACHT
VERLEIHE ICH
DEM

Leutnant Hans Höller

8./Pz.Gren.Rgt. 192

DAS

EISERNE KREUZ
1. KLASSE

Div.-Gef.-St., 14. 6. 1944

(DIENSTSIEGEL)

Generalmajor u. Div.-Kdr.
(DIENSTGRAD UND DIENSTSTELLUNG)

T 4

Dienst grad.	Name	Vorname	geb.	Beruf.	Eintritt in die wehrmacht	Verwendung als:
			1. Gruppe			
Uffz	Klausk	Peter	19.4.19	Bäcker	8.9.39	Gruppenführer
Gren	Jenal	Paul	23.11.23	Bergmann	20.6.42	M.G.Schtz 1
"	Gurski	Siegmund	4.5.23	Landarbeit.	22.5.42	" " " 2
"	Lucht.	Paul	29.9.08	Schlosser	19.5.42	Gew.Schtz.
"	Amend	Johann	8.8.08	Chem.Arbeiter	19.5.42	" "
"	Hubig	Josef	9.8.23	Bergmann	20.6.42	M.G.Schtz. 1
"	Schröder	Günther	29.9.23	Bergmann	20.6.42	" " " 2
"	Sirtl	Josef	15.3.13	Landwirt	15.12.41	Gew.Schtz.
"	Holzner	Johann	25.12.10	Landwirt	22.4.40	" "
Gefr.	Zaderer	Christian	6.11.18	Bäcker+Kondit.	19.12.39	stellv.Gruppenf.
			2. Gruppe			
Uffz	Aust.	Otto	14.9.21	Telegr.Bauhandw.	26.2.40	Gruppenführer
Gren	Michaely	Herbert	24.7.23	Bergmann	20.6.42	M.G.Schtz. 1
"	Erbelding	Arthur	14.10.11	Schlosser	21.4.42	" " " 2
"	Frank	Eugen	19.6.23	Hilfsarbeiter	14.4.42	Gew.Schtz.
"	Buddenborg	Willi	27.1.12	Schneidbrenner	19.5.42	" "
"	Pfeifer	Gerhard	14.9.23	Landwirt	17.4.42	M.G.Schtz 1
"	Dörrenbecher	Oskar	2.2.23	Bergmann	20.6.42	" " " 2
"	Scholle	Erwin	28.1.09	Bohrer	19.5.42	Gew.Schtz.
"	Foebus	Walter	22.7.08	Stellmacher	19.5.42	" "
"	Ohmer	Max	31.3.12	Schäfer	16.1.42	stellv.Gruppenf.

Dienstgr.	Name	Vorname	Geb.	Beruf	Eintritt in die Wehrm.	Verwendung als:
		T 4				
		3. Gruppe				
Uffz.	Hegewald	Wilhelm	4.3.12	Handlungsbevollm.	enter 1930 26.8.35	Gruppen F.
Gren.	Umstätter	Heinrich	24.1.23	Polsterer+Dekorat.	14.4.42	M.G.Sch. 1
"	Schwarz	Fritz	26.6.23	Bauschlosser	14.4.42	" " " 2
"	Haselmann	Josef	9.11.20	Hilfsarbeiter	8.4.41	Gew.Schtz
"	Zimmermann	Johannes	28.12.19	Schlosser	30.8.39	" "
"	Pasch	Josef	4.11.08	Stellmacher	19.5.42	M.G.Schtz 1
"	Thönissen	Anton	23.4.10	Stahlrichter	19.5.42	" " " 2
"	Meindel	Franz	14.8.13	Schuhmacher	14.9.42	Gew.Schtz.
Gefr.	Siegl	Georg	28.4.12	Landw.Arbeiter	24.12.39	" S "
"	Gallistl	Karl	24.9.18	Hilfsarbeiter	26.8.39	stellv.Grpf.F.
		Zugtrupp				
Uffz.	Rupp	Wilhelm	21.12.10	aktiv.	15.11.38	Zugtr.Führer
Gefr.	Kittel	Manfred	8.12.21	Maschinenrichter	4.3.41	Melder
"	Schlindwein	Theodor	16.8.22	Kaufm.Schüler	6.10.40	"
"	Lander	Philipp	2.9.19	Lackierer	26.6.40	"
S.Sold.	Hartmann	Josef	31.12.06	Arbeiter	10.9.42	San.Dienstgr.

Printed in Dunstable, United Kingdom